Antidotes
for
Anxiety

Your Heart Is Stronger Than You Think
How To Be Lazy, Healthy and Fit
How To Get A Good Night's Sleep
You Live As You Breathe
Common Sense Coronary Care and Prevention
Your Life To Enjoy
Mr. Executive: Keep Well—Live Longer
You Can Increase Your Heart Power
Live Longer and Enjoy It
The Doctor Looks At Life
How To Stop Killing Yourself
Heart Worry and Its Cure
What You Can Do for Angina Pectoris and Coronary Occlusion
What You Can Do for High Blood Pressure
How To Master Your Fears
How To Keep Fit Without Exercise
How To Add Years To Your Life
Heart Disease Is Curable
More Years for the Asking
Don't Die Before Your Time

Antidotes for Anxiety

How to Untie Your Bundle of Nerves

By
Peter J. Steincrohn

The Doctor Who Makes 100,000,000
House Calls Every Week

Nash Publishing, Los Angeles

All case histories and letters cited
are from the author's files.
Initials have been used (and often changed)
to protect private identities.

Library of Congress Catalog Card Number:00-000000
Standard Book Number: 8402-1251-8

Published simultaneously in the United States and
Canada by Nash Publishing Corporation,
9255 Sunset Boulevard, Los Angeles, California 90069

Printed in the United States of America.

First Printing.

To my 20 million (give or take a few hundred thousand)
daily readers. But especially to *you*
whose letter or case history may bare your heart
here between these covers.

Contents

Introduction

Sometimes a case history of a medical problem, expressed in the patient's own words, is more revealing than a scientific explanation.

Most people, when faced with an irreversible situation, such as terminal illness, will summon all of their inner resources and face up squarely to it and learn to live with it. However, when they are confronted with a stubborn, puzzling, agonizing anxiety, they suffer frustrations generated by uncertainty.

Here is an example of such a problem:

I am happily married, am 33, enjoy cooking, sewing, golf and reading. We have no financial problems. I do not take drugs except vitamins; don't smoke nor drink.

On to the problem: Fifteen months ago I had what felt like a "flashbulb" go off in my head. On and off since then I've lived as if in a haze. The world seems very unreal. It is an extremely strange and very difficult complaint to describe. It's a feeling of being outside one's own mind; a feeling as if part of the brain may be numbed, paralyzed, in limbo; an unrealness, a feeling of "what's everything all about?" I was told this sensation would soon go away, but it still defies tranquilizers and all other medication. In addition, I live in fear. It takes unnatural resolve for me to leave the house to go shopping or go on an auto trip. The only thing to fear is fear itself? That's me. I get light-headed feelings at the very thought of another "flashbulb" incident. It's fortunate for me that my husband has been patient and loving. Otherwise I would have given up long ago the hope that some day I might still conquer these weird, frightening feelings. Is my condition hopeless?

Millions Suffer Anxiety

This is a fairly good description of the anxiety state. Such nervousness can be so life-depleting that some patients have told me they would gladly sacrifice an arm or leg if they could feel "normal" again.

Millions of Americans suffer silently from anxiety of varying degrees of intensity. Even their families may not recognize the degree of suffering they undergo. They deserve all the help they can get. And I propose to offer as much as I can.

In this book you will read of others in similar predicaments.

As I have said elsewhere, you will improve by a process of osmosis—by soaking up others' experiences, learning what they have suffered, and discovering that recovery is not impossible (no matter how futile and impossible your own problem appears to be.)

Faith in our own eventual improvement comes when we see others "throw away their crutches" and walk again. Anxiety is not, as so many think, an incurable illness. Faith and the will to recover often prevail.

Anxiety is nothing more than prolonged fear. If something frightens you and the fear persists for weeks and months you suffer from chronic anxiety.

I remind those brave souls who look down their noses at their fellows who are scared, to knock on wood or pray that they'll never live in anxiety. For it is true, that however nerveless we appear to be, that not one of us is immune. If the stresses ever get too big and strong, we'll either bend or break our bundle of nerves.

So, the magic words for all of us are: *understanding* and *compassion* for those who suffer from anxiety.

In this book you will learn how to overcome the minor and major anxieties. How to deal with everything from the blues to a "nervous breakdown"; with cyclic tensions and change-of-life adjustments; with boredom and depression; with the frightening symptoms of hypoglycemia (low blood sugar) and hyperventilation (overbreathing); with fears of the number one killer: heart disease; with sleeping pills, tranquilizers, fatigue, tension, the need for sleep, finding a New Way of Life, and how to get along with your doctor.

Promises? Promises? Yes. But they can be fulfilled.

I promise.

—P.J.S.

PRAISE BE!

On some days frustration rises like a stealthy fog that envelops the spirit and makes you wonder if you're making any contribution at all to the life you're part of. For example, before I opened my reader-mail this morning, I asked myself just how much wisdom and comfort I was really bringing to readers out there. I doubted without reason, it seems; for here is at least one letter that acts as much more than a pick-me-up:

> *Dear Dr. Steincrohn:* I am taking time off from my usual daily bout with this unhappy super-charged body and brain of mine, when I try futilely to get some sleep and surcease from my problems. It is not in the least my intention to make this a letter of complaint.
>
> No need to tell you that mankind is plagued by mental illness, the most insidious of all. As a lay-man, I believe without doubt, that many manifestations of mental illness have some physiological origin similar to physical illness. And the time is not far off when the medical profession will discover the causes.
>
> What really prompted this letter was my simple desire to express to you the reverence and warmth I feel toward you as a most humane and know-ledgeable human being. Your love of people and lack of prejudice is uplifting. Thank you deeply for your warmth and sincerity.
>
> Mr. B. (California).

Comment: My hope is that I can spread a similar feeling of warmth and sincerity in the telling of my book.

"May I never see in the patient anything but a fellow creature in pain"

—from The Oath of Maimonides

"How to worry less? Worry more!"

—Steincrohn

I
The Doctor-Patient Partnership

1
How To Untie
Your Bundle of Nerves

"Fear is the curse of man." So said Dostoyevsky.

If this is true of fear, then so is anxiety a fearsome burden. There is a distinction. Fear is something sudden. You either stay to overcome its cause, or run away. A man points a gun at you, a tiger is ready to spring; you face up to the threat or you get out of there—fast. Anxiety is something else again. It is prolonged fear. It lasts for days, weeks or years. It beats you down so that your days are lived in apprehension—even when you should be supremely happy and contented.

Sometimes you know the reason for your prolonged fear. For example, anxiety can plague you because you are concerned about your wife who may be seeking a divorce; about your child who may be seriously ill; about your job; about how you get along with your peers.

At other times, and quite commonly too, it is what we call a free-floating anxiety which digs its shallow trenches around your days and takes pot shots at you. You are concerned, unhappy, frustrated and bewildered—yet you do not know why.

"I have no reason to feel this way," you say. "But I can't get over the premonition that something is going to happen. Something bad."

So you worry. And day-to-day worry adds up to chronic anxiety. And anxiety adds up to unfulfillment. Illness— organic or functional—is the most common reason for anxiety. There is nothing you can mention that equals in importance chronic fear of loss of health and life, whether real or imagined.

Here is a man who is certain that his chest pain is due to coronary artery disease. You examine him from the tip of the longest hair on the top of his head to the longest toe on his foot; head-to-toe inspection and investigation reveal not one iota of evidence that there's anything at all the matter with this man's coronary artery system.

You give him a clean bill of health. Yet he disbelieves. He continues to worry. He says, "How about the man who had a physical, was told he was all right, and dropped dead right after he left the doctor's office?" (This is a standard.)

Anxiety Difficult To Uproot

Once anxiety has burrowed deep into such a man, it often takes a dozen doctors to dig up the anxiety and scatter it to the winds.

Or, here is a woman, passing through her menopause, who is unnaturally anxious about her family. "Whenever my children leave on a date at night, I'm up at all hours until they return. I imagine all kinds of accidents they've been in. I worry about my husband's job; I worry about myself. I'm sure I have cancer of the uterus, but the doctor won't tell me because he doesn't want to frighten me."

And so go the thousands of discordant variations on the melody called anxiety. It can take many forms. These frightened people who bear the curse of anxiety deserve all of our sympathy and attention. Too often they are discarded as hypochondriacs or simply as "pests" by impatient members of their family—and even by doctors themselves (who should know better).

They are as sick as if they were sick. They are as unhappy as if they were suffering terminal illness. In fact, too many of them consider whatever they have as surely being incurable.

Each and every one of us is a bundle of nerves. These are ubiquitous informers which tell the brain everything there is to know about you. Are you concerned about your job? About your health? Your wife? Your children? Your brain is sure to receive instant reports on what is going on in your body and in your mind.

Unfortunately, there is an irritating byproduct of all this nervous activity, which we call anxiety. Every normal (mind you, normal) human being suffers from it in varying degrees.

Of course, anxiety can be normal. For example, when it causes us to turn our head from side to side as we cross a busy street. Or, it can be abnormal when it rises to such intensity that it interferes with a normal, happy way of life.

True Perspective

Simply put, my purpose is to make you aware of various kinds of anxiety so that you can see yourself in true perspective. By comparing yourself with others you will realize whether or not you have minimal fears which do not require the ministrations of a doctor; or, whether you indeed have a nervousness or depression which should quickly impel you to seek professional help.

Anxiety is the end result of nerves hyper-reacting. Now, we realize that you cannot invariably and easily change your environment. Same wife, same children, same job, same problems. It's how well you learn to live with them (and with yourself) that matters.

In a way, this book is a mirror. Look into it—in a good light. Summon the courage to see yourself as you really are. Read of the experience of others who have suffered from anxiety. You will learn how to untie your own bundle of nerves—and how to smooth the frayed ends. I'll help all I can.

Definitions

I'll keep asking and trying to answer.

Anxiety? What is it? Fright? Fear? Apprehension? It is all of these—prolonged. Call it the results of an emotion caused by a signal that danger threatens the body. Or the psyche. Either from the environment or from one's inner mechanism.

Anxiety is prolonged fear. It is flight, but the inner fight continues. It causes actual changes in function: pulse, breathing, blood pressure, weakness, shakiness, sweating, etc. Each of us differs in how we react to the same experience. One survives a plane crash, and immediately gets on the next plane to reach his destination. But another, surviving this experience, vows never again to step aboard a plane.

Exposed to the threat of acute illness, no one is free from anxiety. Personal ego becomes aware of danger. Of course it all depends upon how serious the illness, how long it lasts, and how well-structured the nervous system of the patient. A feather will tip one man over while another withstands the blows of a hammer of fear.

Often, intensity of anxiety depends upon the suddenness of onset. For example, in coronary thrombosis, anxiety can be tremendously overpowering. I have observed brave men turn cowards. Panic spreads terror like ripples widening in a stone-thrown pond.

However, if a person has had indigestion for weeks, he is more prepared for a diagnosis of ulcer or gall bladder trouble without reacting with great anxiety. Even if he has had angina pectoris for months, it is some sort of preparation for the sudden attack of coronary thrombosis. But how you react really depends upon your resilience, unnatural imagination (raising specters of danger), and on your total personality.

Reaction to Acute Anxiety

Picture the driving, strong, demanding man who heads a large organization. He is undisputed "leader" of thousands of workers who depend upon him for livelihood. See him as he confidently guides his business ship. There is no outward evidence of temerity or doubt.

Suddenly the coronary! The heart attack which incapacitates like an unexpected stroke of lightning. How will he react? This is often the test of a man. I have seen them before and after. It is still difficult to pick the "heroes." It is difficult to guess which will regress and become inadequate, unnaturally dependent upon wife, children, friends, nurses and doctors. In some instances, they will act like a child.

Such patients have to learn to grow up again. To be able to relate, as they did before their attack, to the people about them—at home and away. You see, there is a need for emotional as well as structural recovery. It is the doctor's job to realize this: not only do we deal with the patient's illness, but with his reaction to illness. Not only is there need to cure the illness, but to rehabilitate the patient.

More Definitions

Most of the anxieties of life come from turmoil within rather than reaction to visible dangers. Our Ego is in the middle of the struggle between our Id (which continually seeks satisfactions often denied by society) and our Superego (which is our conscience that keeps saying, "No, you mustn't do this—or that").

Anxiety, then, is this morbid anticipation about something that is already happening, or something that is going to happen, but unrecognizable.

All you need is to know that anxiety is due to below-the-surface adjustment to unconscious fears that threaten to throw our entire mechanism out of homeostatic balance—to admit to ourselves that although we are adults, we are not unlike the child who takes a doll or toy to bed, looking for emotional security.

You cannot untie your bundle of nerves without this willingness to agree that you are not free of some degree of anxiety—and not be ashamed of this "weakness." Lives there a man with mind so dead that he doesn't live scared?

Misery is Contagious

This is what this book is about: anxiety. How others have dealt with it and how you can be helped to deal with it. You will read many case histories of various kinds of anxiety problems: how some recovered; how some failed—either because failure was imbedded within themselves or because their doctors failed them.

I hope you will understand that this book is not a substitute for your doctor's advice, or that it equals the effects of long hours of psychotherapy, or years of release on a psychiatrist's couch. All I hope to do is give you a plain, common sense awareness of what anxiety is all about; not a deep, penetrating analysis of the subject—which you can find in specialized textbooks.

Reading what I have to say will give you the assurance human beings get when they realize that they are not alone. Misery loves company. Knowing this is the first essential step in untying your bundle of nerves.

Living in daily anxiety and fear causes more disruption of human values and hopes than almost any other illness. Nervous patients have told me they have received encouragement and help by reading about similar problems in others. For example, listen to this woman:

> Until three years ago the world was my oyster and I loved each day and greeted each new challenge with enthusiasm.
>
> Suddenly all that changed when I had a very frightening experience—numbness in the feet, churning in the stomach, tightness in the chest, weakness all over. For one who had always been so healthy, this was a great shock.
>
> I had been in the habit of taking a yearly physical, so my doctor knew me and my past history really well. Since this happened I have been tested for everything, had three cardiograms, upper and lower GI series, spent a week in the hospital for tests, had Xrays of all parts of the body, was tested for low blood sugar, etc. All the tests indicated that I am in fine physical condition.
>
> I have tried to continue to live normally but these attacks of anxiety recur and without explana-

tion. They can be very frightening. May I list some of my symptoms? Shortness of breath—heart skips—pulsations in the chest—stiff neck and back most of the time (Xrays show no arthritis)—weakness—continual burping and gasiness even on arising—tightness in the chest area.

My doctor says he knows I am not a hypochondriac and that my symptoms are real. He has ruled out menopause as the cause even though I am forty-eight years old. He has prescribed mild tranquilizers. I do not take them often because I don't feel they are the answer.

I am writing to you in the hope that something has escaped us. In a recent column you wrote about anxiety being the cause of so much unhappiness in the world. Can this be treated? I am so discouraged about this condition that I just function at about half of my capacity. I am desperate for help.

(Signed, Mrs. J.)

For reasons I have already mentioned, I think I can help Mrs. J. and thousands of others who are at the "mercy of their nerves." I may not be able to give specific antidotes for each problem; but if you read on you will get help by osmosis—by reading what others have experienced, by learning from their victories and their failures, by gradually becoming more aware of what it is you have to face before you can hope to overcome it.

How a Reader Conquered Anxiety

So many readers of my column write about their stubborn

anxieties. And so many are downhearted, lacking in hope, and certain that the rest of life is doomed to depression and unhappiness. For these unhappy people I make it a point to print, occasionally, letters from other readers who have overcome this apparently incurable state. I am sure it gives them the courage to keep trying. Here is a letter from Canada:

> Like so many others, I have been helped greatly by your column, but have never written to you. I think now I owe a great debt to others who have written, to tell how they conquered emotional illness and recovered to live happy, full lives. Perhaps my letter will help some others who feel that there is no hope of release from fear.
>
> When I felt lowest, I would read copies of your column over and over (I had clipped them from our paper). The knowledge that others who had been down in that dark valley had actually made it back to real life again, helped to keep me going.
>
> Less than two years ago I was still suffering beyond description from a nervous breakdown. I was as low in mind as a human being can get. I thought constantly of suicide and was sure I was going insane, and took more and more sleeping pills. I also started drinking a lot and nearly became an alcoholic.
>
> Incidentally, I am the mother of two young children who at that time were a girl of three and an infant daughter of two months. My reason for telling all this is that when I read the accounts of other people's fears I kept thinking,—They couldn't have been as low as me—until I read all the facts of their illness.

As of now I am a happy, healthy woman. There is no easy recipe. In my case I know it was a slow return to faith in God that brought me back to life. I honestly believe that in many ways I am a better person now for having gone through those horrible dark months.

There is a message in the Bible that reads: "He brought me up also out of a horrible pit, out of the miry clay, and set my feet upon a rock—"(40th Psalms, v.2). I happened to read that in church and thought it described my experience exactly. Also I was helped by a book mentioned by one of your readers. I bought Vincent Peale's *Power of Positive Thinking* and studied it and tried to live it.

I hope, Dr. Steincrohn, I have given some of your anxious readers hope and faith. If they will pray for help at any and all times of the day and night, I am sure they will be helped as I have been.

(Mrs. H.)

Everyday Living a Problem

Blame it on heredity or environment, some nervous systems just can't take it. One man will jump when you say *boo*; another will hardly be startled if you set off a firecracker near him.

So it is on what some have described as the battleground of life. You'll meet one person who is wounded every day by ordinary personal encounters or problems of survival, and you'll see another who binds up even more serious wounds, and goes his way fearlessly facing the future. Here is an example of the former:

One night about two years ago, about six months after I got married, I felt I was sick. I had a checkup. The doctor said I was in perfect health.

Since then I have had several checkups and X-rays. All showed I was in good health. But I still think I am sick. When I am at work, or doing other things such as mowing the lawn, washing the car, I feel fine. But when I quit, I start thinking maybe those doctors are wrong.

It seems that ever since we've been married we've had nothing but money problems, the baby, income tax and other bills. I don't think it's the problems of married life because I love my wife and child. Every time I am away from them I almost go out of my mind. I can't stand crowds. I am afraid of people.

I say to myself, "Is this you? A married man with a baby girl and a wife depending on you? Aren't you man enough to take good care of them? I don't think you are. You should not have got her and the baby. You can't take care of them."

Sometimes I think I'm crazy or going crazy. I am only 20 years old. I don't know what to do. Will I ever get well?

(Mr. X.)

One day I decided to take a personal poll. I stopped 10 strangers (four men, one boy, one girl, four grown women) and asked them: "Right now, what bothers you most. What are you anxious about?"

In substance, the replies:

"Money. My job."

"My health."

"Sickness in the family."

"I'm scared of flunking out."

"My wife is sick."

"My kid is sick."

"I'm scared. Just don't know why."

"Always fighting at home."

"Nothing. I'm a fatalist."

"The bomb."

You will note, Mr. X., that anxiety about finances was answer number 1. I can only guess, but perhaps this is your personal problem, too. When that battered old ship comes in, heading into your harbor loaded with money or offers for a better job, it's likely that your anxiety will lessen. As I said, only a guess—but I've seen it work out before.

What Is Normal?

Two psychiatrists passed each other on the street and one said, "Hello." The other waved his hand and said to himself, "Wonder what he meant by that?" This little joke has deep implications.

Lately people seem to be reading too much into each other's actions. According to one member of a mental health committee, normal people cannot bear the stresses of high position. The implication seems to be that to become a leader, or top administrator, one of the first requirements is a psychopathic makeup. Or, at least the need for being some kind of neurotic.

Isn't that carrying it a bit too far? I've also heard it said that the good actor is the one who is overburdened with complexes and is trying to run away from himself by play-acting. Similarly, that an author takes out his hostilities by creating hateful characters in his novels, putting them through their paces.

I think it's time we stopped trying to find a reason for everything one thinks, says or does. For me there is enough reason for peoples' action in this truth: that all of us want to live as long as we can, be as healthy as we can, be happy, satisfy our egos, and perhaps leave some tiny imprint on the world to give us good reason for having been born. (Even if this gift to posterity is grandchildren.)

Like normal body temperature, there is no exact normal behavior. My normal temperature may be about 98.6 degrees Fahrenheit; yours may be 98 or 99 degrees, or somewhere in between.

Surely a man who gets close to the top in any field of endeavor has more drive than his neighbor who is satisfied to live the existence of a cow. But why label him a neurotic simply because he is a "high normal?" High normal or low normal, very anxious or slightly anxious, let's see if I can help you untie your bundle of nerves.

Mrs. D. writes: "I have a friend who is frankly 'a bundle of nerves.'" Let's hope I can help her, too. She says, "Bridge makes me nervous."

Bridge can be a dangerous game. Most people consider it an excellent sport because it requires little exertion and invariably produces a sense of relaxation and pleasure.

Yet, it is often the precursor of anxiety and tension. Not everyone can withstand the strain. Amiability and good fellowship can, within the hour, turn into irascibility and downright animosity.

Emotions allowed to run amuck are potentially as dangerous as taking your hand off the steering wheel while cruising at 70 miles per hour. Any unexpected obstacle can cause a dangerous crack-up.

It doesn't happen much in poker because you are on your own. Rarely in pinochle because your partner is only an occasional partner. In bridge, you're tied down for consecutive, fateful minutes with a partner—often not of your own choosing. And it is even worse when your regular partner, husband or wife, is guilty of a fateful error.

Are You a Tense Player?

Tensions, anxiety and aggression rapidly mount to the explosion point. Beware. The very foundations of your health and marriage may be vulnerable.

Too many people get too wrapped up in bridge. As it is primarily a game of partners, the temptation and opportunity is always there to inflict silent or outright vituperation upon the "ignorant, stupid, stubborn etc." so-and-so who innocently sits across the table.

Now, there are explosions and implosions. If you explode quite often because of misplays or misbids by the "moron" who is ruining your game, then your temper-ridden body is a good target for a sudden elevation of blood pressure, a stroke, a coronary attack.

On the other hand, if you "implode"—just sit there burning up inwardly without openly emasculating the male partner or cruelly dominating the female partner—the inner tensions and built-up head of steam will plant the seeds of anxiety and tension which certainly won't do your ulcer, heart or arteries any good.

Although I am far from being an expert bridge player

myself, I believe that most bridge players will welcome the gratuitous advice I give you as an expert in medicine. Call them tips about the game, or ground rules if you prefer. They are antidotes against anxiety and emotional outbreaks, and they apply as well whether you are sick or well, single or married, a hard worker or a beachcomber.

Ten Commandments

Here are ten bridge commandments:

1. Keep reminding yourself that it's only a game. (Healthmanship.)

2. Don't play for stakes higher than you can afford.

3. Be patient with "stupid" partners.

4. Remember, the game is as much a test of yourself as a person as it is of your skill.

5. Avoid postmortems mixed with malicious accusations.

6. When your partner fulfills his bid by playing quite well, don't invariably suggest, "You shouldn't have played your etc., etc."

7. An outburst of temper directed against your own husband or wife (before others) may give you vicarious joy and a sense of power and release of hostility, but it is only another brick added to a slowly building wall of resentment.

8. It's not important whether you win or lose, but how you play the game. (Terribly trite but terribly true.)

9. If you can't govern your emotions, switch to chess—or solitaire.

10. To repeat: For the sake of your health and peace of mind, keep reminding yourself (no matter what the provocation) that bridge is only a game—a game—a game! Winning is

not worth the anxiety and guilt feelings you carry away when you rise from the table.

At the Mercy of Our Temperament

A surgical colleague told me the other day that competitive bridge takes more out of him physically and emotionally than standing up to an operating table hour after hour. "I begin to feel anxious as soon as I sit down to play. Wondering if I'll make any mistakes in bidding or play. Or, if a dumb partner will blow the game. One day I'll resolve to give up bridge and take up golf."

I asked him if he'd ever seen an anxious and frustrated golfer wrap a club around a tree trunk—or try to break it over his knee after missing a shot. He said no. "Well," I said, "unless your attitude towards play changes, you'll be doing it, too."

Our games and occupations may change, but we are still at the mercy of our collective temperaments. Nevertheless, anxiety and tension can be overcome with proper application of will power and a workable philosophy of life. Whether bridge—or any other game—masters you depends upon how well you master yourself.

At least 30 million Americans play bridge regularly. Not only does it cause undue anxiety in the susceptible, it may breed violence. It can be a dangerous sport. I have just been reading about the fateful end of a man we shall call Mr. Jones. He and his wife were playing a "friendly" game of contract bridge with neighbors. They bid a small slam. He made a misplay. His apparently docile, quiet wife reached into her handbag, drew a small pistol and shot him dead. Incidentally, she was acquitted when she came to trial. Probably by a jury of bridge buffs. Poor Mr. Jones. He was apparently unaware of the many offshoots of anxiety—how it can cause mayhem as well as ulcers and high blood pressure. Like any other sport, bridge can be exciting, challenging and exhausting. But overlooked by so many is that constant, recurring anxiety while playing is a real threat to the health of those who are not temperamentally suited to play the game. (And to their partners.)

Her Husband a "Bridge-nut"

Consider this nervous wife's problem:

> I need some advice badly. My husband is making a nervous wreck out of me. For the first time in my life I have nervous indigestion. My husband is 48 and this man has never had one tragic thing happen to him; yet he is a constant complainer and fault-finder when we play bridge. He is a nut about the game. He insists that we play at least four or five nights a week. I've grown to hate it. His idea of an evening well-spent is to buy a 6-pack or a 12-pack and spend 6-8 hours a night playing the game. He will not get his mind off himself. He is not interested in anything or anybody else—just himself. I'm surprised people continue to play with us.
>
> He continually badgers me or any of his partners if we have made a mistake. He even does so when we haven't. 'You should have bid it this way—or played it that way.'
>
> He can never forgive nor forget. He can't laugh at anything as being water over the dam. He imagines himself to be persecuted and unappreciated. He wants to be a 'big image' to people but doesn't realize he destroys it all by his actions at

the bridge table.

One day I'm sure he'll run all our friends away because he's becoming such a crashing bore. Our relations think he's becoming a nut. My two brothers won't speak to him. Our four married children are making excuses to spend their holidays elsewhere. My two sons have asked me if he was always like this.

I tell them no. The fact is that he is a tolerant, friendly human being otherwise. It seems that he becomes transformed when he sits down to play bridge. He becomes a devil. And it isn't because of the beer. He can drink when not playing and still be his old sweet self. Doctor, what can I do to shock him out of this?

I told her that the only remedy was to play a finesse—and hope it worked. To tell him that she had given up the game for good. If he insisted that she continue to play she would leave him. Divorce? Yes, divorce. What did he do? Her finesse succeeded. In a sober moment he made a decision, too. He also gave up playing. Now he spends his evenings in a work shop in the basement—wondering why he wasted so many evenings on bridge. And his wife no longer suffers from nervous indigestion.

Endings are not invariably happy ones. For example, consider the following case history:

An Unhappy Ending

I am desperate. My husband beats me. There

must be many other unhappy women like myself who are too ashamed to admit it. Throughout my last two years of marriage I have suffered six or seven terrible beatings and many minor ones. And the small incidents that always triggered these outbursts were arguments that began at the bridge table. All of his terrible frustrations and anger would be directed at me. Mostly when business was bad and he felt himself to be a failure.

Last night he held my head on one hand and began to beat it against the concrete wall of the basement. Right after our friends left following a bridge game. I have never told my parents or anyone else. Everybody adores him. He makes them laugh and acts as if nothing ever bothers him. (He never shows his anger at the table.)

For example, five minutes after my beating in the basement, he was charming and gay when my folks dropped in after the theater. You would think this man was the kindest, happiest and most handsome alive. Other women keep telling me how lucky I am. What shall I do?

On examination it was incredible to see all the bruises. I advised her to talk with her minister or to a marriage counselor. But before doing so, I suggested that she get him to my office for a physical checkup. Opthalmoscopic examination revealed some abnormal pressure which indicated he'd better see a neurologist. An electroencephalogram (brain wave tracing) showed that he had some organic trouble in his brain. X-rays and other examinations led to brain surgery. He had an inoperable brain tumor and died a few months later.

You see, all mental aberrations cannot be charged to the game of bridge. Nevertheless, better keep my ten commandments in mind.

But it is better to be aware that "little" frustrations add up to "big bundles of nerves." Knowing why you feel tense and out of sorts is the first step to relief. For example, have you ever been killed by kindness?

While on a recent visit to New York City I saw a waiter almost killed before my eyes. Yet, like a coward, I sat there speechless, not even offering him one little hope he could cling to.

I was staying at one of the smaller hotels which pride themselves on offering a home atmosphere and on serving fine food to the many people who room there the year round. Among them are retired oldsters (you will never hear me use the euphemism "senior citizens"), sprinkled with a goodly number of widows and widowers.

On that fateful day I sat down at the counter in the restaurant's one remaining empty seat. Next to me sat two women in their late sixties, dressed as if there were on the way to an appointment at the Plaza; and by some strange circumstance waylaid and forced to eat in this place of far less glamour.

They were dressed in black, fingers heavily laden with rings, and their necks encircled with many strands of pearls.

I could not help hearing some of their small talk and chit chat.

Only one waiter was in charge of the entire horseshoe-shaped counter. I counted 16 hungry, impatient people. That waiter was as busy as any I have ever seen. (And that includes me when I waited on tables in the summer before I entered medical school.)

Why only one waiter? Many of the patrons asked the

manager why. He said, "You know George who waits here. Well, he broke his leg. That's why it's all on Fred today. Tomorrow we hope to have someone to help."

But tomorrow was a long way off for Fred. A middle-aged, pale-faced man with puffy rings under his hollow eyes, he was doing his best to satisfy his impatient customers. Worst of all, was one of the women in black.

Her voice was low and cracked, sometimes typically the end result of too many cigarettes and drinks. In order to hear her, he had to come close and cup his ear with a trembling hand.

First, she had him return her beef because it was too rare. He took it perfunctorily and acknowledged her guttural, "Thank you *so* much!"

When he returned it she pointed to her empty glass and asked for a refill of water. "Thank you *so* much!"

A few minutes later she beckoned him. It was salt and pepper she wanted. A simple request from a neighbor would have saved the waiter a long walk from the other end of the counter. He placed the shakers before her. "Thanks *so* much!"

Instead of mustard she wanted vinegar and oil. "Thank you *so* much!"

And so it went on and on. As a doctor I could feel the waiter wilting under the barrage of hypocritical kindness. Paid in full by her "*Thank* you *so* much!" she believed that there was nothing he shouldn't do for her at the slightest request.

At last, they slid off the stools and left. I waited to assess the reactions of the waiter. The repressed tensions and dislike had tightened the muscles of his face. He had to struggle to move his lips. His face was a mask of acute anxiety and frustration.

"Some people kill you with kindness," he said. "I'm almost dead. Do you wonder why I'm a nervous wreck?"

All I could do was nod in complete agreement. He looked at me, thankful that I understood.

For days I kept hearing in my inner ears the ringing reverberations of the words that almost killed him that day: "Thank you *so* much"—"Thank you *so* much"—"Thank you *so* much."

I've made a resolution never to kill anyone with (hypocritical) kindness. Frustration and anxiety are already heavy burdens each human being must carry daily. Why add to the load?

Thoughts and Afterthoughts on Chapter 1

1. Only those who have suffered from a frayed bundle of nerves will agree with Dostoyevsky that "fear is the curse of man."

2. It is a fearsome burden. Either you face up to it or run away.

3. Anxiety is prolonged fear.

4. Illness is the most common reason for anxiety. When you are sick, all other aspirations, dreams, and personal relationships fade into a dark, undistinguishable background of disinterest.

5. Frightened people who bear the curse of anxiety deserve all our sympathy and attention. They are as sick as if they were sick.

6. Have you the courage to see yourself in true perspective?

7. Exposed to the threat of acute illness, no one is free from anxiety. It can be overpowering. I have seen brave men turn cowards.

8. But most of the anxieties of life come from turmoil within rather than reaction to visible dangers. Our Ego is in the middle of the struggle between our Id (which continually seeks satisfactions denied by society) and our Superego (which is our conscience).

9. Anxiety is this morbid anticipation about something that is already happening, or something that is going to happen—but is unrecognizable.

10. You cannot untie your bundle of nerves without a willingness to agree that you are not free of some degree of anxiety—and not be ashamed of this "weakness."

11. It is true that misery loves company. Reading what I have to say will give you the assurance human beings get when they realize they are not alone.

12. Re-read the case history of the anxiety sufferer who recovered and offers faith and hope for those who believe they will never get well.

13. Blame it on heredity or environment (or both): some nervous systems just can't take it. One man will jump when you say *boo*; another will hardly be startled if you set off a firecracker near him.

14. Some common reasons for anxiety: "Money; my job" —"My health"—"Sickness in the family"—"I'm scared of flunking out"—"My wife is sick"—"My kid is sick"—"I'm scared; just don't know why"—"Always fighting at home"— "Scared of nothing; I'm a fatalist"—"The bomb."

15. Are you neurotic? There's no exactly normal behavior.

16. Even the game of bridge may be hazardous by creating anxiety.

17. The "little" frustrations add up to a big bundle of anxiety.

18. Resolve not to "kill anyone with kindness."

2
How Anxiety Grows
in a Doctor's Office

Unintentionally, as a syndicated medical columnist, I conduct an international poll. From all parts of the United States, Canada and some few European countries come thousands of letters every month from readers confessing what patients think of their doctors.

Many praise; others condemn. You will be interested in the number 1 complaint: "The doctor does not give me enough time." Invariably, this is the patient's greatest disappointment after visiting his physician. For example:

Dear Dr. Steincrohn: I am nervous. I need someone to talk to. Someone who will listen. I go to my doctor. He takes all the necessary tests, like xrays, electrocardiograms, laboratory examinations. He is thorough when he examines me.

But how much time does he give me to tell him how I feel? Not more than five minutes a visit. I leave his office feeling worse than when I came.

I do not blame him. His waiting room is full of patients. The poor man looks so tired he probably needs a doctor himself.

But what is the answer? With population in-

creasing and not enough doctors around, how can
we overcome this serious problem? I do not look
forward to having a robot taking care of me. Although, frankly, it's almost close to that already.

(Mrs. W.)

The most eye-opening—and disturbing—part of my job as a
medical columnist is reading letters from other doctors'
patients. I get scores of such letters every day—tens of thousands each year. They're nearly always written by thoughtful,
articulate people who want help with a health problem.

Doctor Too Busy

Why do so many people ask me questions that could be
answered by their own doctors? One reason stands out:
These people feel that their doctors aren't meeting their
problems adequately. Too often they leave their doctors'
offices frustrated, anxious and bewildered. Here is the most
common complaint: *their doctors shortchange them on time*.

To many patients "time" is synonymous with "warmth"
and "care." One reader recently wrote me:

I visited a local doctor two weeks ago. He barely
glanced at me, gave me some pills and said there
was nothing wrong. He didn't even take my blood
pressure—which was probably plenty high, since I
had waited two hours to see him.

I tried to talk to him; it did no good. I was
sicker when I got out of his office than when I
went in. Although I've been to him several times,
he has never taken a medical history. Opponents of

Government medicine say it will hamper the doctor-patient relationship. *What* relationship?

(Mrs. G.)

The doctor-patient relationship is something I stress in my medical column, but the response from readers isn't always heartening. Writing about menopause, for example, I have said, "What you really need is a kindly, sympathetic family doctor to lean on." A reader replied: "Where, oh where does one find such a doctor? Today's family physician herds his patients in and out of his office so fast that if a patient were so rash as to try 'leaning' on him, he'd fall flat on his face."

As these patients see it, some offices have the kind of busy, bustling atmosphere that discourages confidences. The phone rings; an aide pops in; the doctor is visibly distracted by a thousand problems. The patient hesitates to bother him about a "trivial" ailment like a chronic sore throat or to impose on his time by disclosing a secret fear.

One such patient was a mother of three who described herself as happily married but nervous. She wrote that she was continually screaming at her children and slapping them needlessly. "One of my deepest fears", she said, "is that I may inadvertently hurt one of them." She has never told any of her doctors about this secret fear. Why? She doubts that any doctor except a psychiatrist would take the time to listen, "and we don't have that kind of money." So in desperation she wrote to me, though the only help I could offer was the assurance that I'd at least read her letter.

Lack of Communication

Another common complaint: *Their doctors shortchange*

them on information. Even if a physician takes plenty of time to get a good history and do a thorough physical, he may be so closemouthed that the patient turns to a medical columnist for enlightenment. For instance, a worried patient wrote to me: "My doctor tells me I have a hiatal hernia. Isn't that just an ugly name for a tumor? And mightn't it be malignant? Why doesn't my doctor operate to take it out?"

Fear of cancer isn't the only fear that flourishes in the desert of silence between physician and patient. Many patients get sick worrying about their hearts or their minds. I have a letter from a woman describing her headaches, palpitations and feeling of smothering:

"My doctor wrote down everything I told him," she reported. "He examined me from head to toe. Then he patted my shoulder and said, 'It's just your nerves.' That means it's all in my imagination, doesn't it? Yet my symptoms are getting worse all the time. Is my mind going to pieces?" Her doctor could have spared her this anxiety with the simple explanation that nervous tension can cause very real symptoms.

A physician's silence not only fails to erase fears but sometimes actually produces them, as this perceptive housewife noted: "When a doctor seems reluctant to tell me what my trouble is, I begin to suspect that I have something serious and that he's withholding the facts. This type of treatment produces those hypochondriacal tendencies that doctors abhor."

Sometimes the patient interprets the physician's failure to communicate as a brush-off. A woman wrote me about her doctor: "If I do manage to get in a word about something that's bothering me, he brushes it off with, 'Oh, you know. There's the matter of your threescore years.' I'm disgusted!"

The Search For a Good Doctor

One of my correspondents summed up her own and many other patients' feelings about the reticent doctor in these words: "If the average patient could find a doctor who would tell him exactly what type of illness he had, what medicine he was going to get and what results could be expected—well, that patient would think he had met up with an angel."

I am sure that most patients would have just such a high regard for their physicians (and be happier patients for it) if doctors would just follow these two tips:

1. If a patient seems to need "talking time" schedule a separate half-hour session with him—and charge accordingly. Some patients just can't open up when they sense that the doctor is working against the clock and the pressure of a waiting room full of patients.

2. Be generous with medical explanations—in lay language, of course. Use the pictures and diagrams in your library when you think they'll help. Give negative information, too. Make sure your patient knows when he *doesn't* have cancer or heart disease and when it's clear that his ailment *isn't* permanent or degenerative. In short, take the time to listen and to explain. Then maybe *your* patients won't feel the need to consult a medical columnist for the answers.

For some time I have been aware of this deficiency in doctor-patient relations. A few years ago I suggested relief for both physician and anxious patient. I was not surprised at the time that there was no concerted clamor from either public or the medical profession that some form of relief be adopted.

However, I believe the time is drawing closer for an honest reassessment of modern medical practice. Otherwise, the private practice of medicine as we know it today faces a breakdown into an even more impersonal sort of relationship between doctor and patient. This is especially true in an era of mechanical robots.

Need For Doctor's Assistants

You, as the patient, must be heard. Otherwise, your visit to the doctor cannot be considered a satisfactory one—either from your own or the doctor's viewpoint. You must have time to unburden yourself; your doctor must have the time to listen and learn.

But the stumbling block remains: there are only a few hundred thousand doctors responsible for the health of over 200 million Americans.

Here is a possible solution: Train a few hundred thousand mini-doctors. Not MDs but mds. They might be called MDAs (Medical Doctor Associate).

Primarily, their purpose will be to listen fully and patiently to the complaints of the sick. They will have been trained in medical school or in post graduate departments of universities in the fundamentals of physiology, pathology, biology, psychology, psychiatry, so that their actual confrontation with the sick will be medically oriented. A college or nursing degree will be an essential requirement. Also a concentrated one- or two-year course in medical fundamentals which will offer the degree of MDA. Internships will not be required. Neither will diagnosis or treatment be a part of their curriculum.

The MDA's essential purpose will be to delve deeply and unhurriedly into your physical and emotional complaints. To give you the opportunity to express yourself fully; and then turn over to your doctor a summary report. Unburdened by the essential art of history-taking, your doctor will have at least twice as much time to diagnose and treat you and his other patients.

I envision hundreds of thousands of yougsters who would grasp at the opportunity to become MDAs—many who are returning as medics from the armed forces. Within a few years (while medical schools are trying to "catch up") we would have a nation of satisfied patients who have been given sufficient time to ventilate their anxieties; and unencumbered physicians who have been given the time to evaluate the "whole" patient.

For many years now, medical service by physicians has been unable to parallel the rapid growth of the population. Paramedical assistance seems an adequate solution for better medical care. An MDA in the office of every MD will automatically free your doctor from the shackles of time. No longer will you have to complain about "not being heard."

At present, I see no other way to prevent heartless mechanical robots from becoming responsible for the health of millions of Americans. If anxiety is the human being's lot, the cold hands of a robot will not bring him the emotional comfort he craves.

Iatrogenic Disease

Meanwhile, under existing conditions, doctors need to be especially tactful in the care of their patients. In this age of anxiety it doesn't take much to throw many patients into emotional imbalance.

In a book published 20 years ago (now out of print) I wrote about iatrogenic disease—disease produced by doctors.

At that time it was practically an unheard of term. I began one chapter: "Doctors sometimes produce imaginary heart trouble in their patients. To quote Dr. R. D. Gillespie in the British Medical Journal: 'There is a chapter omitted from medical textbooks which might be headed Iatrogenic Disease; that is to say, disease produced by doctors.' "

I went on: "This condition may be found wherever there are doctors and patients—anywhere from Arabia to Zanzibar. It respects no national boundaries—the physician needs to keep reminding himself constantly that what faces him across the desk is not an emotionless, unthinking machine to be repaired, but another anxious human being. He needs to remind himself that he himself on some occasions knew fear and hopelessness when he or a member of his family was sick.

"Remembering, he will tread lightly and watch his step. He will guard against putting even a drop of gasoline on the patient's smouldering fire of anxiety. And unguarded words long silences, quizzical facial expressions—these are the measure of the gasoline."

Why do I reminisce? Because I have been happy to read much lately in the lay press about iatrogenic disease. It is being human to find some small satisfaction in having written about it as long as 20 years ago when the term "iatrogenic" was practically unknown (and unaccepted).

For those of you interested in learning more about it I recommend an excellent article in the August 22, 1970, issue of *Saturday Review.* It was written by the editor, Norman Cousins. It is called: "Can Doctors Cause Disease?" It will benefit doctors as well as their patients. Here are a few pertinent quotes. "The late Dr. Emanuel Libman said: 'A cardinal rule for physicians, ancient even in the time of Hippocrates is *primum non nocere* (first: do no harm).'

"It is the doctor's philosophy of medicine that has to serve as the solid base of his practice. The doctor's respect for life, his special qualities of compassion and tenderness—even under the most devilish of circumstances—these are the vital ingredients of his art."

Having read this article by a layman, doctors will come away better doctors, and patients better patients. As you have been hearing for years, the practice of medicine is an art as well as a science.

Why Procrastination?

Often a concerned wife will say, "I can't understand why my husband keeps putting off examination." Or a husband will say, "I know she's worried about herself. Why doesn't she go to her doctor to find out the trouble?"

I tell them that if I had only one guess I would say it was because they are afraid to face up to the truth. It is natural for any human being to be anxious and concerned about the prospect of possibly being told he has serious heart disease, cancer, emphysema, or one of scores of other threats to his health and life. It is for this reason many sit in discomfort on the picket fence of indecision and procrastination. They prefer not to know. So they sit there hounded by daily fears, thinking they have something serious the matter, but not really knowing.

Anxiety Often an Unnecessary Burden

I am not trying to be Pollyannish when I say that quite often such fears are unnecessary burdens. For example, here is a man with pain in his left shoulder, extending down to his chest. He's afraid to go to the doctor. He thinks he surely has some coronary heart trouble. It turns out to be a bursitis. "If you only knew how much I worried for weeks before coming here," he says.

A young woman with a harmless lump in her breast is sure she is dying of cancer, but later admits she "didn't have the nerve" to find out.

Another woman says, "I'm working up my nerve to go to my doctor, but I'm afraid of his diagnosis. For two to three years I've had immediate urgency to move my bowels after eating. It is like diarrhea coupled with a feeling of constipation. I've been telling myself it's nerves. But there's a history of bowel cancer in my family, and natually I'm afraid that I may have it." Result of examination months later? No cancer. Diarrhea was due to deficient amounts of hydrochloric acid in her stomach.

Such are only a few examples in which the doctor's verdict is good rather than the expected bad. If there is any moral it is this: If in doubt, see your doctor early. The sooner he discovers serious illness the better your chances for recovery.

And what a relief if he tells you, "I can't find a thing wrong that a few pills and special diet won't help." It makes good sense to jump off that uncomfortable picket fence early. Too many anxious patients suffer unnecessary discomfort simply because they are too scared to discover the truth.

Happiness is going to your doctor thinking you have cancer and learning the lump is a benign, fatty tumor. Happiness is having a pain in your chest, and worrying about a coronary attack and having him tell you that it's referred pain from shingles. Happiness is having your uterus out and learning it doesn't mean "the end of the world"—sexually or otherwise. Happiness is having a heart skipping all over the place and learning that the trouble is due to harmless "extrasystoles" or "premature contractions"—often found in the healthiest of hearts. Hundreds of thousands of Americans go through life as invalids or semi-invalids unnecessarily anxious—thinking the worst.

Psychosomatics

Many people still believe that psychosomatics is nothing but a fancy word cooked up by doctors who want to impress patients; or by those who can't discover what's really wrong so fall back on the vague diagnosis: "It's only your nerves."

Although I admit that in many cases "it's only your nerves" is a lazy way of making a diagnosis and missing what's really wrong with the patient, it is also true that psychosomatics is as real now as it was when Hippocrates believed in it about two thousand years ago. Mind and body are inseparable.

A patient complains: "My stomach is always upset lately. I admit that I've had quite a few family worries. But I think it's impossible that 'nerves' are the cause of my trouble. My doctor says they are. He calls it by the highfalutin name, psychosomatics. He has taken all kinds of tests and X-rays. We have even had consultation with the best doctors around here. But nothing shows up but 'nerves' as the cause of my trouble. Is that possible?"

Possible? Yes. If her doctors had said 'nerves' before giving her the complete workup she mentioned, I might say, "Forget psychosomatics until they are as sure as they can be that an ulcer, bad gall bladder or something else isn't causing your trouble." But they've sought—and haven't found. Probably there's something in her history which reinforces their belief that nerves are at the root of her problems. By her own admission she has "family worries."

I recall one businessman, apparently calm and unafraid, who confessed that he invariably vomited before an important conference in which he had to stand up and speak before a board of directors.

I've treated scores of men and women whose migraine headaches could be traced directly to tension in business or family life.

One woman developed a skin eruption whenever her salesman husband returned from his frequent business trips. She used to scratch so hard that she bled. After she was divorced, her skin was as velvety as a baby's. Later she admitted that she disliked him intensely—and that her skin trouble was undoubtedly due to "nerves."

I could go on with hundreds of examples out of my files, but better believe it: Psychosomatics isn't just a fancy word. Like a mountain, it is there—to be climbed. One method is by using psychotherapy.

Everyone has experienced the relief from being able to tell a close friend his troubles: "to get things off his chest." In mild cases of depression or anxiety that's just what the doctor lets the patient do. The doctor listens patiently while the sick and troubled one talks out his troubles—encouraging and reassuring him while the patient slowly gains an insight into what is behind his problems. For the best results, the doctor must be a good listener and the patient an uninhibited talker. If the difficulty is more deep-seated, then a psychiatrist may be necessary for the more probing, lengthy type of psychotherapy known as psychoanalysis. Guided by his analyst, the patient nestles on his couch and undergoes treatment for months or years. Whatever the type of psychotherapy, the patient must talk about himself and the physician must guide him, so he can reconstruct his life, accept himself as a human being, and learn to live with himself. Not always easy. Not always successful. Nevertheless, psychotherapy is a useful instrument in the doctor's little black bag of treatments.

Thoughts and Afterthoughts on Chapter 2

1. Patients' number 1 complaint: "My doctor doesn't give me enough time."

2. Time is synonymous with warmth and care.

3. Lack of communication: "I wish my doctor would tell me exactly what type of illness I have, what medicine to get, and what results can be expected."

4. Busy doctors should reserve time for "talk sessions."

5. Doctors should be generous with medical explanations —if necessary, using pictures and diagrams.

6. Make sure the patient knows what he *doesn't* have as well as what he *does* have.

7. Time is drawing closer for an honest reassessment of medical practice and of the doctor-patient relationship.

8. MDAs (Medical Doctor Associates) may need to be trained to take the load from doctors who are continually fighting the hands of the clock.

9. Iatrogenic disease (disease caused by doctors) continues to be a problem. The physician needs to keep reminding himself constantly that what faces him across the desk is not an emotionless, unthinking machine to be repaired, but another, anxious human being.

10. Anxiety often causes the patient to procrastinate. This is a barrier to recovery.

11. Hundreds of thousands of Americans limp through life as invalids or as semi-invalids unnecessarily anxious—thinking the worst.

12. Psychosomatics isn't just a fancy word.

3

How To Choose
Your Doctor

In these few words I can't even pretend to be able to give you a sure-fire formula for choosing a good doctor. But it is important that I try. For it is true that the anxious patient needs to find one who meshes with his own scarecrow temperament, or it is all a waste of time.

Let me explain. Suppose you know he has graduated from one of our finest medical schools; and that he has had postgraduate hospital training; and that he is no stranger to all the new-fangled medical diagnostic tests and treatments; and that he is the "busiest doctor in town." These are good qualifications—but they are not enough.

A doctor cannot be a *good* doctor unless he is a *good* listener.

Two out of three patients who come to a doctor's office come not because they are physically sick but because they are in emotional turmoil. And even the 33 per cent who are physically ill suffer from a superimposed, large element of anxiety and concern about themselves.

If your doctor is to treat you as a human being and not as a guinea pig, he must take time out to listen patiently to your troubles. Otherwise he cannot help you as much as he might. All the aspirin in the world will not cure your headaches if they are due to the fact that your business is failing. Anti-high blood pressure drugs will fail their mark if your trouble is being intensified by constant bickering and misunder-standing at home. And sedatives and tranquilizers will not promote relaxation and sleep if your "real trouble" is worry over a son or daughter who has made an unhappy marriage, or is on marijuana or heroin.

Only a doctor with large ears can help you. He is the one who reserves sufficient time for your appointment so that you do not feel as if he is rushing you because he has so many patients in his waiting room. You must find a doctor to whom you can talk as a friend as well as a doctor. He must be willing to hear you out in patience and understanding.

Don't Choose Haphazardly

Doctors come in all sizes and shapes—both physically and intellectually. If it's true that you can't judge a book by its cover, it's also true that you can't judge a doctor by the elegance of his office, by the cut of his clothes, or by the shape of his moustache (if he has one).

The kindly, hail-fellow physician may be the one with little heart and compassion. The stern-visaged healer whom you might think has no sympathy at all, may be the one who is all heart.

But the puzzle has more pieces to it than that. There is more involved than understanding and the ability to empa-thize. How about his actual ability? How do you go about determining that?

Well, there are two ways: the proper and the improper.

Here are some of the improper ways to size up a doctor's medical ability. For example, many patients will say: "I just know my doctor must be extra special. His waiting room is always jammed. He *must* be a good doctor. Otherwise, why should he be such a busy man?"

Another says: "I didn't just walk into any doctor's office when I came to this town. I asked my neighbor who he was using. I figured that what's good enough for him should be all right for my family."

Others have given me this reason: "I've heard he's very reasonable. Charges much less than anyone else around here."

There are many other factors that influence choice: "You can always depend upon him. He'll come out to visit you day or night." Or: "He's so friendly." Or: "He's so gentle." Some have actually chosen a doctor because he "doesn't ride around in a Cadillac."

Such methods of choice are the most reckless form of gambling. When you sit in for a friendly game of poker, or bet on some nag at Belmont or Pimlico, you are merely wagering money. However, when you place a bet on a doctor who has nothing more than an MD to recommend him, you may be gambling away your very life and that of your family.

Please remember that the MD and a state certificate give a man the right to treat anyone. But it does not follow that *any* doctor is the man for you or your's. Your job is to look over the field before making your decision (unless, of course, you are faced with an emergency, at which time any doctor is welcome).

Some Dos and Don'ts

Here is a mixture of *dos* and *don'ts* that will help you:

1. If you intend to move to another city, be sure to ask your doctor to recommend a new doctor. If your present

doctor has proved himself to you over the years, it is unlikely he will recommend anyone who is not up to his own standards.

2. Suppose your present physician doesn't know of anyone where you are going? Then better get busy. Finding the proper doctor is more essential than straightening out all the details about getting your phone installed, connecting the gas and checking on the electricity. Yet I'll wager that not more than five out of every hundred are aware of this.

3. If you live in a village or a small town, I guess you won't have much choice. However, if you are in a town or city that has a local medical society, I suggest that you write to the secretary for a list of the qualified men. In other words, find out who are the recognized specialists in the various fields: pediatrics, cardiology, internal medicine, obstetrics and gynecology, dermatology, orthopedics, etc.

The secretary will usually furnish a list of a few names from which to choose. Nobody knows doctors as well as their brother physicians. The medical society will know who is certified in his specialty; and who is qualified to be a member of the American College of Physicians or College of Surgeons. A measuring stick for a good general practitioner is the Academy of General Practice.

4. If you cannot get the information you want from the medical society, you might ask your local hospitals for a list of their active staff. Hospitals are quite jealous about passing out these appointments. If you find a name in which you are interested on one of these lists, chances are that you are on the trail of a reputable physician.

5. In all fairness I want to say that many an MD who is not on a hospital staff or accepted by one of the specialty boards, may be a fine physician. Nevertheless, you can feel more certain of your choice with the man who has "proved himself" to his peers.

6. Now that you have a name or two to choose from, you can fall back on the usual hit-or-miss method that most people use: you can ask your neighbor how she likes Dr. Jones; or, your husband can ask someone at the office if he uses (or has heard of) Dr. Smith. From these people you will get information that will round out your inquiry. In addition to having proof of his scientific ability by your previous investigation, you will now hear the layman's reaction to his willingness to make house calls, night calls. You will know if he is friendly, sympathetic; if he gives you sufficient time at the office; if he is reasonable in his fees.

7. The *don'ts* bear repetition. Don't depend upon hearsay evidence of a doctor's ability. Don't go to a doctor simply because you've heard he is "cheap"—that he doesn't charge much. No doctor, however able, can practice good medicine if he turns out patients at the rate of ten or twelve an hour (at lower fees). Chain-belt methods may make for efficiency in a factory, but usually spell failure when used in a doctor's office. Don't choose the doctor with the overfull waiting room.

8. Here is an important tip: having chosen your family doctor, let him be the one to make referrals to other doctors. In other words, if you need surgery don't *you* do the choosing. He will be better able to know who is best for you. Likewise if you have a skin eruption, a nose or throat condition, a gynecological problem. If the condition is out of his sphere, let him choose the best qualified man. Don't go to the specialist *first*, and tell your family doctor about it later.

9. So many people curl up in fear and frustration when the question of medical consultation arises. If they have had a family doctor for years they are especially concerned about hurting his feelings.

For example, suppose someone in the family has been stricken with a heart ailment. They have complete confidence in their doctor; nevertheless Aunt Tillie or brother Jim would feel better having another medical opinion. What to do? How to go about it?

I have been telling people for years that any doctor worth his salt will consent graciously to a request for consultation. He knows that it is not for lack of confidence, usually. The motivating force is to prevent any "guilt feelings." If the patient does not recover, people want to feel they have "done everything" for their sick one. Consultation is one way of doing that. Another motivation, of course, is the wish to do everything possible for the family member who is critically ill.

Therefore, I suggest that if you ever want consultation, never hesitate to ask for it. And not as a favor from your doctor. It is your right.

10. I hope you remember these suggestions. They come from one who has been in the front lines of practice for over 25 years. If you are sensible in the choice of your doctor, you will increase your odds for good health and longer life.

Unfortunately, the limited number of physicians has narrowed our choice of physicians. These days some doctors are so busy that they will not accept new patients. It almost seems silly to recommend ways to choose a good doctor when most people would be happy to get "any" MD to accept them for treatment. Yet, the principle remains: If at all possible, try to make sure you latch on to a good one. Even though there are not enough doctors to "go around," it's worth the extra effort to discover one who is compassionate as well as able.

How to Get Your Money's Worth

You try to get your money's worth when you buy a house

or a car or piece of furniture. Are you as good a shopper when you go about getting the most valuable commodity of all—your health?

In a drugstore the other day I overheard one man say to another: "Bill, I'm going shopping today. My wife's going to have a baby. We've never needed an obstetrician before. I have a list of three of the best men in town. Just got the names from the medical society. I'm taking off the afternoon to talk to them or to their nurses. The one with the most reasonable fee gets the job. If I can save fifty dollars or more I'll consider it a good afternoon's pay."

His friend's eyes widened. "Hey," he said, "that's a new one. Never heard of anyone doing it. Good idea, but it sure takes more nerve than I've got."

But it shouldn't. Most obstetricians welcome a chat to discuss fees—as do other doctors. One busy man I know admits that his fees are quite high. "I can take care of just so many patients," he says. "If a young man comes along wanting me to deliver his wife and screws up his face when he hears the fee, I gladly refer him to one of the younger, well-trained obstetricians. In that way, everybody is happy. There are no misunderstandings or recriminations."

I believe that most people can be saved the embarrassment and discomfort that comes the first of the month on receiving an unexpectedly large doctor's bill. All they need to remember is that when they engage a doctor they are really "buying health."

You ask the shoe clerk, "How much?" Ask your doctor how much the series of injections is going to cost. How much his fee will be for removing your gall bladder or your son's appendix. Perhaps he can only give you a rough estimate of how much the hospital bill will be (including nurses, laboratory fees, etc.), but at least you will know how much the

operation will cost. Believe it or not the modern doctor has
been conditioned to openly discuss fees. It used to be taboo
years ago. If he doesn't bring up the financial end these days
it is only because he doesn't want to be falsely labeled
"mercenary." Keep remembering that you are the "buyer."
It shouldn't take nerve to ask, "How much?"

Patient's Time Valuable, Too

An acquaintance told me the other day that he had a run-in
with his doctor a few months ago. "I had been going to him
for years. He is a fine fellow and an excellent doctor. But
lately, because he has become so busy, he has got into a bad
habit. I keep my appointment on time but I have to wait
around in his office as much as one or two hours before his
nurse ushers me in. The last time I was there I actually missed
out on a big business proposition at my own office. I gave
him an ultimatum. I told him that my time was worth more
in dollars and cents than his. That if I could not get in within
a reasonable time, I'd have to find a doctor who saw fewer
patients with the idea of giving better service."

I told him I agreed. I was sure that from now on, he
wouldn't be kept cooling his heels so long unnecessarily.
There are times, of course, when an emergency prevents the
doctor from keeping his appointment on time. But when it
becomes a habit, it indicates that you had better tell him how
you feel about it. Usually, he will try to "space" his appointments in the future.

Another way to insure better value from your doctor-visits
is to have a doctor who is unhurried when you at last get into
his inner sanctum. Many patients complain that they get the
"brush-off" in five or ten minutes. "I know my doctor is a

very busy man," they say, "but I don't even get the time to tell him what is really on my mind. The nurse gives me an injection and the next thing I know, I'm outside the office."

If this is true with your own doctor, then it is up to you as the "health buyer" to complain about the service. Having been in practice myself for so many years, I know how distressing it is for a doctor to have to work against the clock day after day. But it can be remedied. In my own case I saw only a limited number of patients a day. Patients found time to "let down their hair"—especially the anxious ones who needed so much reassurance.

Are Doctors Hard-hearted?

I have a friend who says that most doctors get hard-hearted after a few years in practice. They see so much illness and grief that after a while it doesn't "touch them." But I happen to differ with her opinion. I told her that the outer cold facade conceals deep feelings of pity for the sick.

I could go on with a long dissertation and give you examples of so-called hard-hearted doctors who hid their inner feelings by an impassivity of countenance; but I know of no doctor who has thrown more light on this question than the venerated Dr. William Osler who wrote in *Aequanimitas* (1899):

"Imperturbability means coolness and presence of mind under all circumstances, calmness amid storm, clearness of judgment in moments of great peril, immobility, impassiveness, or, to use an old and expressive word, *phlegm*. It is the quality which is most appreciated by the laity though often misunderstood by them; and the physician who has the misfortune to be without it, who betrays indecision and worry and who shows that he is flustered and flurried in ordinary emergencies, loses rapidly the confidence of his patients. . . . From its very nature this precious quality (imperturbability) is liable to be misinterpreted, and the general accusation of hardness, so often brought against the profession, has here its foundation. Now a certain measure of insensibility is not only an advantage, but a positive necessity in the exercise of a calm judgment, and in carrying out delicate operations. Keen sensibility is doubtless a virtue of high order, when it does not interfere with steadiness of hand or coolness of nerve; but for the practitioner in his working-day world, a callousness which only thinks of the good to be effected and goes ahead regardless of smaller considerations, is the preferable quality."

By my own experience I have found that the daily battering on his emotions produced by sharing the miseries of his patients, over a period of years, softens rather than hardens the doctor. How the doctor acts, or what he looks like on the outside, is not a true mirror-image of his inner feelings.

Many patients complain that their doctor is unfeeling. He seems unable to put himself in his patient's shoes. Lack of empathy is evident. Then one day the doctor himself gets sick. After recovery the patient feels he is a changed man. Patience takes the place of former hurried relations; real sympathy takes the place of apparent lack of interest.

One patient said recently: "My doctor changed from a cold potato into a compassionate human being. This happened after he had a lot of serious complications that kept him in the hospital for about six weeks after minor surgery. He almost died. When he resumed practice you wouldn't recognize him as the same doctor. He gives you all the time you want. Doesn't care how many are waiting. He listens carefully. He is kindly and understanding instead of abrupt. Isn't this gratifying?"

It surely is. Neither is it unusual for a doctor who has been ill to see his patients in a new light when he resumes practice. The late Charles W. Mayo, MD said, "I think every doctor ought to be sick early in his career. I'd like to see every young doctor feel pain."

He also said, "When I am your doctor I try to imagine the kind of doctor I'd like if I were you. Then I try to be that kind of doctor." (Another era? Another time?)

I have always believed that no doctor—no matter how skillful—can be a good doctor unless he has a large degree of empathy for his patients. Some are born that way. They don't have to get sick to learn.

Of all patients, the anxious patient needs to find an understanding physician.

Importance of Good "Bedside Manner"

At a dinner party the other night, the discussion, as often happens, came around to the definition of a good doctor. A visiting Canadian sculptor said: "So help me, all my doctor has to do is look at me and I feel better. He's the kindest, most sympathetic human being I've ever met. He has what people don't hear about these days: "Bedside manner." Don't you think that the art of medicine is as important as the science?"

Find a doctor with the proper mixture of the two—science and art—and you have the perfect blend. Don't let him go. I've always believed that bedside manner is important in the doctor-patient relationship. I've often been asked to enumerate some essential qualities the good doctor must have. Here are some of these essential qualities:

As I keep saying, your doctor should be a good listener, and this is most important. He should be frank and friendly. He should be tactful—neither scare you to death nor keep important facts from you. He should be compassionate (there goes that word again).

You should get the feeling that he is truly sorry for you and will try everything to help you get out of any mess you are in. If he is conscientious, you will know you can reach him in an emergency—and not be put off by his nurse or by an answering service. He will tell you if he doesn't make house calls (night or day)—but will also promise that his associate or someone else will get to you if necessary. The good doctor will try hard to keep his appointments. You will not have to hang around in the waiting room for hours leafing through old magazines.

He will have a good sense of humor. (You don't want to be greeted by a grumpy doctor when *you* are filled with complaints.) He is willing to discuss fees without getting uptight. If you or your family become concerned about your illness and would like another opinion, he makes it easy for you to have consultation.

Such are only a few of the attributes that go into making a good bedside manner. I'm sure you can think of more. Patients often ask, "But is there such a doctor around?" I assure you there are many dedicated men and women in the profession. They wear themselves to a frazzle fighting against time to take care of their patients to the best of their ability.

Your job as a member of the patient-doctor partnership is to keep seeking until you find such a doctor. Sometimes it's not easy, but I promise you, all doctors are not interested in just making dough. Their greatest satisfaction and fulfillment comes from treating their patients and helping them.

Does a good bedside manner help? Does the sun rise in the east?

One more necessary requirement: that your doctor be like the Sphinx—see all, hear all, but tell nothing. When the patient confides in him, he should feel that his information is confidential.

Every patient should have implicit faith that he can bring a problem of any sort to his doctor without fear that it will be repeated to another living soul. He should believe that it will not be the future subject of conversation between doctor and wife, the occasion for discussion with other patients or doctors, or be the common gossip at cocktail parties or locker rooms at the club.

I believe that the patient ought to feel that any information he gives his doctor should be as safe as if locked away in a vault. Which means, of course, that your doctor is honor bound not to reveal anything to anybody at all—unless he receives your sanction.

You entrust the key to your doctor; he keeps it in a safe place. As Hippocrates put it in the Hippocratic Oath: "Whatever, in connection with my professional practice, or not in connection with it, I see or hear, in the life of men, which ought not to be spoken abroad, I will not divulge, as reckoning that all such should be kept secret."

However, the unsurpassed definition of a good doctor and of good bedside manner and conduct in the practice of medicine is that given by Rabbi Moses ben Maimon, a Spanish Jew who lived from 1135 to 1204 A.D., and who also practiced medicine in Morroco and Egypt. Here is the Oath of Maimonides:

"The eternal providence has appointed me to watch over the life and health of Thy creatures. May the love for my art actuate me at all times; may neither avarice nor miserliness, nor thirst for glory or for a great reputation engage my mind; for the enemies of truth and philanthropy could easily deceive me and make me forgetful of my lofty aim of doing good to Thy children. May I never see in the patient anything but a fellow creature in pain. Grant me strength, time and opportunity always to correct what I have acquired, always to extend its domain; for knowledge is immense and the spirit of man can extend indefinitely to enrich itself daily with new requirements. Today he can discover his errors of yesterday and tomorrow he may obtain a new light on what he thinks himself sure of today. Oh, God, Thou has appointed me to watch over the life and death of Thy creatures; here am I ready for my vocation and now I turn unto my calling."

Thoughts and Afterthoughts on Chapter 3

1. There is no sure-fire formula for finding a good doctor.

2. A doctor cannot be a *good* doctor unless he is a *good* listener.

3. Don't choose haphazardly. Doctors come in all shapes and sizes—both physically, emotionally and intellectually.

4. The hail-fellow physician may be the one with little heart and compassion; the stern-visaged healer may be the one who is all heart.

5. It does not follow that *any* man (or woman) with an MD after his name is the man for you.

6. Reread the Do's and Don'ts on how to choose a doctor.

7. In medical care, you should learn how to get your money's worth.

8. Complain of inefficient service—like waiting for hours after promptly keeping your appointment.

9. A good bedside manner is still important in these ultrascientific days.

10. No. Most doctors aren't "hard-hearted."

11. Your doctor is honor-bound not to reveal any of your intimate secrets.

12. Hippocrates; and the Oath of Maimonides

4

Anxiety Often Hides Behind Symptoms

One patient said:

> I might have saved myself a lot of money and time and hurt if I had only admitted to my doctor the real reason I came to him. I was afraid. I was anxious. But, as a grown woman, I thought it would be a silly admission of weakness. Don't you think it is true that many anxious patients say "this or that" bothers them, but don't want to admit it's being scared?

I told her she made an important point. I recall many patients, outwardly calm and serene, who I put through long X-ray investigations, scores of laboratory tests, looking for an ulcer or gall bladder trouble as reason for their symptoms. All this rigmarole might have been prevented if they had said at the first visit, "Doctor, I'm here because I suffer from anxiety. I live like a coward. I'm afraid to go out in public, afraid to take an auto trip, afraid to sit in a movie or in church. I don't know what brought this on, but I'm scared of myself and of everything."

Admit Your "Silly Fears"

Many anxious people have "target areas." One will complain of indigestion—gas, fullness after eating, actual pain, etc.—when the real, underlying cause is anxiety. Another will think he has heart disease because he suffers from attacks of sudden palpitation or has heart skips or shortness of breath. Still another has a nervous cough. One has diarrhea, one has constipation—which is the target of his daily apprehensions.

But whatever the symptoms, most anxious patients know that what bothers them most is fear. If that could be washed away they realize that the various symptoms relating to the bowels, heart, head (or anywhere else) would disappear overnight.

The point I want to stress is that if you have the courage to admit "your silly fears" to your doctor right at the start, you will gain early in your fight against your problem. Too many anxious people lose weeks and months of invaluable time while they put their doctors on the wrong diagnostic trail; trying to discover if they really have organic illness like ulcer, gall bladder trouble, heart disease or other ailments.

Keep remembering that doctors don't look upon admissions of anxiety as "silly fears." Why should they, when they know that we all have it in some form or other. The anxiety state is often a stubborn condition to overcome; the sooner it is admitted and recognized, the better.

Get It off Your Chest

Suppose you feel miserable. You are depressed, have pains and can't sleep. Many persons like yourself suffer emotionally and physically; yet take no positive steps to overcome their discomforts. Good blanket-advice is: Get it off your chest. Tell your troubles to a good listener. Sometimes a friend will do. But more often a professional listener is best—doctor, minister, or lawyer—(if your troubles are due to a faulty intermarital relationship).

Here is an example of an anxious patient who found another way:

Dear Dr. Steincrohn: I am one of those unhappy people who keep it to myself. I know I'd feel better telling it to someone. But there is something in my nature that refuses to share my feelings. I hate to expose myself. I'd feel as if I were naked and walking down our main street during the noon hour. All I am concerned with is myself. I can't seem to be interested in others who have troubles more serious than my own. Poor, poor me! That's how it was for months and months.

Then one day I actually stumbled on a remedy. I was in the doldrums, feeling sorry for myself. I happened to pick up a pen that I had just bought to try it out. I doodled a little and first thing I knew I was writing down how I felt. I wrote pages and pages about how nervous I was. How I wasn't sleeping, what I thought of my husband and chil-dren—and anything else that came into my mind.

First thing I knew I had at least ten pages of written material. I couldn't believe it. I sat down to read what I had put down. It was miraculous, the effect it had on me. Like being my own psychia-trist.

I reread it again, then tore it up into small pieces so nobody could read it. I felt as if I had taken a supertranquilizer. For days I was a different person. Now, whenever I feel "down" I use the same technique: I write it all down—and tear it all up. I believe this simple procedure will help many of your despondent readers.

Mrs. B.

Comment: I agree. I recommend it. Others have been helped. Of course, if it doesn't work, one can always fall back on professional help. But it's worth trying. Talking it out with yourself (on paper) often makes life seem more worthwhile. It is like a petcock that lets out the stored-up steam in a boiler—like guilt, hostility, self-incrimination, anger, resentment and some of the other bad emotions.

Good and Bad Emotions

For thousands of years both doctors and their patients have realized that emotions exert a profound influence on their health. High blood pressure, heart disease, ulcer, diabetes, arthritis, colitis, and scores of other diseases are somehow tied in with how we feel emotionally.

Resentment can bore a hole in your stomach. Anger can light the fuse in an aching joint. Tension can start the anvils pounding out a headache. Anxiety can spill more sugar in the diabetic.

Recently I was asked: "I suppose everyone knows that getting upset and letting the emotions run riot is not good for the health. But what are the bad emotions? I've heard so much about good and bad emotions that I'm not sure which is which. Would you be good enough to list them? Then I'll know just where I fit into the picture."

I offered the inquirer a list which I said was far from being complete:

Bad Emotions: anxiety, wrath, ire, indignation, resentment, fury, rage, scorn, displeasure, passion, excitement, violence, madness, turbulence, irritation, vexation, temper, peevishness, petulance, exasperation, impatience, animosity, offense and fretfulness.

Good Emotions: mildness, gentility, calmness, good nature, jollity, enjoyment, patience, forbearance, gentleness, placidity, pleasantness, agreeability, love, gratitude, happiness, contentment, peace.

Psychosomatics

Put all emotions into one bag, mix thoroughly, and try to separate and identify, and you have what is commonly known as "psychosomatics." What affects the mind affects the body; and what affects the body affects the mind. Anybody who has ever had a headache or toothache will testify to the truth of that.

I am often asked if psychosomatics is being overdone. My own opinion is that it is "underdone." If the doctor will take the time for a complete history and become acquainted with his patient, he will often find that emotions and not disease are making his patient ill.

If you can learn to neutralize anxiety, or at least remove excess apprehension, you will have taken the one giant step towards a lifetime of fulfillment and happiness.

At the head of the list of bad emotions (and not only because it begins with the letter A) I place *Anxiety*. It is the thorn in the side of living.

For years I have observed patients who complained of

chronic headaches. Only those people were cured completely or helped who at last admitted that they were likely due to tension. Interpersonal relationships with spouse, boss, friends or children triggered and exploded their headaches. "They give me a pain in the neck," was a common complaint. What that actually meant was that their neck muscles contracted hard on nerves and blood vessels.

Taking aspirin, applying heat and massage helped only temporarily. Honest inventory was essential to improvement. Also an expression of their anxiety to a compassionate listener—preferably the doctor. And the admission that they had feelings of guilt, shame, inadequacy, helplessness or envy. Whatever such reasons, they at last added up to emotional conflicts such as frustration, hostility, anger and anxiety. I discovered that many of these patients were perfectionists: rigid, worrying too much about their health, jobs and family.

Write That Book!

> *Dear Dr. Steincrohn:* Tuesday night my mother called me and suggested I read your column in Monday night's *Sacramento Bee*. I thumbed through the paper and found it on page A-16. I saw the heading and knew exactly why she had advised me to read it.
>
> To make a long story short, I am 20. My husband and I just lost our first child. I was in my sixth month of pregnancy. I have always been what I consider to be a healthy person. Never suffered more than the common cold or German measles up until my miscarriage.
>
> I began to have fears that I am really sick inside. "Am I going to die? Was the miscarriage due to my heart?"

I'll tell you doctor, it's really strange how your mind plays tricks on you. My husband began telling me I was becoming a hypochondriac. But I really was having chest pains and stomach pains and this and that.

After repeated trips to the doctor and endless nights of lying awake worrying, I finally confessed my fears to my doctor. Not until then did he realize how much I had been worrying. I had kept it from him. At last I explained that my nerves were as jumpy as the Prize Frog at Angels Camp and then some.

Anyway, a long talk with him, a physical going over and just plain putting everything in the right perspective helped me come to the realization that I'm really Okay. And when I stopped beating my head against the wall and told myself to relax about it all, well you've probably guessed by now —no more chest pains. I feel great. I look eagerly now to many years of good health, more pregnancies and a less nervous husband.

But the main reason I'm writing this is to ask you, Dr. Steincrohn, that some day you write that book about Anxiety. I'm sure there are many people that may be benefitted by it and many minds set at ease. I'm so glad those months of worrying are over for me. I can look confidently to the future now and not lie awake night after night worrying about myself.

(Mrs. O.—Sacramento, California)

Note: Here it is, Mrs. O. Like many others who have written to me about their anxieties, I consider you a co-author with an intense desire to be helpful to those who live half-lives of frustration, anxiety and hopelessness.

I have many co-authors—the thousands of anxious patients I have treated during my practice. I learned from them what it is to suffer daily with no hope. Many who recovered from their chronic anxiety gave me practical tips that were helpful in my management of other sufferers. So the only credit—if any—that I take from writing this book I share willingly with those who not only suffered themselves, but were intent on helping others.

In many instances I have realized that a doctor can learn much from his patients. Often, their advice is even more practical and helpful than his own. Having lived through it, they *knew*. So my ears have been open. Whenever advice seemed potentially helpful to others, I never asked for top billing. I willingly and freely said to some distressed soul, "Here is what I heard from another patient. It helped her, perhaps her advice will be more helpful than mine."

For example, here is what I consider advice better and more graphically given than I could give myself. It was offered by a patient trying to help a 30-year-old friend suffering so badly from the symptoms of anxiety that she was appalled by the very thought of having to live until 70. She said that she was going to butt in with suggestions—even though unasked. I asked her to put them down on paper so I could transmit her suggestions to her friend, and to others.

First: You've been told what's wrong. Nothing. So stop doctor-shopping. No one has an instant cure for nervousness. Keep on taking the tranquilizers your doctor has prescribed until you are accustomed to being calm. Then keep a few at hand for flare-ups if they should occur. Never take more than the doctor prescribes, or you'll find yourself climbing walls for a few uncomfortable hours!

Have your husband talk to your doctor because your husband's support is essential. By this time he probably thinks you are a nut! Or worse!

You can alleviate your own symptoms. Remember your body has breathed successfully without your active help. So stop consciously breathing. I know that hyperventilation is panic-making, but remember you will not die! Your doctor will tell you what to do to overcome the episode of apparently uncontrollable fear. (More about hyperventilation elsewhere.)

Second: And this is the difficult part because from here on out it's up to you. However, unless you want to spend the rest of your life in a state of panic, you will act now. (Well, you don't want a divorce and a bunch of neurotic kids, do you? After all, don't you set the tone of your household?)

Sit down, look at yourself in a mirror and say to yourself: I am a reasonably intelligent, introspective woman who worries too much (never mind about what). I am no longer going to punish my family because I have this weakness. Having done this, decide what the important things in your life are and ruthlessly drop the rest. Or, at least declare a moratorium. If the list is not reduced so your family can be happy, healthy, well-fed and well-clothed, you aren't the woman I take you for.

Third: Since your activities are somewhat circumscribed (and we all crawl before we run) and since, above all, the children should not suffer, decide between your husband and yourself how you will share your responsibilities. Daddy: movies, dinners at a restaurant, visiting Grandma, Sunday drives, etc. Mommy: Homework helping, cookie-baking with the kids, reading stories, nature walks, chats, etc. Family: Entertaining friends, drive-in movies, zoos, picnics, marshmallow roasts. The list is endless.

Fourth: Stop always thinking about yourself. This is most difficult. This is where you must be really ruthless. To come out of yourself turn on a talk-show or an all-news station on the radio. Get involved in daytime TV, if you have the time. Read whenever you get the opportunity. If you can't concentrate, then read out loud.

Tell stories to your pre-schoolers. Make them up. They'll think you are a genius. But until you can handle your thoughts don't allow time to think them. If it takes you a long while to get to sleep, keep redecorating your house in your mind or building a new one. In any case, do not mull and mull about how unlucky you are.

Fifth: Pamper yourself. Slim down if you need to. Make it a project. Color your hair. Try new make-up. Bathe in goat's milk! Do something every day to please only one person—you!

If you can afford it, hire a high school girl as a mother's helper in the afternoons as often as you can—while you do what? Milk that goat? Nap? Bone chicken breasts to stuff? Whatever pleases you—just you.

I have assumed during all this that your husband

has been reasonable. He has stopped being dismayed and confused (the conference with the doctor should have helped). He is no longer sneering or nagging. He at last realizes that you are truly not being obstreperous; that he is not going to continue for years to live in this totally unsatisfactory manner.

Up and at 'em my girl. It's up to you to do the dirty work. Don't despair. As a fracture heals slowly, so will you eventually. It takes time, energy and perseverance.

My last words of advice for you, my dear. Do you remember the enthusiastic, emotionally, secure, happy person your husband married? Don't you remember that it was impossible to be depressed because you were always smiling and laughing? Well, resurrect her! She's only sick—not buried. You may get cramps in your cheeks, but both you and your husband will be happy and grateful to see her smile again.

Sorry about that—it was almost my last word. I repeat, it will take time for you to rejoin the human race. Don't rush it. Test the water; if it's too cold, wait a while. But don't become, while waiting, such a self-satisfied cowardly recluse that you are a bore. Keep testing but don't keep talking about it. That bores everyone around you. Let your problem be only your own and husband's secret. Mostly yours.

I know I may have seemed harsh and unsympathetic at times, but really what is there to do but tell the truth? There are no panaceas for anxiety. Nevertheless, it can be overcome with the help of a sympathetic doctor, a supporting family; but it has to be contained before inertia and lethargy become a fixed way of life.

I know that panic paralyzes. But that was over 10 years ago. Using the methods I have suggested to you, I can now smile and laugh. I cry only at a sad movie—which is a heck of a lot more than I was able to do at the age of 30.

Believe me, chronic anxiety is not a hopeless and permanent burden.

(Mrs. B.)

Take it from one who has been through it. And from having seen many recover like Mrs. B., take it from me, too.

But what is important is not to hide behind your symptoms.

"Happy families are all alike; every unhappy family is unhappy in its own way." So begins Tolstoy's novel *Anna Karenina*.

I recall many patients whose illnesses were stubborn problems because they were ashamed to confess what was really bothering them. Instead of taking their doctor into their confidence, they consciously and unconsciously put up roadblocks against his efforts to help.

One apparently happy woman suffered severe attacks of chronic skin disorder which reddened and excoriated the skin of her entire body. The best skin specialists were stumped. They couldn't find the cause; therefore, their treatments were ineffectual.

After a few years of suffering the tortures of constant itching and disfigurement she finally confessed. She wondered if the unhappy relationship which had developed between her husband and herself might be the cause. "What makes it worse," she said, "is that I have had to put forward a happy face all the while. Underneath was a tragic mask. The community thinks we are a happily married couple."

I asked her, "Why didn't you tell this to your doctors earlier?" The answer was the one doctors often hear: "I was too ashamed to tell anyone." A marriage counselor saved their marriage. And, incidentally, cured her skin trouble. In her case, the skin irritation had been visible evidence of inner irritation and marital unhappiness.

There was an executive who developed stomach cramps, which lasted on and off for months. He spent thousands of dollars on trips to various clinics to diagnose the trouble. Not once had he confessed to a doctor that concern about his wife might be the cause. She was a chronic alcoholic and had been running around with other men. For the sake of his children, he refused to bring his problem out into the open.

At last he told me about it. He returned about three months after his divorce saying, "I can eat nails. Haven't had a stomach pain since I fixed what was really bothering me."

If there is a moral, it is this: There's no guarantee that telling your doctor "everything" will cure your anxiety or illness. Nevertheless, it is true that thousands of patients are suffering unnecessary anxiety because they keep important information from their doctors.

Keep remembering that MD also stands for medical detective. Don't withhold any clues, however unimportant they may seem to you. Let him decide—and there is greater likelihood that he will run down and capture the source of your anxiety.

Thoughts and Afterthoughts on Chapter 4

1. Admit your "silly fears."
2. Otherwise, you put your doctor on the wrong diagnostic

trail.

3. "Get if off your chest." Sometimes a friend will do. But more often a professional listener and adviser—doctor, minister, or lawyer (if your troubles are financial or due to faulty intermarital relationship).

4. One way to get rid of some anxieties is to "write them down."

5. Emotions exert a profound effect on health.

6. *Bad Emotions:* wrath, ire, indignation, resentment, fury, rage, scorn, displeasure, passion, excitement, violence, madness, turbulence, irritation, vexation, temper, peevishness, petulance, exasperation, impatience, animosity, offense, fretfulness and *Anxiety* (last, but not least).

7. *Good Emotions:* mildness, gentility, calmness, good nature, jollity, enjoyment, patience, forbearance, gentleness, placidity, pleasantness, agreeability, love, gratitude, happiness, contentment, peace.

8. A doctor can learn much from his patients Often their advice is even more practical and helpful than his own. Having lived through anxiety, they *know*.

9. Stop doctor-shopping. Jump off the medical merry-go-round. If in doubt, ask for consultation.

10. Reread the case history of the woman who discovered that chronic anxiety is not a hopeless and permanent burden.

11. Don't hide behind your symptoms. Don't deceive your doctor. Remember Tolstoy's: "Happy families are all alike; every unhappy family is unhappy in its own way." MD also stands for medical detective. So do not withhold clues from your doctor.

II
Your Heart's in Your Own Hands

5
How To Live
With Coronary Disease—
and Without It

Perpetual motion? Consider your heart. It begins to beat months before you are born; and continues to beat at least once every second, every day, every year of your life.

It is an untiring organ, beating about 100,000 times daily —approximately 40,000,000 times a year. Unlike a clock it does not need rewinding. With only a fraction of a second's rest after every beat, it pumps, and pumps and pumps.

Although unglamorously designated as a pump, I think we should glorify its importance as the most essential organ in the body. Its job is to propel oxygen and nourishment to every near and distant cell (of the many billions) in the body.

When the heart becomes abnormal, other organs necessarily become abnormal. Do you wonder why most apprehensive people are likely to become anxious about their heart? Why they become cardiophobes?

A Connecticut business man told me, "Not until I had my coronary attack did I realize how much everything depends upon a sturdy heart. For weeks I felt like a vegetable until it began pumping like it used to. When we're healthy, too many of us take the heart for granted."

Your Coronary Arteries Are Your Lifelines

Many things can go wrong with a pump; the most usual reason for failure of the human pump is trouble with its own coronary arteries. Their important function is to keep the heart itself alive and functioning normally.

"Just what and where are the coronary arteries?" many anxious people ask. There are actually two coronary arteries, the right and the left. They originate in an area between the junction of the large blood vessel called the aorta and the heart muscle itself.

They run along on the heart's outside surface. Each coronary divides into two large branches. These, in turn, subdivide into numerous smaller branches. They arborize, like trees, and supply every area of the heart's muscle with oxygenated (fresh) blood.

Of all the body's circulation systems, the coronary circulation is the shortest. The heart pumps only about 5 per cent of all the body's blood through the coronary arteries themselves. You might say that the coronary system is like a small trunkline between two large railroads—the systemic (general body) and pulmonary (lung) trunklines.

Fearful as you may be you should know what may go wrong with a coronary artery. The unknown intensifies our anxiety.

For example, the word "arteriosclerosis" (hardening of the arteries) is a common term. But a special type of hardening which commonly affects the coronary arteries (as well as those of the brain, kidneys and elsewhere) is called "atherosclerosis". As a Philadelphia lawyer once told me, "This gets more and more confusing." But it is really not difficult.

All it means is that the inner coat of a coronary artery has become thickened and roughened. Cholesterol, calcium and fatty materials have piled up abnormally and gradually (or suddenly) and have closed off the artery.

Result? Sudden closure and deprivation of oxygen: coronary thrombosis, commonly known as "heart attack." Gradual closure: angina pectoris. (I'll describe these conditions later on.)

We don't know all we need to know about cholesterol metabolism, but we are certain it is in some way tied in with coronary disease, as are other fats in the body.

Neither do we know exactly how other diseases and habits influence atherosclerosis and coronary artery disease. But we know that they do: heredity, high blood pressure, diabetes, hypothyroidism, over-or-under-exercise, tobacco, excess alcohol, emotional stress.

One day, and the sooner the better, we hope we will discover how to prevent and treat atherosclerosis. Until then we had better mind our Ps and Qs and learn the ABCs of coronary disease.

If you learn how to maintain the efficiency of the coronary arteries, you increase your chances for better health and longer life. And you won't be living in daily anxiety, simply because they are less mysterious threats.

How To Prevent Coronary Disease

"My father, two brothers and an uncle died before the age of 45 of coronary attacks. I can't change bad heredity, can I? Then what's the sense of taking care of myself?"

Shrugging his shoulders, the 40-year-old president of a manufacturing plant outside of Hartford sat back, lit another cigarette with a quick flick of his lighter and inhaled deeply. "I smoke at least two packs a day. Why not enjoy them in the few years I have left?"

I could understand his frustration and surrender. I admitted that bad heredity could not be disregarded. For example, in the *New England Journal of Medicine*, Dr. Paul D. White stated: "Coronary artery disease was nearly four times as prevalent among siblings [those having the same parents] of individuals with coronary artery disease as among siblings of persons without it."

Nevertheless, I told the patient I had seen so many exceptions, that any man who goes out of his way to "invite" an attack isn't being reasonable or sensible. Whether heredity is good or bad, there are many things the patient can do to prevent or delay a heart attack.

A New Way of Life

For example, we know that the man who is overweight, suffers from high blood pressure and/or diabetes, smokes or drinks excessively, has high cholesterol, and lives in tension is a prime candidate for an attack of coronary thrombosis.

I recall another patient in his early 40s who had good heredity—yet suffered from this complication of diseases and bad habits. He came in one day saying, "I've made up my mind I want to live. Not only for myself, but for my wife and kids. I know I've been killing myself. Tell me what to do to cooperate."

He finished his cigarette, stamped it out in the ash tray and tossed his pack of cigarettes into my waste basket. A good start. But he was a good finisher, too.

He returned regularly for the treatment of his obesity, hypertension, diabetes, nervous tension and high cholesterol level.

He dieted and lost 35 pounds. The low saturated-fat content in his diet also reduced his cholesterol. Modern drugs brought his pressure down to normal. Pills and diet controlled his diabetes. He lightened his office duties and gave up many civic affairs and interests, all of which lessened his previous tension. Even when apparently well he came in twice a year for routine checkups.

Although the odds were against him ever reaching the age of 50, this apparently doomed man lived to age 67. His resolve to live a New Way of Life was the answer.

No Mysterious Formula for Survival

Many ask for some mysterious formula that will effectually delay the onset of coronary disease. Unfortunately, we have none. But we can offer common sense preventive measures:

1. If you are fat—reduce.

2. If your blood cholesterol level is high—follow your doctor's low saturated-fat diet (cut down on eggs, cheeses, butter, cream, fatty meats, etc.)

3. If you have high blood pressure take the newer miracle drugs as prescribed.

4. If you have diabetes, take your insulin (or special pills) as directed, and try not to go off on eating binges.

5. If you live in tension, find ways to cut corners and relax.

6. If you drink too much, cut down or stop.

7. If you smoke, *Stop.*

8. Exercise? In moderation. Jogging and other methods should not be undertaken without your doctor's permission.

In thousands of cases, such practical, down-to-earth care has prevented or delayed heart attacks.

It is the doctor's job to diagnose and treat; but the patient has a part in it—to cooperate.

Heart Attack: Modern Diagnosis and Treatment

During a heart attack, chest pain is the most common and evident symptom. Yet, the doctor must never misjudge pain. It may be due to an unsuspected condition outside the heart. Often, anxious people are difficult to convince that they are not having a heart attack.

Here is a man with constricting chest pain. Is it due to an attack of coronary thrombosis? No. The cause: hiatal hernia.

Here is another man, doubled up with chest pain. The cause: an attack of gall bladder colic.

And here is still another who "looks like he may be a coronary." But his chest pain turns out to be due to a duodenal ulcer that has kicked up its heels.

Likewise, referred pains to the chest may be due to other noncardiac conditions—spinal arthritis (with pressure on the nerves leading to the chest); severe shoulder bursitis; shingles developing on the chest and causing severe pain before the skin breaks out with the telltale blebs.

But perhaps worst of all is the absence of pain—the "silent coronary." In such patients there is no history of pain at all. Just a little gas or "indigestion." Nothing else. Such apparently mild attacks may turn out to be the most serious, because their presence is unsuspected. The patient keeps on working and is more liable to suffer complications that may threaten his life.

The Typical Heart Attack

However, in spite of the vagaries of chest pain, it still remains the outstanding symptom of the heart attack—when a closed-off coronary artery deprives a section of heart muscle of its normal supply of blood and oxygen, the damaged heart cries out its warning with a plea for help. It's cry is *pain*.

During the typical, severe heart attack the pain spreads across the chest and, maybe, down one or both arms. The patient is covered by a layer of sweat. He is in near collapse. His blood pressure plummets. His heart beat becomes weak and thready, his pulse irregular. He may have nausea and vomiting.

For such a patient, his best chance for recovery is immediate admittance to a hospital's Coronary Care Unit. Here, surrounded by special machines for diagnosis and treatment; by technicians, nurses and heart specialists, any sudden complication can be met with counter-measures within minutes.

During the first forty-eight hours—and during the first two weeks—time is of the essence. Life may depend upon quick action. For example, the heart's rhythm may become crazily upset; immediate treatment with electric shock or special heart stimulants will quickly bring it back to normal cadence.

Modern treatment of coronary attacks is capable of saving hundreds of thousands of lives every year. Whether or not oxygen, blood thinners, prolonged sleep therapy (a newer development in management) are used in treatment will depend upon the doctor's judgment.

Early Diagnosis is Essential

But most important of all is early and correct diagnosis. As I have indicated, the untypical or atypical attack may be overlooked because it is so "mild." (No coronary attack is "mild.")

Here, for example, is a man admitted to the hospital because he has only slight chest pains, some nausea and "not feeling just right." His doctor is suspicious it may be a heart attack. He takes an electrocardiogram. It is negative. Another ECG the next day: negative.

A few years ago he might have been discharged as not having had a heart attack. Now we know better. We keep taking "serial" ECGs (every day or every other day) for at least ten days. In some such cases I have not observed the telltale ECG changes until the second week.

Meanwhile the apparently well patient becomes irked with bed rest. You almost have to sit on him to keep him quiet until you are certain it *is* or *isn't* a heart attack. In addition to serial ECGs we use "enzyme blood tests" which help indicate whether or not the heart muscle has been damaged by closure of a coronary artery. For safety's sake we should reverse the usual law procedure and substitute medical procedure. In other words, any suspected heart should be labeled "guilty" until proven innocent.

Angina Pectoris

Observe this middle-aged man. You see him walking quite briskly along the main street. But for no apparent reason he suddenly stops. It is as if he has pushed down on his brakes and skidded to a halt. He now appears to be staring into the display window of a store.

If you watch him closely you will see that he has no interest in the display. He stands still except for inserting a nitroglycerine tablet under his tongue. He does so furtively so nobody will see. Perhaps he clutches his chest. Within a few minutes after absolute immobility he resumes his walk. This time, more slowly.

By now you are undoubtedly aware you have been watching a man undergoing an attack of chest pain due to coronary disease: angina pectoris.

This may occur in patients whose coronary arteries have gradually become narrowed due to atherosclerosis (the nature of which I have sketched earlier). Unlike the attack of coronary thrombosis, the pain in the anginal patient lasts only for a few minutes. And unlike the former, the coronary artery involved is only partially occluded—and not suddenly and completely shut off by a thrombus (clot).

We know that the seriousness of anginal attacks vary. Some patients have chest constriction only once or twice a week. Others may have as many as a dozen or more seizures a day. We also know that any angina patient who suddenly begins to have increasing numbers of attacks daily is more liable to come down with an attack of coronary thrombosis. Therefore, he should see his doctor for more ECGs and other evaluations.

The clinical diagnosis of angina pectoris is usually easy. The patient complains of chest pain after exertion which extends down one or both arms. The attack is usually more likely if the patient exerts after a heavy meal or after excitement. (Some patients have anginal attacks only during intercourse. Taking a nitroglycerine tablet before the act often prevents the onset of chest pain.)

However, there are times when diagnosis is difficult. The patient's electrocardiograms may be normal. Even special ECGs taken after a Master two-step test may be equivocal.

Newer X-ray procedures outlining the coronary arteries may be necessary to establish the diagnosis.

Some angina patients have no arm pains at all. Still others may complain only of constriction around a wrist after exertion. I recall one patient who always had a "toothache" after extreme exertion. This was an atypical anginal attack. The toothache would disappear after the patient rested for a few minutes.

How to Manage Angina

Once the diagnosis has been made, what can the patient do to help himself? It makes sense to try to neutralize the conditions which caused or aggravated the atherosclerosis in the first place.

Here are some commonsense preventive measures: (they deserve repetition)

If you have high blood pressure follow through in its treatment. (High blood pressure aggravates coronary disease.)

If you have a high level of cholesterol in your blood cooperate with your doctor's suggestions in following a low fat diet.

If you have diabetes mellitus, treat it conscientiously.

If you live in tension, try to manage your job and home life so you "untense."

Do you smoke? QUIT.

Do you overexercise or underexercise? Let your doctor plan your daily exertions for you. Moderation is the answer.

Some few patients are afraid to take nitroglycerine. The name connotes some kind of explosive. I tell them to think of it as a "glycerine" tablet rather than as a "nitro" tablet. Often this removes their anxiety. Another tip: buy nitroglycerine in small amounts. Stale nitroglycerine loses its effectiveness.

Other patients have found less need for nitroglycerine tablets to control pain by taking an ounce or two of liquor daily (in divided tablespoon doses, like medicine). You might try this. If you keep the intake within limits it is unlikely you will become addicted to alcohol.

Suppose you have tried every known medical regime for the treatment of angina. Suppose attacks continue or even increase in number and severity? Then I believe you should have your cardiologist call in a heart surgeon to discuss your case. Many new heart operative procedures have been devised to bring added circulation to the heart. For example, grafting a part of a leg vein to bypass an occluded coronary artery. Yesterday I met such a man. Before operation he could not walk 100 yards without having chest pain. Now he says he plays 18 holes of golf three times a week in complete comfort.

Unfortunately, every angina patient is not a fit candidate for such surgery. But you may be the lucky one. In obstinate angina, you deserve surgical consideration.

Every Wife a Potential Florence Nightingale

During her husband's coronary attack the wife looks on him in helpless fear. She cannot relieve him by ministering to him. All she can do is call for the doctor and an ambulance to get him to the hospital as soon as possible.

But her responsibility does not end there. It is just beginning. During convalescence and months and years that follow she must enact the role of a Florence Nightingale. Common sense, compassion and understanding are three essential ingredients. She must not coddle and spoil him; yet not be too aloof and disinterested. She must try to walk the middle road; not being overprotective—which often produces undue anxiety in the patient—and she must never criticize him for becoming too "lazy."

Emotional reactions to a heart attack differ. Some patients become happy philosophers while others go to pieces.

I recall a friend who had a sunny, happy disposition before his coronary attack. During his convalescence, and for years later, he was grouchy, unhappy and unkind to his family. He developed fears and mental quirks. Fortunately for him and for her, his wife had an angelic disposition and put up with him, doing her best to keep the family together. "He's not the same man I married," she said. "But after all, he has been deathly sick. It's not his fault."

Ways to Keep Your Husband Alive

Hundreds of women have asked me how they can help their husbands stay alive and be happy after a coronary attack. Here are some practical suggestions I have made to them. Admittedly, the partner of a coronary patient has a big job on her (or his) hands.

It begins when he is still in the hospital. She should cooperate with the nurse in keeping visitors away during the crucial first weeks. Well-meaning but premature visitation has produced many serious setbacks in some coronary patients.

If you asked me what is the one most important factor in keeping your husband well I would say: do all you can to remove stress and tension from his life. He should come home to a haven of relaxation. Don't greet him at the door when he arrives from work with tales of woe. Let him sit down and relax with a drink for a half-hour before dinner. Don't rush him into eating the minute he gets home "so dinner won't get cold."

Let him win his little battles so long as you win the war (having a live husband around longer).

Sacrifice some of your social activities. If he is too tired at night, better cancel the party.

Forget Mrs. Jones. Don't force him into working too hard so you can have new furs or a new car.

As his wife you need to have complete understanding of sexual problems that may arise. Have compassion for one whose sexual drive has been weakened, and convince the highly sexed man that lessened sexual activity is for his own good—and not the result of lost desire or love for him.

Don't tempt him with tasty dishes. Don't offer him second helpings even though you are intensely proud of your cooking ability. Remember that excess fat is a nemesis to coronary patients. One man who kept gaining weight after his attack said, "You may think I'm giving you an excuse, but I'm not. When I'm away from home I keep my caloric intake way down. But when I get home my wife is continually pushing food in front of me. Why don't I just nibble at it? I don't want to hurt her feelings, she's such a wonderful cook."

Be a Gentle Nag

I also believe that the wife of a coronary patient should be a gentle nag. She shouldn't keep quiet when he is endangering himself. If he is smoking too much she should let him know it. Likewise if he has reverted to working too hard and too late. If he becomes too lazy she should try to influence him to exercise moderately. On the other hand, if he becomes too active physically, she should try to slow him down.

Months after an attack many a man forgets about its implications as a threat to life and resumes his former work habits. It's the wife's job to try to get him to remember—and to take things easier.

Such men are often too conscientious. They think their business will collapse without their personal direction. They forget that their business "went on as usual" while they were out of circulation for three to six months.

Perhaps many women will think that what I have set down here is too great a sacrifice to make in taking care of a coronary patient. Why keep nagging him? As I have often said and keep repeating: It's much better to be a (gently) nagging wife and keep your husband alive rather than become a "nagless widow."

More Practical Tips on How to Live with Coronary Disease

If you are a coronary patient don't try to diagnose or treat yourself. Don't forsake your doctor. Entrust treatment to him. (If in doubt ask for consultation.) However, I think you will agree that often time stands between you and your physician. When you are in his office the hands of the clock often thumb their nose at you.

For this reason alone, you sometimes can't ask questions—or find answers—that mean so much to you. Lack of complete communication is often due to lack of time—(too many patients waiting in the outer room). Therefore, I offer some tips that will supplement the work of your own doctor. They will make you a better and more cooperative patient. I have already mentioned some of them previously, but not exactly

in the same way. Coronary heart disease is Public Enemy
Number 1. You cannot learn too much about how to put up
your mitts to defend yourself against it. Therefore, let's take
a new look at some more practical tips for survival:

1. *"But I was feeling so good."* It is human to get careless
at such a time. Patients cancel their appointments for the
necessary checkup because they feel good, or they revert to
many former bad habits. Control is essential. Don't tear
down in an hour or day what took so many months and years
of care to build. It's true that many a patient dies on account
of his disposition rather than on account of his disease.

2. *Never overeat.* A full stomach increases the heart's work
at least 30 per cent. It puts too much of a strain on already
weakened coronary arteries. Make it a habit to rest at least a
half-hour after eating. Six small meals a day are better than
taking one overly large evening meal. Don't indulge in
"blockbuster meals."

3. *Learn to control your emotions.* I believe that the
easy-going patient will outlast the one who has outbursts of
temper or "inbursts" of resentment. Tension is the great
enemy of the coronary patient—as it is for the ulcer or
hypertensive patient. For this reason I advise that many
patients take tranquilizers to get over some rough spots.

4. *Job change.* Many coronary patients are able to return to
their former work. Some, however, cannot stand the old
strain. For them, change of job (if possible) will prevent early
complications such as more frequent anginal attacks or another attack of coronary thrombosis. In most cases it is
simpler to return to the same job but learn to cut corners—
not in efficiency but in not taking on extra work. Incidentally, moonlighting is "out."

5. *Luncheon.* Take time out for it. Don't eat off the top of
your desk to "save time." Gobbling a stale cheese sandwich is

no substitute for a relaxing lunch with friends to break up the tensions of the business day.

6. *Vacations*. They are necessities—not luxuries.

7. *Retirement*. Ideally, retirement should be prepared for years in advance. Develop hobbies, physical, psychological and financial resources that will take the pressure off after enforced rest following a heart attack. You may need a change of environment. However, do not just pick everything up and move without trial residence in the new location.

8. *Learn to be a snoozer*. It takes practice. Set aside time after lunch or after dinner for a short nap. It will reinvigorate you more than anything else can. I feel certain that the daily nap has prolonged the lives of many patients by cutting the cords of daily tension.

9. *Don't let the telephone or clock bedevil you.* Few instruments of modern life so constrict us.

10. *ABOVE ALL HAVE FAITH.* This is a powerful antidote against illness. Keep repeating and believing: I *will* get well. If you *believe*, you help your doctor and yourself.

Unsung Heroes

Many bear their suffering heroically; their courage is not trumpeted to the world. But there are many other unsung heroes and heroines: those who day by day, take care of loved ones whose illnesses make great demands on their own lives. Like many brave patients, neither do these bystanders wear medals. Here is an example:

> I found that once I changed my attitude toward
> my husband and his illness (no easy task), there

was noticeable and steady improvement. Our deadliest of all enemies, *fear*, may have taken hold first, and this is most difficult to contend with.

If his head were swathed in bandages or if his body were in a cast, it would be easier to accept, because this is physical evidence of injury and hurt. But we "heart" wives must look beyond the physical evidence of injury, and into the psyche.

My husband's heart attack left him with severe angina pectoris. I massage my husband's back, neck, feet, etc., until my arms burned with pain. For a long time I resented this ritual. But when I turned this "chore" into an unselfish act of love, I no longer welled with resentment. For months I went nowhere because my husband didn't like to be left alone. At first, more resentment on my part. Because he turned into a persistent faultfinder and nagger and would not take on any social obligations. Talking, suggesting, philosophizing falls on deaf ears; and because we do love and do care, our patience dwindles faster.

Then it came to me that he needed my understanding. I learned to take one day at a time; renewed my sense of humor; exercised patience beyond all comprehension; encouraged him; didn't press him. Nothing else mattered. It became a team effort. I looked for no rewards in the form of praise or appreciation. My husband is still alive. And we're sliding into home plate after striking out many, many times at bat.

Is there a Heart's Anonymous organization? Some day I'll start one.

Thoughts and Afterthoughts on Chapter 5

1. Although an unglamorous pump, your heart is the closest marvel to perpetual motion.

2. Your coronary arteries are your lifelines.

3. Atherosclerosis is the common enemy of mankind.

4. We do not know how other diseases and habits influence atherosclerosis and coronary artery disease, but we do know the following exert an influence: heredity, high blood pressure, diabetes, hypothyroidism, overexercise or underexercise, tobacco, excess alcohol, emotional stress.

5. We don't know all we need to know about cholesterol.

6. A new way of life to prevent coronary disease.

7. If you are fat—reduce. If your blood cholesterol level is high—take a low saturated diet. If your blood pressure is high take medicines to reduce it. If you have diabetes, take insulin and a special diet. If you live in tension, find ways to cut corners and relax. If you drink too much, cut down. If you smoke, STOP. Exercise? In moderation.

8. It is the doctor's job to diagnose and treat; the patient's to cooperate.

9. Chest pain, although the most common symptom in heart attack, may simulate other conditions: arthritis, duodenal ulcer, gall bladder attack, hiatal hernia.

10. But sometimes there are "silent attacks" in which coronary disease is overlooked.

11. Early diagnosis is essential in attack of coronary thrombosis.

12. Review methods used in managing angina pectoris.

13. Every wife is a potential Florence Nightingale.

6
Maybe Your Heart Trouble Is Imaginary

Having read about the anxiety reactions to real (organic) heart trouble, you can understand why a patient might become terribly upset after a heart attack. But there is such a condition as imaginary heart trouble, as distinct from organic heart disease. And when I mention "imaginary" I do not do so in a derogatory sense.

I am not intending to tell a patient, "Oh, you're nothing but a hypochondriac. All you're doing is imagining that your heart is bad." For, in my experience, more people suffer heart symptoms who do not actually have heart disease than those who have either coronary disease, hypertensive heart, rheumatic heart and scores of other actual heart conditions.

Some days as many as three out of every four patients who come to the office do so with heart symptoms—yet they do not have organic involvement. They may have heart skips, shortness of breath, swelling of ankles, cough, indigestion, chest pain. At least fifteen million Americans suffer needlessly from heart *trouble*, but not from actual heart *disease*. They should be treated with compassion and understanding. They're scared. Scared to death. They need special handling —like an important package in the mail.

Recently, this complaint:

> I have a very serious problem that is wrecking
> my health. I am the mother of four children and
> am only 33. I continue to fear that I have heart
> disease although three doctors—one a heart
> specialist—have taken all kinds of tests, and all are
> negative. They all say that the muscles and nerves
> on my left side are causing the pain and that my
> heart is all right. But I can't believe them. I think
> they're keeping the bad news from me not to scare
> me.
>
> I've had aching and soreness through my chest
> and back on the left side for a year and a half. I am
> very nervous but think it's because I never feel
> good and am afraid something terrible is wrong. I
> know it's not normal to be checking my pulse and
> taking my temperature all the time. Can nerves
> really cause pains and fear and anxiety like I have?

I told her that "nerves" can simulate almost any kind of
disease. Keep going to the one of the three doctors who
doesn't say, "It's only your nerves—forget it." You need
someone to lean on until you get over your fears. It may take
months before you lose your anxiety—or only days. I wonder
if you would be as fearful as you are if your chest pains were
on your right side instead of on your left? I've often said, if
some people didn't know the difference between left and
right, there might be less imaginary heart trouble.

Incidentally, the heart isn't "way over on the left," it is
really in the left-middle of the chest. Most so-called heart
pains that are felt over the left chest aren't heart pains at all.
Someday your doctor will be able to convince you that what
I say is true.

"Questionable" Heart Disease

Down, boy! Down, boy! Come down from that ivory tower. Nothing makes me so anxious to come down and "mingle" as when I hear a plea such as the following from an unhappy, completely frustrated person.

> I am at my wit's end. I pray that you can advise me. I have been having chest pains, occasionally radiating down my left arm. At times I feel a sort of pressure in the chest and a shortness of breath.
>
> I don't have these feelings often. They come on when I'm sitting and not exerting, as well as when I walk fast. I have had regular cardiograms taken and the doctor keeps saying, "they are not good and not bad"—whatever that means. Recently I had a two-step cardiogram and nearly died after having to go back and forth over those steps 47 times. At the age of 52, I should have had the good sense to quit half way. But I was anxious to find out what was wrong, so I kept on climbing. It took me a day to recover from that exertion.
>
> And what report did I get after the two-step test? The same answer: "Not good and not bad." What kind of an answer is that? Must I go through the rest of my life wondering whether or not I really do have heart disease? Stomach and gall bladder X-rays have been negative. I seem to be all right except for this irritating and worrysome answer: "Not good and not bad." Any advice will be appreciated by a lady who is beginning to feel unhappy about the whole business.

As I said, here I come leaping down from my ivory tower

without parachute—I'm so anxious to stand beside you and give you support. Whenever a patient receives a questionable, half-hearted diagnosis, I am tempted to ask his doctor if he ever heard of iatrogenic disease (discussed elsewhere). In your present state of mind you have the right to ask for consultation so you will learn whether you do or do not have specific changes in your electrocardiograms. You deserve to know. If I received a verdict of "not good and not bad" I'd feel as upset as you by such an equivocal reply.

Incidentally, you bring up an important point about the two-step ECG test. Recently, during a routine physical checkup, my own doctor—a close friend—ordered one for me, too. Halfway through it I felt like you did—*exhausted*. I wanted to quit. Nevertheless, I kept climbing up and down the steps for the prescribed number of trips.

In my case, the report was: "Swell. Your tracing's normal." I was happy to hear it. Nevertheless, I told my colleague that if I'd had a few more steps to climb I'd probably have come down with a heart attack. The Master two-step test is often essential. But when it isn't, why risk a heart attack while exerting on the steps? At least I got a specific reply: "You tracing's normal." If I had been told: "Your tracing is not good and not bad," I would have put my good friend on the spot: "Is it or isn't it normal?"

Some Patients Difficult to Convince

Eliminating a patient's anxiety about his heart is not invariably a simple matter. In spite of assurance from the doctor that the "heart is all right," many fearful patients continue to believe that their heart pump is defective.

A 20-year-old girl said: "I've been having heart skips for

over a year. Just about every day. I've been to at least half a dozen doctors. They all say the same thing: 'You don't have heart disease. It's nerves and anxiety.' All the ECGs, X-rays and laboratory tests have been normal. Yet, I keep worrying about myself. Whenever a skip slaps my chest or turns over in my throat I feel as if I'm going to go crazy or die. Can't six doctors be wrong?"

On the same day a 33-year-old housewife complained: "I think I have heart disease. I get severe pains in my left chest at times, get real dizzy, feel faint and almost black out. During the past six months I have been to a diagnostic clinic in our city, and have had ECGs, blood and kidney tests, cholesterol examinations. The works. All the doctors say there is nothing wrong with my heart. But I'm scared to death to do anything around the house for fear it might kill me."

I told them they were active members in a society of frightened people we call cardiophobes who were difficult to convince they had normal hearts. I agreed that heart skips (called extrasystoles or premature contractions) can be disconcerting and frightening. But I emphasized that skips may occur in the healthiest of hearts. I asked them to have faith that one day they would disappear as suddenly as they came. Medicines and habit control (no smoking, less coffee etc.) would be important, but faith in the doctor is just as important. After weeks of calm reassurance both at last lost their skips and their abnormal heart fears.

Anxiety about Heart Murmurs

One patient reacts with panic to chest pain; another to heart skips or palpitation; and still another to the pronouncement: "you have a heart murmur." There's something about a "leaky" heart that instills fear and an element of oncoming doom in the susceptible.

A young woman was told she has a murmur. Her doctor said, "Forget about it." He gave her no medicine. He told her to live without physical restrictions because it was a functional murmur and of no consequence. But seeds of fear, when planted in an already anxious mind grow to be enormous plants. She lived scared.

I tried to reassure her. I said I was certain that her doctor would have restricted her physical activities if he really believed that the murmur was an indication of a weakened heart. He would have prescribed medicine and advised her how to conduct herself instead of telling her to "forget it." There are all kinds of murmurs, I said. It was likely her doctor believed hers to be functional (not due to disease).

Even though heart valves may be normal in many people, blood surging over the heart valves causes all kinds of sounds (heard with the aid of the stethoscope) which we call murmurs. People with these functional murmurs can go on living their lives as other people do who have no murmurs.

Frightened people require time and patience during an examination. We talked for a while, which in itself is an important part of the examination. I found that she had a minimal murmur of no consequence. X-rays showed no heart enlargement; ECG tests were normal. Careful inventory showed no evidence of heart disease. When it was over I told her that it is true that murmurs may occur in some patients who have hypertensive heart disease or rheumatic heart disease or congenital heart disease. But my examination showed she was free from all of these diseases.

I said to her, "What is really tragic is that so many thousands of Americans limp through life unnecessarily, because they keep thinking that they have heart disease—simply because some doctor has told them they have a murmur. Take you, for instance. You have given up tennis, which you love to play so much. You've given up socializing because you are afraid to stay out late. You are beginning to live like a vegetable. I'll tell it to you now, and not keep repeating it, because repetition doesn't help: your heart is a normal heart. Would I tell you to go out this very day to play a few sets of tennis if I didn't truly believe it?"

She was one of the fortunate ones. A complete cardiac examination and a long talk convinced her that she was a healthy young lady. Within 24 hours she was her normal self again.

I wish this formula was universally effective. It isn't. Too many continue to worry about themselves and the "murmur" in spite of assurances from dozens of doctors they visit. It is for this reason that I believe doctors should resolve never to mention "murmur" to a patient if they have found it is an innocuous one. If the heart is normal why plant unnecessary anxiety in the mind of a nervous patient?

Heart Anxiety No Respector of Age

The fear of heart trouble is not limited to the young or to the old. I have seen it in teenagers as well as in the aging and the aged. When there is a threat to the "life-pump" people react with fear. The length and breadth of the anxiety are unpredictable.

Here is a businessman of 49 who says:

> I have had heart palpitation occasionally since I was 20. It has ruined my life. Although I am a

successful man financially, I have had to forego my
social life and such satisfying relaxation and good
fellowship as golf. I live in daily fear. I got up this
morning asking myself, "Will this be my last day?"
Since I have become older my heart not only beats
irregularly but seems to stall. Then I feel as if I'm
going to black out.

Other symptoms which cause me concern are
fullness and pressure in the chest; a feeling as if the
heart is rubbing against my chest; also a sound of a
squeak or squiggle as it beats. When it pounds it
creates an awful fear.

I think it's possible that I had unrecognized
rheumatic fever when a child, as I remember I used
to have leg aches. I've been worried about heart
damage ever since. I had an ECG about six weeks a
go. The doctor said it was normal and to forget the
whole thing. But my symptoms are still with me.
Shall I forget the whole thing?

Forget? Easier said than done. However, I asked him this
question. Did you have a complete cardiac workup? Too
many remain scared because the doctor has only spent a few
minutes during examination, which consisted only of the
laying on of stethoscope. They wonder how any doctor could
be sure unless he had given them a careful, unhurried examination. When you get home, I said, get in touch with your
family doctor and ask for consultation with a cardiologist.
(Not that a good family practitioner can't do the job. It all
depends upon the time given, as well as on the physician's
training for the work.) Besides, you will feel more convinced
if the examination is performed by a specialist in internal
medicine or cardiology. No good family doctor will refuse

consultation if the patient's welfare is at stake.

The specialist your family doctor decides on, must take the time to take a complete history. Let him decide, I said, whether or nor the leg-aches in childhood were really due to growing pains sometimes associated with rheumatic fever. But remember this, too: not every patient who has rheumatic fever gets heart complications.

Let's assume that all examinations are negative. If your doctor says, "Not guilty. Your heart's okay," then you have a difficult job to do yourself to contribute to your well-being. You have to be able to forget it.

But as I said, it's easier said than done. That is why so many millions of people with strong hearts live in heart-anxiety and suffer needlessly. They drag through life instead of skipping through it. Unhappy and anxious, they live like cardiac invalids even though they have healthy hearts.

For example:

> Yes, I am 38 years old, and what a mess. It all began when I was only 21 in the Air Force. Suddenly, while in my car coming home on a three-day pass, I began to get rapid heart beats. My heart pounded like a trip-hammer. It kept on like that for over two hours. Then suddenly stopped racing. I went into the hospital. They said it was my nerves and gave me a shot.
>
> Since then I've had heart skips on and off. Sometimes they disappear for a few days or weeks, but always return. I've awakened in the middle of the night with skips that scared me to death. When I get up in the morning they may be gone but come back in the afternoon or evening. Each time it happens I'm sure I'm going to have a heart

attack. I can't forget my heart. Think about it all the time.

I have a wife and three boys. I feel as if I'm a burden on them. I don't ever want to go any place. Never play with my kids or even go on a picnic once in a while. I never take a vacation because I'm afraid I'll get sick and be too far away from a doctor. You can imagine how much fun my family has!

I wonder if you'll believe I've been to at least 50 doctors in my lifetime—and not one has told me I have anything wrong with my heart. Yet I keep changing, hoping one will tell me there's something wrong. Can you imagine such a silly feeling? I want one to substantiate my fears. Just one to say, "Yes, there's something the matter with your heart." I have been in the hospital three times and have spent a lot of money my family might have used. But I get the same answer: no heart disease. Nobody has helped me. All they say is "forget it." I wish I could.

Thought and Afterthoughts on Chapter 6

1. More people suffer from the symptoms of imaginary heart disease than from actual organic heart disease.

2. Three out of four patients who think they have heart disease haven't.

3. No patient should receive a questionable, halfhearted diagnosis which leaves him in doubt and trepidation.

4. Eliminating a patient's heart anxiety is not invariably a simple matter.

5. In spite of assurance that the "heart is all right" many fearful patients continue to believe that their heart pump is defective.

6. Heart skips and palpitations in a normal heart can be disconcerting.

7. Heart murmur? There's something about a "leaky" heart that instills fear in the susceptible—even though the heart is normal and the murmur is a functional one.

8. Frightened people require time and patience during an examination.

9. Heart anxiety is no respector of age—it may occur in the very young and in the aged.

10. When in doubt, a heart specialist should be called into consultation.

III
Anxious?
Check Your Blood Sugar, Thyroid and Hyperventilation

7

Hypoglycemia
(Low Blood Sugar)
May Cause Anxiety

My husband has a problem. For several years he has had spells in which he becomes pale, sweat breaks out all over his head, he feels faint, and once almost lost consciousness for a few minutes. His doctor had him in the hospital for three days. He took many tests including brain waves. No blood sugar studies were done. According to the doctor everything was negative. His final conclusion: "You're just a bundle of nerves."

We have a happy homelife, my husband's work is satisfactory, and he has several hobbies. He has never acted like a nervous man. I keep thinking there must be some other reason than "just nerves."

Her suspicions were correct. Blood sugar studies showed that he had hypoglycemia. Proper diet improved his condition. No longer did he complain of these spells of weakness and faintness.

On another day, I received the following questions and complaints:

I was recently advised by my doctor that I have hypoglycemia. What are the chances for curing this ailment?

Another: My doctor says I have low blood sugar. He suggests eating five times a day. No medicine was prescribed. I still have uncomfortable weakness and trembling.

Another: A few months ago I had a glucose tolerance test and my sugar went down to 55 by the third hour. My doctor put me on a diet but is too busy to explain what it is all about. I no longer feel nervous and tense. Only occasionally light-headed in mid-afternoon. Will you explain?

Another: Why are more doctors not aware of hypoglycemia? When a person has all the symptoms associated with it, why do doctors treat him for years for allergies or look for everything else in the book? A glucose tolerance test would either prove or disprove the presence of the condition. Will you please discuss "below normal blood sugar" and its treatment?

It is significant that these four requests came on the same day. They indicate the increasing awareness of low blood sugar as a possible cause of many disagreeable symptoms like trembling, nervousness, fainting, dizziness, weakness, chronic anxiety and, in severe cases, convulsions and unconsciousness.

Surprisingly, some doctors still minimize the effects of hypoglycemia. They say the concept is exaggerated. Maybe so. But too many of the innocent suffer because the guilty go free. Low blood sugar deserves a trial before the patient is dismissed.

Hypoglycemia Can Cause Neurosis

Many patients with hypoglycemia who might have been helped are treated for months and years as neurotics, when a blood sugar tolerance test might have revealed the true cause of symptoms.

We do not know what causes hypoglycemia in most cases. Therefore, we call it idiopathic (of unknown origin) hypoglycemia.

In rare cases we discover that the cause is an "islet" tumor in the pancreas which secretes an abnormal amount of insulin, burning too much sugar and depleting the blood of necessary carbohydrates. Operation to remove the tumor almost immediately removes the symptoms. Sometimes, diabetic patients who normally have high blood sugars are subjected to sudden attacks of hypoglycemia when there are discrepencies in their diet or insulin administration. Whatever the underlying reason, we now realize that low blood sugar is still too often overlooked as a cause of nervous symptoms.

Dear Dr. Steincrohn: I read recently with extreme interest a letter from a 34-year-old woman concerning herself and her 28-year-old brother. Among the symptoms listed were chronic fatigue, depression, a feeling of panic, nervousness, fogginess, confusion and a weak feeling to the point of nearly "passing out."

Seven or eight months ago this desperate plea for help could well have been my own and my husband's. We had both suffered similar symptoms, with several added ones for years. We had made the rounds from doctor to doctor with the same results: "It's just your nerves. You're not as young as you used to be." (My husband is 41 and I am 31.)

Neither of us felt we were quite ready for the psychiatrist's couch nor did we feel that old age had descended upon us. Yet we knew our symptoms were real and could find no one who could or would give us a reason.

We were at our wits' end when I decided to return to a doctor who had attended our family when we lived in another neighborhood. When we told him our symptoms he immediately arranged for glucose tolerance tests. Diagnosis: hypoglycemia. He immediately put us on the appropriate high protein, low carbohydrate diet and for a while gave us injections of adrenal cortex. We began to improve within a few weeks.

We are still on the diet, and my husband and I are practically back to normal. We are so much improved it seems like a miracle.

As I understand it, hypoglycemia is still very much overlooked by many physicians. Our doctor told of a patient with low blood sugar who had been seeing a psychiatrist for over a year—and didn't improve until the diagnosis of hypoglycemia was made.

After what my husband and I went through emotionally and physically and financially I simply write to you in the hope that someone else might possibly profit from our experience.

Mrs. C.

Doctors Disagree

During the past year or two, many books, newspaper

columns and magazine articles have informed millions of readers about low blood sugar. Yet, in confrontation with this problem, many are still not sure how to manage it.

Unfortunately, in some cases this is due to doctors who disagree. Some still prescribe sugar; others say, "stay away from it."

> Both my husband who is 23 years old and my mother who is 64 have been diagnosed by separate doctors as having low blood sugar. The glucose tolerance test was used by each doctor to make the diagnosis. My husband was told to eat four small high-protein meals a day and to avoid sweets. But my mother was advised by her doctor to eat a piece of candy whenever she felt weak or dizzy. Nothing about eating a high protein diet. My husband felt better; my mother didn't. Are there different ways of treating hypoglycemia, or is one of the doctors wrong? How does one make the correct choice?
>
> Mrs. K.

I think it will help you make your decision if you realize that only during the past few years has it become apparent that patients with low blood sugar should take high protein diets, rather than try to raise an abnormally low blood sugar by feeding on carbohydrates.

Too Much Sugar Lowers Blood Sugar

Unfortunately, some doctors still are not aware that too much sugar in the diet subsequently lowers the blood sugar instead of raising it. Sugar stimulates the pancreas to secrete insulin, which burns the sugar. In patients with idiopathic hypoglycemia (low blood sugar of unknown cause—the most common form), the pancreas responds by oversecreting insulin. The result is abnormally low blood sugar causing the common symptoms of nervousness, anxiety, dizziness, weakness, extreme hunger, faintness and similar symptoms.

The reason a high protein diet helps is that not so much insulin is called upon to regulate smaller amounts of sugar in the diet. Although it is true we give some patients sugar by mouth or into a vein to overcome a sudden fall in blood sugar, the overall plan is to keep patients on a high protein diet and medication rather than on a high carbohydrate regime. In managing hypoglycemia it's vitally important that the patient's intake of carbohydrates be restricted.

Another woman said recently:

I have just been through an ordeal of being called a neurotic for months, when all the while I had been suffering from undiagnosed hypoglycemia. Yes, when your blood sugar level is low it can cause all sorts of awful sensations from the crawling, ant-on-skin sensation to actual convulsions and even coma. The funny thing is you have to knock the doctors over the head with a sledge hammer to get the diagnosis. (I practically had to beg mine to take a glucose tolerance test.) Oh, yes, they are careful to diagnose diabetes, but you have to end up with nervous tremors and fears before they will even consider low blood sugar. While I was in the hospital I spoke with three others who had hypoglycemia. One said, "I have a chilly feeling come in my head." Another said, "I feel like snakes are crawling in my stomach." And the third said, "I feel like water is running all over me." As for me, I felt like I was passing out. I would go into a panic to prevent myself from doing so. You might be interested to know that each and every one of us lost our "crazy" symptoms after we gave up sweets.

Suffered as Psychiatric Patient

Earlier I mentioned the doctor who told about a patient who, unknowingly suffering from hypoglycemia, had suffered for years as a psychiatric patient. I have seen a few such patients in my own practice. Here is a history of a similar case. It was given to me by a patient who knows that I am interested in hypoglycemia.

Since early childhood I have been struck down frequently by illness. The symptoms were usually the same—nervousness, indigestion, headaches, craving for sweets, ravenous appetite, nightmares, sweating and chilliness, insomnia and anxiety.

After I had been married and had given birth to three children I continued to be plagued with insomnia and nightmares. One night I had a convulsion, but was conscious, extremely cold and perspired, with a fear I might become violent. I asked for orange juice, drank it, and quickly revived. Each day was an endless purgatory. I had constant fears of going violent, committing suicide. Only my religion sustained me.

I was treated for months as a psychiatric patient. But I kept noticing that whenever my husband

gave me orange juice the spell would end. And
drinking milk between meals and before bedtime
lessened the spells. I learned eventually that taking
a glass of milk at 2 A.M. put an end to them
completely.

Not until a few months ago did I learn that I
have hypoglycemia. A high-protein diet and frequent small meals have transformed me into a
normal person. I have given up the psychiatric
couch and returned to my own bed—sans nightmares, insomnia and all the other frightening symptoms.

(Mrs. A.)

All Patients Do Not Suffer Extreme Discomforts

Thankfully, most patients who suffer from low blood
sugar do not have such extreme discomforts. Many simply
drag themselves through life without energy to support them
for the business, home and social requirements of normal
living. Others are "just plain scared" all the time and don't
know why.

Whenever I am confronted with a person who is abnormally anxious, I ask: "Have you had a glucose tolerance test?
First make sure that an abnormally low blood sugar is not
the culprit. If it is, we can shackle him and make you feel
much better."

Sometimes there seems to be reason enough to overlook
hypoglycemia. For example, when a person has undergone
long convalescence from severe illness or operation, fatigue
and nervousness might readily be ascribed to them.

Since January 1966 I have had two colon operations, a hysterectomy, a bladder repair, two cysts (benign) removed from my breast, and shingles on my forehead. Between my general practitioner and my surgeon I was able to feel like a human being again—except that I was forever tired and exhausted. This was passed off as being due to having undergone so much surgery in such a short time.

For two years, during which time I developed a bleeding ulcer, I didn't concern myself with my fatigue and off-and-on dizzy spells. When my ulcer healed my fatigue and nervousness were attributed to the menopause. (I am 53, have no wrinkles and no signs of wear and tear except gray hair.)

One day I started shaking—inside and out. My doctor called it "nerves." He prescribed tranquilizers which didn't help.

At the next visit he suggested blood tests to check on my blood sugar. I had a six-hour blood sugar curve made. At the four-hour level it went down to 35. The doctor regulated my diet. No sugar, minimum starches, lots of meat, cheese, vegetables, very little fruit. Within weeks I began to feel like myself. My strength came back and I have lost the shakes and nervousness. I hope what I have told you helps some poor souls, mislabeled neurotics, who have been suffering from undiagnosed "hidden hypoglycemia."

(Mrs. H.)

Time for a Closer Look

It is time to take a closer look at what I have been telling you about hypoglycemia. Having read the case histories of patients who have been helped so much by merely going on a high protein diet, it would not surprise me to learn that many anxious people believe now that they may have found the open sesame to all their nervous complaints. "I'll have a blood sugar tolerance test, hope my blood sugar is low, and presto! I'll be healed within weeks of these frustrating symptoms that have dogged me for years."

Although it is true that recognizing and treating low blood sugar patients helps many overcome their anxiety, I want to stress that it is not a cure-all. For example, some doctors still believe that hypoglycemia is still a rather infrequent condition. They say that only a few people who complain of nervousness, depression and fatigue have a low blood sugar to explain their symptoms. These doctors think that many patients who may have hypoglycemia also have emotional problems—and it is difficult to tell whether they complain because of their low blood sugar or because they can't simply tolerate their emotional turmoil. They say that many people have all these uncomfortable symptoms of anxiety even though tests show their blood sugar levels are normal.

Not Hedging

Now, I am not hedging when I say I agree with them, too. A distinction must be made. But it is difficult to agree with those almost fanatical believers who ascribe all kinds of symptoms and disease to low blood sugar: asthma, alcoholism, ulcer, hay fever, drug addiction and many others. This is going too far.

Nevertheless, I think we are not going far enough if we lightly pass over, with a wave of the hand, and minimize the importance of blood sugar investigations entirely. The pendulum often swings widely and crazily in the practice of medicine. There are the believers and the disbelievers. The former at least give the patient the benefit of the doubt; the latter often refuse to order a glucose tolerance test because their minds are made up. Obstinate refusal often closes their eyes to an effective diagnosis and potentially helpful treatment.

So my advice to the anxious is that they have the benefit of blood sugar tests. Time will tell if hypoglycemia plays an important hand in their suffering. If your doctor still insists that it's "silly" to go to the trouble, then you have the right to ask for consultation.

The Glucose Tolerance Curve

In the past doctors hoped to make the diagnosis by taking a fasting blood sugar test. One test. Later we learned that reading a sugar curve is essential. You come to the doctor's office or to the laboratory, on a fasting stomach. The first blood sugar test is taken by withdrawing a specimen of blood. Then you are given a measured glucose solution to drink. An hour later another blood sample is taken. Then four or five more samples taken at intervals of an hour, and each measured for the amount of blood sugar. The blood sugar readings are put on a chart and connected: this is the blood sugar tolerance curve. If abnormally high, it signifies diabetes mellitus; if abnormally low, the diagnosis is hypoglycemia. It's as simple as that. If you suffer from anxiety, it seems worth it to get at least this off your mind—especially since it may be the means to recovery.

"Yes, I can see the need for a blood sugar curve", says one nervous patient. "But I still don't understand just how low blood sugar causes all these horrible symptoms."

Well, here is a brief explanation. Normally, the fasting blood sugar reading is anywhere from 70-100 milligrams of sugar per cubic centimeter of blood. After you eat, it may rise to 140-150. But if it gets to 170 or higher we suspect diabetes. If the hourly test shows that it later gets far below the 65-70 mark, then we label it hypoglycemia.

Now why should a low blood sugar cause symptoms? Because the brain is so sensitive when deprived of nutrition and oxygen. Without proper amounts of blood sugar the brain cannot absorb its oxygen, and it rebels. This is why the low blood sugar patient gets nervous, jittery, anxious and restless. He drinks a glass of orange juice or takes a candy, and symptoms disappear temporarily because the blood sugar has been raised and the brain handles its oxygen supply.

It all seems so simple, but it isn't. Although the pancreas which secretes insulin is usually the main factor in blood sugar regulation, we know that there may be other offenders: the pituitary and adrenal glands regulate sugar production, too. So does the liver, whose job it is to store unused sugar as glycogen. For these reason, we tell you to eat frequent meals, stop smoking, stop coffee, stop wines and cocktails. One or all may contribute to unnatural falls in blood sugar. I walk the middle road about hypoglycemia, but I recognize that each anxiety sufferer deserves study of his blood sugar.

Thoughts and Afterthoughts on Chapter 7

1. There is an increasing awareness of hypoglycemia. However, this blood sugar deficiency is still often overlooked.

2. Common symptoms of low blood sugar are: nervousness, trembling, faintness, dizziness, weakness, chronic anxiety, convulsions. In severe cases, unconsciousness.

3. Some doctors still minimize the effects of hypogly-cemia.

4. Low blood sugar may cause a neurosis.

5. In rare cases the cause of drop in blood sugar is an "islet" tumor of the pancreas which oversecretes insulin. Operation can cure this condition. Usually, the cause is unknown and we call it "idiopathic hypoglycemia."

6. Only during the past few years has it become evident that patients with low blood sugar do better on a high protein diet rather than on a high carbohydrate intake.

7. A patient suffered as a psychiatric patient for years because her condition of hypoglycemia was undiagnosed.

8. Most patients who have abnormally low blood sugar do not suffer extreme discomforts. But they drag themselves through life without energy to support them for the normal business, home and social requirement. Others are "just plain scared" and do not know why.

9. Most anxious persons should have the benefit of a blood sugar tolerance test. Taking a fasting blood sugar test is insufficient for the diagnosis of hypoglycemia.

8
Does Your Thyroid Gland Need a Tune-Up?

Here sits a woman who says she is always tired. And here sits a man who complains of extreme fatigue and nervousness from day to day. There isn't a day in the life of the busy doctor when he doesn't hear men and women, who live their lives in daily tension and anxiety, ask for "something" to help their nervousness and fatigue. In some cases you can simply charge it up to that vague yet fully encompassing term, "anxiety state," and try to discover the emotional basis for the trouble. But often the tiredness and anxiety are due to organic problems.

I'm always so tired and nervous I'm really getting sick of myself. My husband and children, I'm sure, consider me nothing but a "drag." I am only in my early 30s and the mother of three youngsters. For several years now I have been plagued by physical symptoms as well as nervousness. Every part of my body seems affected.

I can handle most of the feelings I get, but I suffer most from the following: I am always exhausted. My mind feels dull. I can't seem to think straight and make decisions. My skin is getting dry and my hair is thinning and falling out. My eyes are puffy, even though I get enough sleep. I'm always cold. Wear a sweater when the rest are so warm they keep saying, "How can you wear a sweater in this hot weather?"

I try to keep my home running on schedule and also try to keep active in Community and Church work. My friends, or even my family, hardly know how awful I feel most of the time. Last month I threw away every tranquilizer I had in the house. I wanted to fight it my own way. But I'm losing. Whatever I do to try to overcome my anxiety and these tired feelings fails.

How Is the Thyroid?

Any third-year medical student hearing this history would immediately become suspicious of some trouble in this woman's thyroid gland. In this case, is it too lazy? Isn't it putting out enough hormone to keep the engine running effectively?

Not too many years ago, we would have overlooked the possibility of thyroid deficiency in tired and nervous people just as we do now the possibility that they might have a low blood sugar count. But gradually the profession has become more aware that the thyroid gland's dysfunction might cause many symptoms that were attributed to "nerves." All internists and many general practitioners have installed basal metabolism machines in their offices. In many stubborn cases of anxiety and fatigue, we are happy to discover that a low metabolism is the predominant cause. We give the patient thyroid extract, and within months there is a happy transformation for the better. The tired patient becomes peppy. Anxiety lessens as physical reserve renews itself.

Today fewer cases of thyroid trouble are overlooked, because we have newer ways of determining thyroid dysfunction. When your doctor does a physical, he orders blood tests. Invariably included are tests for thyroid function. Some are called protein-bound-iodine tests. Others, "T3" tests. Whichever are used is not so important as being aware that the thyroid should not be overlooked in the examination.

The Lazy Thyroid

The lazy thyroid is the type of gland that we call hypo-active. The condition that results is hypothyroidism. We need to give the thyroid a boost by prescribing thyroid hormone. This can be taken in pill form. Depending upon the degree of subnormal activity, we prescribe anywhere from one to three or four grains a day. Some patients have to take it for years. But the medicine is relatively cheap, and the bother of taking the pills is small compared with how much relief and stamina they bring to the patient.

The mind clears. Hair becomes less brittle, the tired look in the eyes disappears, and that awful feeling of always being cold vanishes. Sweaters are discarded. Anxiety and fatigue lessen. Many such patients say, "I've been given a new lease on life."

If I were asked to choose the one most common complaint I've heard from patients it would be "I'm tired." People suffer from pain, cough, nervousness, headaches and innumerable other disagreeable sensations—but fatigue leads the list. Survival in this world drains our energies.

Fatigue is found in the healthy as well as in the sick.

Nevertheless, if you are inordinately "tired all the time" I think you should have your doctor find the real reason (emotional or physical) for your discomfort.

Continually Exhausted

I am only twenty-five, have no reason that I know of to feel tired and anxious, yet I am continually exhausted and a chronic worrier. I'm even exhausted on days when I don't have to clean the house, market, or socialize too much.

This has been going on for a few years. Worse this year. As I feel healthy otherwise, I haven't seen our family doctor about it. I've been taking vitamins, iron and eating well-balanced meals. Even resting in bed for two hours every afternoon hasn't helped.

Sometimes I'm so tired it's an effort to eat. And so nervous it's impossible to swallow. Recently my husband has called my attention to the fact that my eye-lids are drooping. I've looked in the mirror and noticed it, too. To put it mildly I'm tired all over. I know it's about time I went to my doctor. I'll make an appointment. But meanwhile I'm disturbed about what may be wrong.

As I've said fatigue and anxiety are common complaints. These can be found in perfectly healthy individuals whose life scheme is off the beam: due to emotional problems, financial difficulties, or to overworking, undervacationing, etc. These reasons may apply to you.

Among other tests, you should give the doctor the opportunity to check on your thyroid and on your blood sugar—in addition to ruling out any other possible organic disease.

For example, with your suspicious history of extreme exhaustion, unaffected by rest periods, your doctor will want to make certain you do not have a condition called "myasthenia gravis." This is a disorder (cause unknown) in which there is some defect in nerve-impulse transmission between nerves and muscles. Muscles become abnormally weak. Even breathing, swallowing, and keeping the eyes open become taxing efforts. (Eyelids droop.)

There are special tests to diagnose the disease. In treatment, certain "anti-cholergenic" drugs are often effective in restoring energy. In some cases, removal of the thymus gland has helped.

Patients who have complained of being dead-tired are often amazed at the surge of energy which follows either medical or surgical treatment. Sometimes improvement is only temporary.

But proper diagnosis and treatment have undoubtedly helped thousands of people who suffered from "unexplained tiredness and nervousness." Myasthenia is often overlooked— but as in hypoglycemia and in thyroid disease, doctors are becoming more alert in discovering and managing this illness. Nevertheless, myasthenia is nowhere near as common a cause of fatigue and nervousness as is thyroid dysfunction.

The Hyperactive Thyroid Gland

What is this thyroid gland? Can one feel it? See it?

Although it's the largest purely endocrine gland, it weighs less than an ounce. It is shaped like a butterfly, a wing of it on each side of the midline of the neck, between the voice box and the wind-pipe. Normally, you cannot see it or feel it. It is the storehouse of the body's iodine and of the thyroid hormone which the blood distributes to every part of the body. Whether the gland is underactive, overactive or normal depends upon how much hormone it liberates.

A lazy thyroid is not the only threat to the normal function of the body. Sometimes the gland becomes quietly berserk and oversecretes. This is called hyperthyroidism. Even the medical student can recognize the typical patient. Here is a case history:

> I was a perfectly normal woman until I turned thirty-five. Then, for some reason I couldn't understand, I began to become irritable, overanxious and undescribably nervous. Even my hands and fingers would shake when I tried to light a cigarette. I felt warm all the time. Never wore a coat in winter. I could feel my heart palpitating and skipping all over the place. I had a tremendous appetite but still lost weight. I'd have alternating spells of constipation and diarrhea. When I'd walk up stairs my legs would feel dead tired.
>
> A friend first called attention to the fact that my eyes were stary. Later on they actually began to bulge a little. They made me have a constantly frightened look. And I also noticed that my neck seemed to be swollen. Especially on one side.
>
> My husband said I was becoming insufferable to him and to our three children because I was so jittery and nervous. He insisted that I see our doctor.
>
> No sooner did I walk into his office than he

asked me to sit down so he could take my pulse (which was running away) and feel my neck. He said, "I'll have to investigate further, but my hunch is that your thyroid's overactive." The laboratory tests proved he was right. About six weeks later I had a thyroidectomy. Within a month after it was removed, I began to feel like a new person. My husband said, "Now you're like the girl I married."

"Masked Hyperthyroidism"

This is the typical history of a patient with exopthalmic goiter. The reason for anxiety becomes quite evident—even to a layman who can only guess at the reason for the change in a person's actions.

But what is important to know is that there must be thousands of unsuspected cases of anxiety due to "masked hyperthyroidism." There is no eye enlargement, neither is there enlargement of the neck. Yet the patient has rapid pulse, slight finger tremor, loses weight and strength, complains of anxiety. No age is exempt. But there are many in their 60s and 70s who complain of nervousness for which no apparent cause can be found—yet the thyroid is overlooked. In the aging, the thyroid may be either underactive or overactive without any overriding symptoms that point distinctly to the correct diagnosis. In some, a little thyroid hormone transforms them into healthier and happier beings; in others, a few drops of iodine daily or some other specialized "antithyroid" drugs to combat overactivity do the job.

No diagnosis is complete unless the doctor actually feels the patient's neck carefully for nodules or enlargement in the thyroid gland. Benign nodules should be removed to lessen the chance of cancer of the thyroid (which is relatively rare). Sometimes the concern about cancer of the thyroid is unwarranted:

Hashimoto's Disease

I guess I'm more worried about my thyroid gland than anything else. And the worry is about cancer. I am 47 and have felt well except for a slight cough and pressure in my throat. My doctor has stuck a needle into the swelling in my neck and assures me it isn't cancer. He calls my condition Hashimoto's disease. I have just begun to take pills for it. Is an operation necessary? I suppose I shouldn't be so anxious, but seeing the swelling in my neck every time I look in the mirror doesn't help.

Hashimoto's disease is a chronic inflammation of the thyroid—not too commonly found. It occurs most often in middle-aged women and is supposed to be caused by some "auto-immune" disorder. As in your case, it may produce pressure symptoms such as cough and heaviness in the throat. If the gland becomes quite large it may interfere with normal swallowing and even produce hoarseness.

The usual treatment is giving thyroid extract (which is probably what your pills contain). Often the thyroid gland become smaller after months of such treatment. But if the pressure symptoms remain, sometimes surgery is used to relieve the condition. I hope what I have said relieves your anxiety about the probability of cancer.

Anxiety and Fatigue Deserve Early Investigation

Whether anxiety is about something specific (cancer, in this case) or is "free-floating" I hope you are beginning to understand that it deserves early investigation by a doctor. Too many people stumble and crawl through life, living at much less than their potential capacity, simply because they do not take the time to discover the underlying reasons for their emotional or physical disabilities.

Is the reason hypoglycemia? Hypothyroidism? Hyperthyroidism? Or any one of scores of other conditions we can cure—or at least help? Are you a procrastinator? Then it is more likely you will go on feeling anxious and tired. Self-treatment with vitamins and other "tonics" may be as ineffective as pouring water into a pot with holes in the bottom. In other words, anxiety should not be accepted as a necessary evil that cannot be exorcised.

One word I do not use in diagnosis is "borderline." A condition *is* or *isn't*.

For example, when a man comes in complaining of chest pains, the diagnosis must be either angina pectoris or no angina. Not "borderline angina."

If there is a question of an ulcer, it is or isn't present. "Borderline ulcer" doesn't mean anything except not having resolved suspicions one way or another.

Some doctors may not agree, but I call it hedging on a diagnosis. Not being sure. (And the patient should not be burdened with such doubts). Sometimes we are stumped and must learn to say, "I don't know." But that's not hedging. Just a statement of fact. Saying one has a "borderline" this or that gets us (and the patient) nowhere.

This is especially true in the diagnosis of irritability and nervousness possibly due to an underactive or overactive thyroid gland. We have tests that will help make the correct diagnosis one way or the other. It is important to know if the thyroid gland actually needs tuning.

Thoughts and Afterthoughts on Chapter 8

1. Tired and nervous? Don't overlook your thyroid gland.

2. The lazy thyroid is the hypoactive gland we find in hypothyroidism. Usual symptoms are exhaustion, nervousness, dullness, puffy eyes, brittle hair, dry skin and uncomfortableness in cold weather.

3. If you are tired all the time suspect your thyroid gland. But be sure your symptoms are not due to emotional problems, financial difficulties, overworking, undervacationing, insomnia.

4. Also be sure you do not have unsuspected myasthenia gravis. There are special tests to diagnose this disease.

5. The normal thyroid gland cannot be seen or felt. In cases of hyperthyroidism (overactivity) there may be a nodule or evident enlargement of the gland in the neck.

6. Symptoms of overactivity of the thyroid are: nervousness, anxiety, rapid irregular pulse, palpitation, diarrhea, muscle weakness, hand tremor, loss of weight despite a large appetite.

7. Anxiety and fatigue deserve early investigation.

8. The treatment for an underactive thyroid is thyroid hormone; for an overactive gland, either medication or operation.

9

Faulty Breathing
Aggravates Anxiety

There are moments when breathing
becomes a love affair with God.
—Ben Hecht

People don't seem to be using this simile anymore: "It's as easy as breathing." I guess one reason is that when one has seen a heart patient, or one who suffers from asthma or emphysema, fight for his breath, one never forgets it.

Breathing may be natural, free-and-easy for normal people, but it's certainly a big problem when the breathing apparatus becomes disarranged—or simply goes out of whack.

Nevertheless, too many still take breathing for granted. I don't mean that people should become self-conscious about every intake and output of air. First thing we know, we'd all become too self-conscious, and foul up the apparatus.

Yet, I believe that we should all be aware of a breathing problem we call "hyperventilation." Basically, all it means is overbreathing. Many people who have anxiety suffer from overbreathing and do not suspect it. They overbreathe unconsciously by taking rapid shallow breaths when nervous, which only intensifies the nervousness. They sigh or yawn often.

They complain: "I can't seem to take a good breath. It isn't as satisfying as it used to be." Some complain of being "short of breath" when it is not that at all.

What hyperventilation does is create an imbalance of oxygen and carbon dioxide in the blood. Too much and too rapid breathing forces out an unnatural amount of carbon dioxide. As a result the carbon dioxide tensions in the alveoli (of the lungs) and in the blood become abnormally low. This produces a lessened blood and oxygen supply to the brain and the rest of the organs.

Then come such symptoms as faintness, rapid pulse, perspiration, numbness in hands and feet, and extreme anxiety. Rebreathing into a paper bag for a few minutes often makes these symptoms disappear (by rebuilding the carbon dioxide balance.)

I have helped many anxious patients by teaching them how to breathe. Anxiety and breathing are so tied-in that helping the one often improves the other. Many have given up tranquilizers, sleeping pills and other sedative medications after they learned how to breathe normally. Every chronically nervous person should check with his or her physician to make certain that hyperventilation isn't complicating the picture. This relatively simple procedure doesn't invariably help all nervous patients. However, overcoming hyperventilation (and the reason for it) has saved many an anxious patient from years of unnecessary suffering.

Hyperventilation in a Youngster

Although most patients do not know that they occasionally overbreathe, in some instances they do. In fact, sometimes the syndrome has been brought on because of a youthful fad. It seems ridiculous that a youngster would bring on such discomfort, but it has happened.

Six years ago when I was in high school it was an almost unnoticed fad for kids to make themselves "black-out" by hyperventilating and then holding their breath and tensing their abdominal muscles.

I never did this with other kids, but later I began it as an escape from difficult or unpleasant situations. I did well in school, had friends and other good marks of "adjustment," but I was always looking for an escape from—well, anything—or just diversion or maybe attention.

First it was pretty mild, but then it started to scare me. But I could not make myself stop breathing fast and deep. I'd get hysterical, numb in my hands and feet, and cry out with horrible headaches. When someone found me, my pulse was really scrambled and I couldn't talk.

My folks sent me to a neurologist who took a brain wave tracing (EEG). He concluded I had hyperventilation. My family doctor prescribed tranquilizers. At times I'd have to rebreathe for a few minutes into a paper bag to stop the extreme spells. Now I'm okay since I am able to control my rapid and deep breathing.

Most Patients Unaware of Overbreathing

This has been an example of conscious overbreathing. Admittedly, a silly manoeuvre. Most anxiety sufferers who also overbreathe do not realize that this pernicious habit is contributing to their fears and other uncomfortable symptoms.

Here is a woman who sits tensely in her chair as she relates her complaints. She holds the sides of the chair until her knuckles are white. She speaks in a low, soft voice—as if she would be frightened to death if she heard herself speak louder.

"Will I ever get over being scared? Will these fears of mine go away eventually? I'm afraid to go to work. Afraid to go to church. Afraid to sit through an entire movie because I suddenly get the urge to run out because everything is closing in on me. I'm disheartened. Wonder why I should get out of bed in the morning because every day I have to fight to face the world. I feel I have a hopelessness that will never end."

I watched her as she spoke. I noticed that she sighed a lot, and quite often put up her hand to cover a yawn. Meanwhile you could see her chest go up and down rapidly. Unquestionably, she was overbreathing.

I asked her, "Do you have any trouble breathing?" Her face lit up, alive for the first time, as she said, "I'm awfully glad you asked that. Yes. I have trouble filling my lungs with air. I can't take a full breath. I find myself breathing fast at times to make up for the air I lose. Yes, I'm glad you asked."

Some Practical Advice

After complete examination, there was no evidence of organic disease. I asked her, "Do your hands and feet get numb when these nervous spells come on? Does your heart race? Do you feel faint?"

She said, "Yes. How did you know that?"

"Because," I said, "you're suffering from a specific syndrome we doctors call hyperventilation. You have a bad breathing habit. You don't realize you have it or how important it is.''

Like most patients confronted with this statement, she acted completely frustrated. She said she had no bad habits that she knew of. Would I explain what I meant?

"If I could make your heart race, and make your hands and feet feel numb right now, and give you the jitters—would you believe I know what I am talking about?'' She nodded.

"Then let's conduct an experiment. Do what I tell you to do and within a minute or two you'll have all the symptoms you've been telling me about. Ready? I want you to breathe as deeply and fast as you can—at least 30 times a minute—for one or two minutes. By the end of that time you'll have your symptoms.''

She sat there breathing fast and deep. Within a minute her face became taut, she clutched her chest, and looked up with frightened eyes. "I'm having an attack. The same as I always get when I'm scared to death. My feet and hands are numb and my heart's racing.''

I gave her a brown paper bag to rebreathe in, and within a minute or two her symptoms had disappeared.

She looked at me in disbelief. I said, "There's the proof. One of your problems is overbreathing. The only difference is that you do not sit down ordinarily to take rapid, deep breaths; you do so unconsciously. You're a shallow-chest breather. Over the long run it produces similar symptoms. Until you become more conscious of your breathing—catch yourself in the habit—you'll continue to be having these bad, scary spells.''

She Improves

She was a cooperative patient. A good student. She learned

her lessons. Within weeks she was having fewer attacks of hyperventilation because she would catch herself in time to prevent these episodes of rapid breathing. She stopped sighing and yawning so much, too.

Although she did not miraculously lose all of her nervous attitudes and discomforts, she declared that she was at least "75 per cent better." I had explained to her that over-breathing may only be one of the side effects of anxiety itself. But like the chicken and the egg and which came first, it is often difficult to know whether it is the anxiety that produces the rapid breathing or whether the hyperventilation is the instigator of the anxiety. Nevertheless, it is evident that whichever comes first, any patient suffering from anxiety would undoubtedly be helped if we could teach him how to breathe—and remove such scary symptoms as trembling, numb hands and feet, heart palpitation, fearsome jitters—and actual panic.

Those who suffer from "anxiety state" feel a hopelessness that it will never end. Their fears are known only to themselves and to their doctors. Perhaps your own neighbor or associate in business suffers from such extreme anxieties—for while many wear the masks of happy faces, they suffer daily fears.

Anxiety Is Not a Hopeless Burden

About a year later the woman with hyperventilation came in for a short check up. "But I'm really here only for a social call," she said. "Simply to let you see how an anxious person can become normal again. You know how close I was to a nervous breakdown only a dozen or so months back. I was severely depressed. Thought I would never get better. I became completely dependent upon people around me. Because, you see, I had lost my identity. I could not find myself within myself. How could I when I was living daily with all these senseless fears? I don't have to explain to you how tough life can be under such circumstances. I needed faith and strength, and that simple experiment in your office gave it to me. Since I've stopped overbreathing I have been able to face fears one at a time, not letting them overcome me. I keep conquering them again and again until they have become smaller and smaller. Many have disappeared. My special reason for being here today is so you can see me. How I look. How I feel. Perhaps my case history will help others to 'believe' that anxiety can be overcome; that they can 'reblossom' into normal human beings again."

I promised I'd tell her story. She got up and walked out proudly, confidently and upright—the way our creator has meant us to walk.

Some People Indifferent to Anxiety

But there are some who think that too much time and wasted energy is spent on anxious people. On the very day that our "reborn" anxious patient was in the office, came one interested only in her arthritis.

"Why don't doctors find a cure for it?" she asked. "I'm sick and tired of swallowing aspirin. But what makes me even more impatient is hearing and reading what the medical profession keeps saying about anxiety. Why should people who "imagine" illness be given so much more time and sympathy than those of us who actually suffer pain?"

I told her that there are all kinds of pain—and that sometimes mental anguish supersedes the physical. Anxiety imaginary? Hardly. There are all degrees of fear. In its extreme form it can make living merely existence—a daily nightmare. Ask the one who is afraid to sit in church or in the movies or take part in a game of bridge. Or too frightened to sit in a restaurant or too fearful to ride in a car. Fear comes in multivarious forms. Everybody's scared—if not afraid of illness or depressed by financial problems, there is the "bomb" in the background that colors (discolors?) our lives more than we realize.

I agreed that arthritis—and heart disease, diabetes, hypertension, etc.—are more discomforting physically than chronic anxiety. But ask the nervous person which he thinks is worse. The majority say, "Give me peace of mind and freedom from fears and anxieties and I'd gladly swap for an ulcer or heart attack. This daily battle to keep my sanity is devitalizing. I'm so scared I can't work and can't sleep—and am a burden to my family and friends."

For these reasons, I told my patient suffering from the aches of arthritis (which I admitted were surely distressing) I keep asking family members and friends to be patient with those who suffer from anxiety. Sympathy and understanding often help as much as tranquilizers.

We look for every way in which we can help them bear up under their daily burdens. If overcoming hyperventilation, for example, will lift the burden completely or partially—fine. Sometimes it's as simple as that to discover a remedy. But more often it takes more than that—a complete study and understanding of the one who lives in anxiety.

Thoughts and Afterthoughts on Chapter 9

1. "It's as easy as breathing" doesn't apply to everyone.

When the breathing apparatus becomes disarranged, patients with heart disease, asthma, emphysema fight for breath.

2. Too many still take breathing for granted. As a result many overlook "hyperventilation" (overbreathing)—which is often tied in with anxiety.

3. Symptoms of hyperventilation: extreme anxiety, faintness, rapid pulse, perspiration, numbness in hands and feet. Rebreathing into a paper bag often aborts the attack.

4. Many anxious patients are completely unaware that they overbreathe.

5. The symptoms of overbreathing can be turned on within a minute or two after rapid, deep breathing. This convinces the patient how important overbreathing is in causing his discomforts and anxiety. It is proof, dramatic and unforgettable, that hyperventilation is something worth overcoming.

6. I agree that arthritis, heart disease, diabetes, hypertension are more discomforting physically than chronic anxiety. But ask the nervous person in a hyperventilation attack which he thinks is worse.

7. Hyperventilation isn't the only answer to anxiety, but it is, nevertheless, an important one.

IV
Why Many Women Suffer Anxiety

10
How Premenstrual
(Cyclic) Tension Induces Fear

Are you a "Sweet Sandra" for about three weeks every month? And a "Horrible Hannah" during the other 7-10 days? For the most part is your house a home? And the rest of the time only a house filled with turmoil?

If so, I can venture a guess at what is causing all the unhappiness. Probably "premenstrual (cyclic) tension" is at the bottom of it all.

For thousands of years there have been days every month when otherwise-contented husbands have called their wives veritable "witches" (a euphemism). They could not understand what came over their wives every month. Children, brought up by a sweet and understanding mother, hid in a corner or locked themselves in the bathroom to escape the sudden temper tantrums and unreasonableness that came up like thunder out of the sea.

Not until the early 1930s, when the premenstrual syndrome was first described, did doctors awaken to the truth that many women are the prisoners of glandular imbalance. They just can't help being "witches" any less than a match will light up if you strike it.

I recall scores of husbands and children who used to complain, "I can't understand what comes over mother for a

few days every month." Although we haven't the entire
answer yet, we do know these things: about a week before
the menstrual period some women are thrown off balance
because their ovaries secrete proportionally less of a hormone
called progesterone in relation to the amount of estrogens
secreted. As a result there is a disturbance in fluid retention;
too much water remains in the tissues. When this edema
affects the brain, there is reason enough for increased emotional instability.

Common Symptoms

Here are some common symptoms which such women will
recognize: fatigue, extreme sensitivity (bursting into tears at
the slightest provocation), inability to concentrate, overwhelmed by the usual amount of housework, anxiety, depression, sometimes increased activity, nervousness, headaches,
bloating, aches and pains "all over," craving for sweets, and
generally increased appetite, weakness, faintness, trembling
and nausea. Quite a collection of miserable sensations, and
fortunately not all found in every woman suffering from
cyclic tension.

If some of these recur every month like clockwork—and
disappear almost immediately after the onset of actual menstruation, chances are you are a victim of premenstrual
tension.

Don't just charge it off to "woman's nature" and let it go
at that without trying to overcome it. Tell your symptoms to
your doctor, however denigrating. In many cases, such treatment may prevent divorce and provide better relationships
with your children.

One very conservative estimate is that about 40-50,000

women in the United States suffer from premenstrual tension. When you consider how much unhappiness the condition causes in interpersonal relations, I think you will agree—although it isn't a serious condition as far as health and life are concerned—that it is certainly important enough to do something constructive about it.

The doctor's job is to make the diagnosis after hearing your story—and not dismiss it as "just nerves." He will give you progesterone hormone to counteract the glandular imbalance; he will give you medicines (diuretics) whose prime purpose is to remove excess fluids from your body (a quick way of losing that unnatural weight), and he will probably prescribe a mild sedative or tranquilizer to help overcome your nervous symptoms.

You will discover that perhaps there's no reason why you shouldn't be a Sweet Sandra all month; instead of turning into a Horrible Hannah periodically.

Many Women Are Still Unaware

I am 30 years old and have four children. I get awfully upset about a week before my periods. I hate myself because I become a burden to my husband and children. I don't know how they stand me month after month. But after I go through this nervous, cranky (bitchy, if you will) week, I am my old sweet self again. But along with the nervous feelings, I get depressed, tearful, full of anger and plain meanness. My nature is not at all like this ordinarily. I have fought it with all my strength, but I can't seem to lick it. I've thought of seeing a psychiatrist, but I think I'll try our family doctor first. It may sound plain stupid that I have not consulted him before this, but I thought it would be silly to bother him—considering all the really serious problems he has to take care of. But lately I seem to feel bloated at the same time. My clothes feel too tight. And my legs swell. It's time to go.

Her Clothes Hardly Fit

It is not unusual for vanity to drive a patient to a doctor while she remains reconciled to unnaturally uncomfortable symptoms. When something interferes with wearing a favorite suit or dress, then it's time. No more procrastinating!

> More than any of my friends, I suffer from nervousness and bloating about a week before my periods. I get so fat my clothes hardly fit. I get tired of hearing my friends (friends?) keep saying, "Been putting on a little weight, haven't you?"
>
> Then after my period I feel calm again, and the excess fat disappears. Can you explain, and also advise what I can do?

I've already said most of it, but it bears some repetition. You can be sure I *won't* say this: Why worry about it? Why get so upset when you know it's only a part of woman's lot to put up, every month, with a "natural" phenomenon?

Too many of us doctors used to say something like that in the past, and advise nothing to take that might alleviate the discomforts. But now we know that you are not imagining it when you say that your clothes don't fit. The bathroom scales prove it. And remember it isn't an increase in fat; but an increase in water retention. When the period is over, you do not lose extra fat, you lose excess fluid. And the lessened edema in your brain also lessens your irritability and tension.

You may have other complications at the time. In some women there is a fall in blood sugar. Therefore, a high protein, low carbohydrate diet helps. So does a low salt intake, in decreasing edema (swelling due to water). In some women I have observed a low metabolic rate complicating the cyclic tension. Taking a grain or two of thyroid extract helped control the periodic, uncomfortable sessions.

Blame it all on a temporary upset in the glandular system, probably set off by an imbalance in the sex hormones. As a result the pituitary, thyroid and adrenal glands get out of tune. When they play bad music, you can't help being out of tune yourself.

Perhaps what I have already said will help, and bring comfort to the following woman, whose case history resembles so many others:

A Similar Plea

Please do me and so many other women a favor and write about the crazy, mixed up time a woman has before her period. Husbands just don't know what it's like. It's hard to explain to them, when you don't know yourself what's wrong—although I've heard it has something to do with hormonal changes.

It is really hurting our marriage. We can't go on much longer. He won't go to my doctor with me. He thinks it's silly, and that all the trouble is in my

head. What can I do? About a week before my
period I get neurotic and upset about every little
thing. I try very hard to control my temper and
tears, but it's still one endless battle every month.
We have two children, five and three. Everyone
catches it—even the poor innocent kids. They look
at me as if they don't recognize me any more. As if
I'm an ogre. What bothers me especially is that I'm
usually an easy-going friendly person at other times
of the month. I with you'd explain such episodes
to husbands. Maybe some of them will be more
patient and understanding towards their wives.

So I keep telling husbands. All they have to do is open
their eyes and ears, and see and listen—and understand. But
wives have at least one responsibility. Not to try to fight it
alone, but to seek the help of their doctor long before cyclic
tension becomes a problem for the entire family.

And another point. I also call it cyclic tension instead of
premenstrual tension for this reason: even long after menses
have ceased, and a woman is in, and past her menopause,
cyclic changes in personality and well-being may continue to
plague her. It may all be tied in with chronic anxiety, but
whatever the cause, it deserves a doctor's observation and
advice.

Thoughts and Afterthoughts on Chapter 10

1. Are you a "Sweet Sandra" for three weeks a month and
a "Horrible Hannah" the other 7-10 days?
2. Perhaps premenstrual (cyclic) tension is the cause.
3. Scores of husbands and children cannot understand why

the wife and mother has these changes in personality every month. Blame it on an imbalance in glands due to hormone secretions by the ovaries.

4. Some common symptoms: fatigue, extreme sensitivity (bursting into tears at slightest provocation), inability to concentrate, overwhelmed by the usual amount of housework, anxiety, depression, nervousness, headaches, bloating, aches and pains "all over," craving for sweets and generally increased appetite, weakness, faintness, trembling and nausea. Quite a collection of miserable sensations. Not all found in every woman suffering from cyclic tension.

5. Don't charge it all up to "mother nature" and let it go untreated.

6. Your doctor will prescribe medicines to relieve the abnormal amount of edema (water) in the tissues. He will prescribe hormones to counteract glandular imbalance; and tranquilizers to help overcome some of the nervous symptoms.

7. For the sake of themselves, their husbands and children, wives have the responsibility to seek help to overcome unnatural anxiety during these monthly periods.

11
Hysterectomy:
Cause of Unnecessary
Apprehension

Only an unfeeling, unimaginative, completely indifferent person approaches any operation without anxiety. Whether it's the child who is told he has to have his tonsils and adenoids removed, or the elderly patient who faces a hip operation after fracture—whatever the age, there is the fear of anesthesia, operation, afterpain or complications. But there are psychological hurts, too:

I have a problem you may think silly, but it is very real to me. I had to have four operations and this one makes five. They took out tubes, womb and one and one-half ovaries.

Of course, you know I can't have children now. But I have been fortunate. Before this operation was necessary I gave birth to four beautiful children. Now that they are growing up, I feel useless. I am only 35.

My problem is that my husband thinks I am not a whole woman now. He told me so. The word "useless" is a mild one, nevertheless, I feel dead and empty inside. I know his words are something I'll never forget. I'll never forgive him for the hurt he has caused me by saying I'm no longer a "whole woman." I love him and could forgive him for anything except this.

Here is my silly question: Is there any way to have an operation to somehow replace these organs by plastic surgery so I can be whole again and be able to carry another child? I'd do anything to be whole again.

I told her that now, at least, plastic surgery could not give her a new uterus, tubes or ovaries. But considering what the new heart surgery has accomplished, in medicine it's no longer proper to say anything is "impossible." Nevertheless, I suggested that she had better forget the nonsense of not being a whole woman.

Having already borne four children, how much more proof did she need to convince her of her womanhood? Even women who have never had children aren't necessarily "useless."

I told her she was undoubtedly suffering from the effects of postoperative depression which some women undergo after hysterectomy. Usually it passes within a few months.

As for her husband, some day his own problems may knock some sense into him. For example, when he has to bear up under the psychological aftereffects of a prostatectomy, he'll know better than to go labeling a wife "useless" simply because she has had her uterus removed.

Many Men Understand

These days when there is so much unfortunate misunderstanding about the hysterectomy operation and its consequences, it is a fact that most understanding husbands are helpful to their wives after a hysterectomy:

> I've heard and seen many women after they had their hysterectomies. In spite of the experience as a registered nurse, when it came my turn, at the age of 33, and the mother of three children (7, 8 and 9), I was scared and conjured up all kinds of fears about malignancy and other complications— physical and emotional. I just "knew" I had a malignancy.

> Following the hysterectomy I learned that I had suffered only from endometriosis which had spread to the ovarian tissue as well. Within three months I was completely recovered—no pain nor aching, no sweats or hot flashes, no backaches, no emotional problems such as depression.

> My only moment of regret came before the surgery when I knew I would definitely have no more children. But my understanding husband kindly and firmly pointed out that we intended to have no more children anyway, and that having the surgery would certainly improve me as a wife and mother, rather than "de-sex" me.

> Many women overlook their greatest source of comfort and understanding—their husband. Most men accept the facts of hysterectomy with very matter-of-fact attitudes, and are often themselves relieved. The difference in relationships after such surgery can be remarkable.

> It appears to me to be foolish not to discuss frankly these things with the person most closely involved besides yourself. With marriage being a

partnership it's unfair to deprive yourself of your
strongest ally—your husband.

Younger Women Worry More About Hysterectomy

If you asked ten women which type of operation they
feared most it is likely that the majority (or all) would
answer: hysterectomy.

Perhaps I should say, If you asked ten *younger*
women. . . . For I have found that the woman past her menopause is much more philosophical about the removal of her
uterus. She has already had her children. She is not as
concerned about its effects upon her figure, her sexual desires
or its psychological impact. The younger woman faced with
hysterectomy invariably has some degree of anxiety.

> I've just been told I have a hysterectomy to look
> forward to. As I'm 26, have only two children (we
> planned on having at least four) I am concerned.
>
> I understand that when one has uterus and
> ovaries removed, one loses sexual interest, becomes
> fat, cranky and ages rapidly. This is a dim prospect,
> I think you will agree. But I have no choice. I
> understand that large fibroids and excessive
> bleeding make the operation mandatory. Like any-
> one about to undergo surgery, I'll appreciate any
> words from you that may keep my spirits up.

I said that things are not as bleak as you imagine. First,
let's get an important definition out of the way. Hysterectomy means removal of only the uterus. If your ovaries are
healthy, your doctor will not remove them unless there is a

significant reason to do so.

Now, if only the uterus is removed, you can expect little or no change in your hormonal status. Except for psychological reactions it will not follow that the operation will change your sexual desire or feminine qualities. In fact, the sexual desire is increased in many women who are now free from the possibility of having any more children.

The operation should not produce any changes in your voice, hair or skin. As for the psychological reactions (depression, nervousness etc.) they will depend upon each individual's response to hysterectomy. It is difficult to predict. I have seen many young women, without offspring, take it more calmly than older women who already have raised a large family.

So my suggestion to you is that you take your operation in stride. You are young, you have a family, and there's little likelihood you'll age prematurely. Even if you also require operation on your ovaries, your doctor can prescribe hormones to help take up the slack.

Although anxiety about looks and premature aging are common fears about the hysterectomy operation, in many it is the doubts about its effects upon sex drive: women are concerned about how it will affect relations with their husbands:

> Although my doctor is conservative, he now advises that I have a hysterectomy. I hate to think of it as I'm only 37. Fortunately, we have five children. My trouble is chronic fibroids that have begun to grow and cause me to bleed so much I've become anemic. What has really concerned me is the effect the operation will have on our sexual relations. My husband and I are perfectly happy.

But I'm too much of a prude to ask my own doctor if the operation will make me lose my own desire for sex. And suppose the surgeon finds something also wrong with my ovaries? Suppose they have to come out, too? Will that complicate things even more?

What has really put doubts and fears into me is a friend who said I may as well say goodbye to the good old days after the operation. I'm worried for my husband as much as I am for myself.

I said that where life and health are concerned, sometimes I think that good friends become bad liabilities rather than assets. They may mean well but arouse unnecessary apprehensions. It seems needless to say it again and again, but isn't it more sensible to take the advice of a trained physician than to depend on the hearsay evidence and suggestions of well-meaning friends who have no inkling of what the problem is all about?

Let's suppose that your ovaries as well as your uterus are removed. Is it inevitable that you will lose your sex drive? Ask your doctor. Hardly a day goes by when he isn't asked this question, so don't feel self-conscious about talking frankly with him.

It's likely he will tell you that removal of ovaries and uterus (or uterus alone) will not necessarily diminish desire or accomplishment. Mainly, psychological reactions in some women are the cause of sexual problems after hysterectomy or ovarian operation.

If your doctor feels that you will need some hormone therapy after operation, that will take care of any hormonal deficiencies. Most women I've talked to after they had hysterectomy said that sexual pleasure increased rather than decreased after such surgery. Reason? Freedom from fear of unwanted pregnancy.

Nervous After Recent Hysterectomy

An anesthetist puts you to sleep. The surgeon snips off your appendix or removes a gall bladder filled with stones. Not pleasant, most people will agree. But within a few weeks after surgery all is forgotten. Just an uncomfortable interruption in one's normal way of life. But not so in many instances, when the organ removed is the uterus—symbol of motherhood and womanhood. As I've said, not only is the sense of loss a physical one, but one of psychological impact that throws some women into a depression:

> I am fair, fat and forty, but instead of having my gall bladder out, I am one of those unfortunate women who have had a hysterectomy. I'm a woman no longer with a uterus. The operation was fairly simple as all I had was a bleeding fibroid, but I've become a nervous wreck since the operation. Like a bird, I feel that my womanhood flew out of the window on the morning of my operation. I've come to believe that my husband doesn't love me any more because something was taken out of my sex life. Am I being silly? Is this a passing phase? Will I get over it?

In the majority of cases: just the "temporary blues." Most patients who have had the uterus removed soon realize that losing this organ, so closely associated with a woman's reproductive life, is not a catastrophe—especially after the childbearing age. I repeat: it is a passing phase. A woman about your age said a few days ago:

> I'm glad it's out. At first I was concerned about many things; such as sex, nervous reactions and hot flashes. But our sexual adjustment, which was good before my operation, is now even better.
>
> I feel relaxed and happy. All I can tell my friends is that a hysterectomy is not so bad as they've imagined it. I advise them to think of it as just another operation—and nothing to cry over.

Human Kindness

People like to help people. Is there a man who has had a headache who hasn't at some time been offered an aspirin or something similar by a sympathetic neighbor? Is there a person who has been blue who has never been offered a sedative or tranquilizer by a well-meaning friend with the words, "These are wonderful. They quiet me down. Take them with my compliments." Is there a student, concerned about his final exams and willing to stay up all night to study who hasn't been offered black coffee or a pep pill by a roommate to keep him awake?

All are evidences of human kindness and helpfulness. But as I have often said, we do a disservice rather than a favor in giving others medication we take ourselves. The aspirin you take may send another into shock. The tranquilizers you offer may make a habitual user out of your friend. The pep pill may make an addict out of the one you offer to help. Back-fence advice and offers of help should be on everyone's conscience. For it may do more harm than good.

Nevertheless, kindly people will go on offering help—and in most cases—actually succeeding in giving relief.

Another way some people try to help others who are "down" is by writing to me and suggesting that I relate their experiences so that the anxious one can find relief and hope by learning how others have overcome similar problems.

For example, letters keep coming in from hysterectomy patients who want to help those faced with the problem of undergoing this operation. For example, there was the Mrs. X. who was depressed about having to have a hysterectomy because of fears she wouldn't feel like a "whole woman" any longer. I was asked to send her the following letter:

Letter to Mrs. X.

> *Dear Dr. Steincrohn:*
> I hope you will be able to forward this letter to a Mrs. X.; she wrote a letter which appeared in your column in our *Baltimore Sun* tonight. She said she was quite depressed about having a hysterectomy and felt like she wouldn't be a "whole woman" any longer.
> Dear Mrs. X:
> When I was 21 years old I wanted to have my tubes tied. I had three children before I was 20 and although I love kids, the thought of maybe 20-25 more years of childbearing terrified me. I had visions of ending up with 10-15 children. Because of laws at the time I was not able to have this done as I wasn't old enough and would have had to have four living children. I had two more children by the time I was 26. One died soon after birth. So

now I had four children. Laws had changed and by that time I was now able to have the operation to remove my uterus. (Besides I was developing some fibroids that were growing fast.)

Well, I had my operation and I still feel that it was one of the best things that ever happened to me for numerous reasons. To start off with our sex life—it is now so much more natural because I don't have to worry about becoming pregnant. Secondly, I can do anything I want all year long; such as swimming, hiking and things like that without having to worry about whether or not my monthly period is going to interfere with my activities. This alone was worth the operation!

My children are almost grown. They are 18, 15, 14 and 7. I find, now that I don't have any toddlers, that I can devote more time to my husband. When the kids were little, if we couldn't get a babysitter (which happened quite often) he went off without me. Now that we have our own babysitter, very seldom if ever does he leave me home. I can also devote more time to him since I don't have crying babies to attend to. Very seldom does he ever see me with curlers in my hair or looking dowdy.

As for myself personally, what a difference this operation has made. When my children were small I had given up almost everything that I had done. Now that I have more free time I'm getting back to the things that I enjoy such as oil painting, reading, baking, and my herb garden. I can go out and window shop or take lunch with a friend while the kids are in school. I can pick up "at the drop of a hat" and run off to a flea market or an auction if a friend calls and says, "Let's go." I've been blessed with four healthy children and I am still young and healthy enough at 33 to really enjoy life. What more can any woman want?

Anyway, Mrs. X., being able to have more babies does not make a woman "whole." Now that you have more time, devote it to your husband. Do little things that you did for him before the babies came. If you go around thinking that you are not a "whole" woman then chances are that you will not be; not because of your operation, but because of your attitude.

Just don't let yourself get so low that you can't pull yourself up again. Then you cease becoming any kind of woman and become a drudge. I hope I've helped you some, Mrs. X.

(Signed, another Mrs. X.)

What I (and others) have been trying to say is that hysterectomy is not as simple as a tonsillectomy; but neither is it an amputation or mutilation.

Thoughts and Afterthoughts on Chapter 11

1. Only an indifferent person approaches operation without anxiety.

2. If you asked ten women which type of operation they feared most it is likely that the majority (or all) would answer: hysterectomy.

3. There's the groundless fear that everyone becomes fat, cranky, and ages rapidly after hysterectomy.

4. When only the uterus is removed there is little or no change in hormonal status—the reaction is mainly psychological.

5. The operation should not produce any changes in voice, hair or skin.

6. It is difficult to predict each individual's psychological reaction to operation. I have seen many young women without offspring take it more calmly than older women who already have raised a family.

7. Many women are concerned about their sex drive and how their husband will react after hysterectomy.

8. Good friends often become liabilities rather than assets because they arouse apprehensions about the operation.

9. If your doctor feels that you will need some hormonal therapy after operation on uterus and/or ovaries, they will take care of any deficiencies.

10. Many patients have said that sexual vigor and pleasure have increased after hysterectomy. Reason? Freedom from fear of unwanted pregnancy.

11. For some, hysterectomy is the removal of the symbol of motherhood and womanhood. But most soon realize it is not a catastrophe.

12. Reread Mrs. X's advice to Mrs. X.

12
Change of Life
(Male and Female)

Change of life is considered to be a natural phenomenon. From the time they are little girls, the female learns that there will come an "era" in life when menstruation will cease—and they will be "changed" from young women to older women. This, they will be told later on, is due to the natural slowing in function of the ovaries, which will secrete less and less of the vital "youthful" hormones.

Unlike hysterectomy and oophorectomy (removal of ovaries) which interrupt the normal course of events and produce an "unnatural" change, menopause is nature's normal way of lessening and finally interrupting woman's reproductive powers.

Most women navigate the troublesome waters of menopause without being thrown overboard into physical or psychological trauma. They sail serenely along, contented and comfortable. Many women say that the menopausal years are the most satisfactory of life—no longer burdened with recurring monthly menses, rearing of children, or other responsibilities that the young married years entail.

But there are exceptions. Some women complain about the change. They become nervous. Depressed. Lose interest in life. Suffer from hot flashes. Many have sexual difficulties—

psychological or physical. For them menopause is not a "party." Yet, much can be done to make them comfortable. If there are no contraindications to such therapy, the administration of hormones helps them. It reduces the hot flashes and produces a sense of well-being. Tranquilizers and sleeping pills help get them over the rough spots until they are able to adjust.

What I have been saying is now mostly old-hat to women. The menopause has been so much discussed—formally and informally—that they know what to expect and how to overcome it. Except for cases of extreme depression (involutional melancholia) most women can cope with the menopause as just another phase of existence that is a normal part of aging.

Is There a Male Change of Life?

But the male of the species is not so well prepared for change of life. Not having had monthly periods which ultimately stop, he has not had any specific proof that he is a different man than he was when in his teens and young adulthood. In fact, he can't be sure because even some doctors aren't sure that there is a male change of life similar to that of woman's.

As one man put it recently: "Is or isn't there such a condition as male change of life? I went to one doctor who pooh-poohs the idea, yet my family doctor says there is definite evidence of what he calls the male change of life or "male climacteric."

A wife asks:

> Is there such a thing as male change of life? Our family doctor doesn't believe in it. I understand

that some doctors do. I believe there are definite signs that my husband has "changed." He is only 52, yet he is gradually becoming impotent, very unsure of himself and anxious. He has become very nervous about his job, about our kids, and about the world in general. In other words, he is quite depressed. At times he even says, "I suddenly get warm all over"—as if he were having a hot flash.

But our doctor refuses to take him seriously. He tells him that what he needs is a vacation. Doesn't give him any tranquilizers or any tonics. As he doesn't get any sleep and complains of loss of vigor and strength to do a good day's work, don't you think it's possible he may be going through a kind of change?

Such are variations of hundreds of similar questions that patients ask doctors. And they are still unanswered because doctors disagree. Put the good physicians in a room and ask them to discuss male climacteric and difference of opinion might be split right down the middle. In some groupings, the percentage might be 60-40 or 70-30—for or against. I happen to be one of those who believes that men go through a male climacteric as do women through their menopause. A woman's change usually comes during her middle or late forties; the male climacteric appears, usually, during the fifties.

There is no specific, rigid dividing-line of age groups. As most women are not greatly affected by the menopause, so most men pass through their 50s and 60s without complaint. But some men do get nervous and irritable. They may also complain of flashes. They become anxious and fearful. They lose confidence. They lose sleep. They become depressed.

When these symptoms are more than passing discomforts

(especially when depression intensifies) it may be necessary to have psychiatric help. But most often the family doctor can manage the problem with male hormones, tranquilizers and reassurances.

Is male change of life due to hormonal changes or to psychological problems? We are not certain. But my opinion is that such symptoms should not be minimized. Such men do not "imagine" their symptoms any more than women do who are having discomfort due to change of life.

The male change is not so dramatic as it is in some women. Nevertheless, like women, they may also suffer from such symptoms as sweats, hot flashes, generalized weakness, lack of drive and energy, emotional instability, depression, lack of potency and less ability to concentrate. I believe that when a man has such symptoms they should not be passed off lightly with such advice as "you need a vacation"—"don't take yourself so seriously"—"pull yourself together." What's important is to recognize the underlying cause as possible male climacteric (change of life).

Of course, the doctor should consider other possibilities as the cause of the man's symptoms: like atherosclerosis of the brain arteries, psychoneurosis, or trouble due to organic disease. However, I have seen too many proved cases of male climacteric to believe this clinical entity should be brushed aside. Male hormones can decline in function, as well as female hormones.

The Study of Male Mid-life

Man, formerly the forgotten one of the species, is now being subjected to study of his earlier years—long before there is any question as to whether or not he "changes" due to his glands.

I have recently received a release from the U.S. Department of Health, Education and Welfare regarding a proposed study of the American male between the ages of 35-45. According to Dr. Daniel J. Levinson, Professor of Psychology at Yale University, this is the decade he regards as the turning point of man's life, the transition from early adulthood to middle age.

According to HEW News: "Much has been written about the middle-aged woman. Her plastic surgery, cosmetics, diets, sex life, and hormones are widely discussed in the mass media. Middle-aged men, in comparison, are rather shadowy figures."

Between the ages of 35-45 a man "usually reaches the culmination of his youthful aspirations, both in his career and personal life. This is also the decade when a man faces many new crises."

Dr. Levinson says: "A man at 40 may feel trapped and impotent both at work, where his skills have become obsolescent and where he feels crushed under the weight of a bureaucratic machinery, and at home, where his wife makes unwelcome demands and his adolescent children question his values and his paternal authority. On the other hand, he may find in one domain the sustenance and strength needed to deal with the problems of the other."

Aging at whatever age, is a personal challenge to the individual. Change of life occurs during every year of a lifetime. While much importance has been placed on the later years of change, I have always believed that possibly the most significant and trying "change" occurs during adolescence. I think these are the difficult years of adjustment to "changing times."

But whatever the age groups involved, as human beings we should be aware the "change" produces emotional currents that cause various types of personality eruptions that we should try to understand in others—and forgive. Confused and anxious and frustrated each individual should be given the understanding he craves, whether he admits the need for it or not. It is no symptom of physical or moral weakness to admit that one is anxious. There's no shame in being scared.

An Anxious Man

> I cannot understand my constant tenseness. I clench my jaws till my teeth ache. And for no apparent reason. Lately I have felt fear and panic. It feels as though something horrible is about to happen. I wake up suddenly in the night or early morning—in a sweat.
>
> I've recently sold my successful business. Our children are grown and happily married. I cannot understand why I cannot just be happy and feel relaxed. I am 56. I worry about everything. The world, our country. I keep as much of this to myself as I can, but I recognize that others realize I'm in some sort of depression. I jump at every noise. I used to be a happy and optimistic person. Is there a reason for all this?

In his case, yes. The male climacteric. Tranquilizers, hormones and reassurance did much to relieve his anxiety within three months.

Thoughts and Afterthoughts on Chapter 12

1. *Change of life is a natural phenomenon.*
2. Unlike hysterectomy and oophorectomy (removal of

ovaries) which interrupt the normal course of events and produce "unnatural" change, menopause is nature's normal way of lessening and finally interrupting woman's reproductive powers.

3. Most women meet the challenge of menopause without being thrown into physical or psychological trauma. In fact, many say the menopausal years are the most satisfactory of life—no longer burdened with recurring monthly menses, rearing of children or other responsibilities that the young married years entail.

4. But there are exceptions. Come complain of nervousness, depression. They lose interest in life, suffer from hot flashes and sexual difficulties. Administration of hormones and tranquilizers helps. In severe depression (involutional melancholia) shock treatment may be necessary to bring improvement.

5. There is difference of opinion, but I believe there is male change of life—the "male climacteric." Man can change too. Why not? This is the reason men in their fifties may become nervous and irritable; have hot flashes; lose confidence; lose sleep; and become depressed.

6. Whether or not the male change is due to hormonal imbalance or is strictly psychological is not so important as recognizing there is really such a syndrome in the male.

7. As in women, the male change can be helped by reassurance, hormones and tranquilizers.

V
Depression

13
Minor Depressions: The Blues

"I'm naturally a cheerful person, but every once in a while I get into the dumps for no apparent reason. I'm only in my thirties and know I'm not going through the change."

Not knowing how "dumpy" you get, nor how often or how deeply depressed, I can't give you a specific explanation. But in a general way I can say that every normal person has his blue days—for no apparent reason. Nothing apparent seems to provoke them.

But as sure as the sun rises and sets and the tide comes in and goes out, all of us normal people have this uncontrollable rhythm in our lives. I say "normal" because I am not referring to severe psychoses in which the swings are so wide and prolonged and deep that they interfere with normal existence.

One businessman said recently, "I can't understand it. I made a sale a few days ago that netted me thousands of dollars. All the news I heard on that day was just perfect. You'd think I'd be the happiest man on earth. Yet, I acted as if a dog bit me, or that I'd lost my best friend and all my money. I was simply down. I was blue. My spirits were low. This lasted for about a day, then I was my old, optimistic, happy self again. I haven't marked it down on the calendar but I think I get a blue day at least once a month. Is that bad?"

I told him that it is the intensity and frequency of depression moods that are important. Short dips in the normal line of everyday outlook on life are experienced by most of us. Like the beat of our heart, they are beyond our control. It is part of the body's normal metabolism.

Sometimes I've found it is related to body temperature, which seems to be lower on "blue days." Some people feel better and more efficient in the morning; others, in the late afternoon or evening. I tell people who have important problems to work out to try this experiment: take your temperature every hour for a day or two. Keep a chart. Then try to channel your important work into those hours when your temperature readings are higher. It's important to learn during what time of day you are most efficient. Your thermometer may tell you.

It is all a part of the mysterious truth that our enthusiasms and life forces ebb and flow like the tide. Unless the "dumps" are severe enough to interfere with normal way of life, I doubt that they are anything to be concerned about. However, if they last long and sink deeper, it would be wise to talk to your doctor.

Weekend Blues

I dread the weekends in our home. The children are grown and away, and only my husband and myself now occupy our large house. He is a hard-working executive, still in his early 50s. He dispenses gloom and depression which begins on Friday nights and doesn't end until Monday morning. Yet during the week he is high-spirited and easy to be with. But come those dreadful weekends and he mopes and worries and makes life miserable for both of us. How do you explain this? Is there an answer to this problem?

I told her that many women shared her complaint— droopy-in-the-spirit husbands on weekends. One of my favorite authors is William Saroyan. I like to read him because he has such a penetrating insight into human beings and their relations with one another. For example, in a short piece called *Sunday Is Hell* he writes: "Sunday is the day people go quietly mad, one way or another."

Now, what did he mean? For one thing, it expresses the truth that for most people it is a trying task to unwind from our daily duties. We work along at full speed during the week, heavy foot on the accelerator, but don't know just how to gently apply the brakes so we slow down easily and painlessly in the vacuum of workless days.

Your husband, like many others, suffers from "weekend blues." He is like an unhappy fish out of water. He misses the oxygen-giving energy he finds in his work. So he mopes around the house. Your job, as I see it, is to try to plan weekend activities in advance to fill the void. A social engagement on Saturday night; a movie or short car trip on Sunday. Maybe you can get him interested in playing golf. Or, taking a long drive to see the children and grandchildren.

Whatever the remedy, mental, physical or emotional, it seems he needs your help to overcome his weekend depression. You asked for the answer. It is efficient planning on how to fill those hours which can get to be quite depressing if they remain empty.

It is true that many men are quite content to be left alone

on weekends so they can relax and quietly read or putter around the house. But if he isn't the type to enjoy such leisure for two days each week, then you can help him overcome the blues by remembering that: "Sunday is the day people go quietly mad, one way or another."

Boredom and Depression

My doctor tells me that I am in the middle of my change. In addition to having hot flashes and excessive perspiration, I have been a bit depressed. He suggests that I take some hormones and special medicines that will make me feel more comfortable. But I hate to do so. Isn't feeling this way natural during the change?

It seems to me that every day is the same. Every night I go to bed and sleep until morning. Then I have my cup of coffee and pack a lunch for my husband. He says, "Have a nice day," then we kiss goodbye and out the door he goes to the same place he has worked in for years—to the same job he did yesterday and will do tomorrow.

My children eat their breakfast and off to work they go, too. Then I put on the radio, hear the same commercials and do the same dishes, make the same beds, put in some wash and click on the TV set. Then I'm alone again, seeing the same furniture, vacuuming the same carpet and fixing the children's lunch again.

I don't talk very much or see friends or go anywhere. Around five o'clock I make dinner and set the table with the same dishes. After dinner, I wash the dishes, watch TV and go to bed. Then it's morning again and it's everything the same all over. I often picture millions of people doing the same things over and over for years and years. The only thing that ever changes is the weather. I feel like "here I go again" every day of my life. What do you think?

I said: I think it's time to follow your doctor's advice. My guess is that you are in more than a mild depression like the weekend blues. You are bored, and boredom I've found, is often tied in with depression. Untreated it may become more intense. I think you will admit you are in a rut. You need to be helped out so you will begin to take an interest outside of yourself; an interest in other people and in other things. Otherwise, giving you a "lift" will require longer and more complicated treatment than your doctor can offer now.

Often the distinction between "normal blues" and serious depression is one only a physician can make. Depression is too serious to go undiagnosed and untreated.

Choking and Difficulty in Swallowing

In spite of all recent information about the relationship between emotions and disease, it is often hard to convince the sick individual that he is not suffering organic trouble.

For example, here is a patient with Globus hystericus, in which the predominant symptoms may be choking and difficulty in swallowing. You make all sorts of tests to rule out actual organic disease, but you find none. You tell the patient that the discomfort is likely due to emotional problems. But you have a difficult time getting him to believe you. Here is another extremely nervous person who has been complaining of heart skips. You study him carefully with all sorts of tests and examinations, and you find he has a healthy heart. Unfortunately, it may take months or years to convince such a patient that there's nothing radically wrong. You have a job on your hands to convince him that he has what some patients call a "nervous heart."

And so it goes for spastic bowel which may be due to tensions built up at work or at home; yet the patient is convinced that he has ulcer or cancer. There are worried patients who believe that their tension headaches are really due to brain tumor. There are patients with asthma whose attacks are set off as if by a fuse of emotional discharge.

Outward Appearances Often Hide the Blues

A chic, smiling saleslady behind the counter at a department store greets you cheerfully. "What a happy individual," you may say to yourself.

A robust, hale-and-heart pharmacist fills your prescription and says, "Hope this fixes you up. Good luck."

Yet, I have treated two such individuals who were suffering the torments of daily anxiety. They kept their emotional hangups to themselves. Similarly, thousands suffer in silence. Others tell:

> For the past three years I have suffered from extreme anxiety. All my days were blue days. Now I feel that I am at my worst. I started out by being nervous following some surgery. I later found that my difficult breathing was due to allergies. I am now receiving a shot a week to combat mold, dust,

pollen and similar allergies.

This, however, doesn't seem to be my problem. Once about three years ago while eating I seemed to feel that some food particles were lodged in my throat. Ever since I seem to be prone to have this same feeling while eating.

I am at the point now where I am almost afraid to swallow anything. It seems as if I feel secure in knowing that there may be a doctor nearby while I am eating. However, if I am in a drive-in restaurant —or where I feel I can't receive this security—I almost panic. My anxiety seems to be in the form of choking on something—food, saliva, or anything. Liquids don't seem to bother me at all. I have a terrible fear of death associated with my choking on something.

Why? I'm not afraid of cancer, heart disease, or of anything else—only choking. Everything just seems to stick in my throat. Is it nerves? However hard I try to combat this problem, I fail.

Otherwise, I am a relatively healthy 28-year-old woman with a very nice family. I have plenty of money, love, and security with both friends and family. My daughter is five and healthy and happy. But I feel that I am all alone in this problem. I feel, blue day after day.

I have never told my family or family doctor how I feel. It seems so silly. Now I'm afraid to go on vacation, afraid to eat in restaurants, I'm afraid of being afraid.

Adversity gets most people down—for a while, anyway. But there are some hardy sufferers, who refuse to surrender.

Chin up, they force themselves to smile and push on; as if it is a natural thing in life to find obstacles which obstruct an effortless and smooth passage.

The other day a formerly "blue" person said to me:

> Having been through anxiety for months, it fills me with pity when I meet someone who is hanging on for dear life in spite of fears and disheartenment.
>
> I have experienced tragedy, humiliation, death, sickness and poverty. My life has been full of tragic experiences which I have long since ceased to speak of, except when I can help someone else by so doing.
>
> In spite of my troubles I have six children, many friends. I worship God, love people and do not think we were all born to suffer. I have learned what true happiness is. I maintain that anyone can have it if they want it badly enough. From my adversity I have learned that one must forget about oneself, serve God, serve your fellow man, develop your mind, improve your education, and cultivate spirituality.
>
> I told a friend last week—and she is already feeling a little better for it—that her trouble is that she has lost faith in herself. I told her to pray to God and ask His help as if the world depended on it; then go out into the world and act as if it depended on her. I told her to laugh at discouragement, smile in the face of adversity, and pray some more for endurance—and for God's sake—being living.
>
> It worked for me. It's working for her.

Thoughts and Afterthoughts on Chapter 13

1. Every normal person has his blue days.

2. It is the intensity, depth and frequency of depression moods that are important.

3. Many dread the week-end blues. For example, William Saroyan wrote: "Sunday is the day people go quietly mad, one way or another."

4. Boredom also creates depression.

5. Untreated, apparently innocuous blues may become more serious depression. Therefore, early treatment is often advisable.

14
Nervous Breakdown

"My husband is having a nervous breakdown. Do you have any suggestions or any special medicine that might help?"

Nervous breakdown? What is it? Like rheumatism it is a "wastebasket" term. For example, rheumatism may signify that the patient is suffering from osteoarthritis, the common form of arthritis fround in so many persons after forty. Or, it may be rheumatoid arthritis, which may begin at any age, and is an entirely different form of rheumatic disease. Or, it may be gouty arthritis. Or, it may be one of scores of other different types of arthritis. Or, it may even be due to bursitis, myositis (muscle inflammation) or to many other aches and pains man is heir to.

Likewise, "nervous breakdown" is a wide, encompassing blanket that covers many conditions. Generalizations are troublesome. They may mean one thing to some people and something entirely different to others.

Here are two examples:

The first was a fine young man who was rising fast in a large manufacturing plant. In fact, the president of the concern had hopes that the hard-working, intelligent fellow would one day become his executive vice-president.

As the weeks went by, his executive brethren began to

notice a change in the young fellow's personality. Instead of the quiet, industrious, efficient, popular fellow he had been, he became difficult to work with—ordering everyone around in an arrogant manner. He developed what one co-worker termed a "napoleonic complex."

At the time no one realized how close to the truth that was. Not until a few months passed was the unfortunate young man admitted to a hospital with a nervous breakdown. This so-called breakdown was due to a major psychosis. It has now lasted over two years and he is still too ill to be discharged.

The other was a fortyish business manager whose assistant had come down with a coronary attack. While he was convalescing, the manager had to work 12-15 hours a day at high tension. After a few weeks of this extreme pressure he "cracked." His boss insisted that he take a sea trip to get over his "nervous breakdown." When he returned, refreshed and rested, he was completely well. Now that his assistant had returned, the pressure was off.

These two instances are the extremes of nervous breakdowns. The wide chasm between having a psychosis develop and being simply worn out emotionally and physically by overwork accounts for the hundreds of variations of nervous breakdown.

Facing the Truth

Sometimes the reason for the patient's symptoms is not so easy to discover. He suddenly or slowly develops what we call an anxiety state. He becomes unduly frightened of himself and of his surroundings. He can't sit in a restaurant or a movie or in church without suddenly developing an urge to "get out of there" because of his fears. He can't feel at ease in crowds.

He has a variety of common anxieties. If these feelings last for months, some people might describe it as nervous breakdown, too.

Some improve—with or without help—when they at last recognize what they were and what they are. For example, one man who suffered through a few years of a nervous breakdown began to feel better only after he realized that his problems included being a too "nice guy," being unable to express true feelings, especially anger, turning bottled-up emotions against his own body, having extreme anxiety, depression and guilt—and looking back frankly on a childhood of an unloving, unprotecting, unrewarding mother and a no-account father. Not until he was able to face these disheartening and disrupting truths was he able to come out of his nervous breakdown and function happily in society again.

The Fear of Psychiatrists

I am in a nervous breakdown. I am terribly afraid of people—therefore have no friends. Even when I have to go to the store I get so nervous and tense I start shaking.

I ask myself why I feel this way. I'm nice looking, there's nothing queer about me, but I'm afraid people are going to laugh at me. Because of this, I'm making my 5-year-old girl the same way. She is afraid of children and sits in the back yard rather than play. I get into periods of depression and feel I'm hopeless.

I'm 22 years old, have a wonderful husband and two great kids. What makes me feel this way? My doctor says I'll get over these feelings but I don't know when. My husband tells me to grow up. He also says "for people to like you, you have to like them." Well, I do like people.

If I weren't so afraid of everything I'd like to join the Red Cross and help other people. And most of all, lead my own children down the right road of life.

Mine probably sounds like an absurd problem, but it means everything to me—to my husband and to my children. I've asked our family doctor if I should see a psychiatrist. He says forget it. Time will take care of it. But how long can I hold out?

The cause of such anxiety as your's, your "nervous breakdown," may lie deep down inside yourself. If your family doctor can't find the reasons and offer more help than he has, then I agree that he should refer you to a psychiatrist. As you must know from personal experience, people who suffer from "nerves" often suffer more intensely than those who have organic illness. Too many patients (and doctors) use the psychiatrist as the last resort—when, often, he should be the first. They wait for their medical doctors to recommend psychiatric therapy—while the family doctor is standing in the way of getting such help. Many doctors procrastinate, I suppose, because they do not want to frighten their already anxious patients.

They do not want the patient to think he is "going crazy." The patient waits and waits for help. None comes. In this pitiful stalemate the patient suffers, his spouse suffers, his children suffer, homes are broken, and suicide statistics increase.

Nervous breakdowns which are severe emotional disturbances are properly the concern of all medical doctors. Many patients need the help of psychiatrists early—and not late, after many months and years of suffering.

For many, psychiatry is the best hope. I have seen many patients helped by psychiatrists who could not be helped by regular practitioners of medicine. They are not infallible. But who is?

Emotional Illness Not Taboo

Emotional illness is no longer the skeleton hidden in the closet. You and I have become more honest in consideration of "shameful" illnesses. Not too long ago taboos loomed large in prohibiting a frank discussion of some of our ills. For example, if there was "TB in the family" it was hushed up. The words "gonorrhea" and "syphilis" never appeared in newspapers or magazines. Woe to the announcer who used them on the air.

And so it is with emotional illness—with major or minor emotional sickness. If there was a psychosis like schizophrenia, it was kept a secret between doctor and family. If someone was being treated for a "nervous breakdown" due to lesser emotional illness, such patients were away "on vacation" until they recovered. There are still remnants of such taboos.

> My husband is not the same. He has been very nervous and upset. He is unbearable around the house. Lately I have heard rumors they are going to let him go at the office because he has become so obstreperous. I keep begging him to go to our doctor. He refuses. He says, "What do you think I

am, *crazy*? Do you think I'm going to advertise that I'm having a nervous breakdown?" Otherwise he seems healthy. He eats and sleeps well. He hasn't lost any weight. But he simply is not himself. He is only 38. We have five fine children and everything to live for. What next?

I suggested that if he wouldn't go to the doctor then she'd better bring the doctor to him. As emotional illness covers quite a large range of disturbances, early diagnosis is essential. So is treatment. Procrastination only makes things worse. There are no taboos about calling for medical help when one breaks a leg or comes down with pneumonia. "Nervous breakdown" deserves equal attention. The psychiatrist who "sets" your mind is as important as the orthopedist who sets a bone fracture.

Compassion for the Emotionally Sick

Most nervous people have a major complaint: they are not understood. All they want from family and associates is simple understanding and compassion. Nothing more, nothing less.

I would like to tell you about the reaction of so many people toward a breakdown or any kind of mental or emotional problem. I have been there myself. When I was in the hospital, often the subject of returning to "society" was raised.

It was pathetic to observe the fear, anxiety, and apprehension that arose when people brought themselves to thinking about going back home. Even those who said they didn't care what people said or did to them, really were frightened more than the others who hoped the family and friends wouldn't just turn their backs on them and run.

I remember commenting myself that if people were cruel in words or deeds that we should feel compassion for them, because they lacked human understanding and were missing much of what life is all about.

I can plainly see that these are really unhappy people. They are all wrapped up in their own little world. I truly feel sorry for them.

While I was in the hospital I met some of the most genuine people I have ever known. They all had different problems, of course, but their personalities were such that you couldn't help but love them—warm, understanding, kind, genuine, and sincere.

Yet I am afraid that these sensitive people are the very ones that break under the cruel acts and words administered by unthinking individuals in our society. How I wish I could help people understand how much their words bite and their actions destroy other human beings.

The plea for compassion and understanding when one is emotionally sick is made so often that it becomes a bore. People get tired of hearing it. Many still have a transient feeling of superiority when they can say of a co-worker: "Oh, Jim? He's out of circulation for a while. Having a nervous breakdown."

I'll repeat what I've been saying periodically: Remember that none of us is exempt. We may bend or break when our own bundle of nerves is subjected to unnatural strains and pressures.

Thoughts and Afterthoughts on Chapter 14

1. "Nervous breakdown"—like rheumatism—is a waste-basket term.

2. Review the case history of the young executive whose nervous breakdown was in reality a psychosis, and of the manager who simply needed a vacation to untie his bundle of nerves.

3. If the family physician cannot manage the patient's nervous breakdown—whatever the cause—he should refer him to a psychiatrist.

5. Too often the patient waits and waits too long for help; and so does the doctor.

6. Emotional illness is no longer a taboo subject of conversation; it is no longer the skeleton in the closet.

7. I'll repeat: none of us is exempt. We may bend or break when our bundle of nerves is subjected to unnatural strains and pressures.

15
Major Depressions

What is meant by the term "depression"? Does it mean the blues—or what? Healthy individuals are often unaware of how many apparently well persons suffer from emotional upheavals. These sick people exist on a stage whose backdrop is a black curtain that hems them in and prevents ordinary exuberances and joys of daily life. For a while, at least, they are the lost generation.

I hope and pray that you can help me. I've been told that my trouble is depression. But I've always thought that depression means that one is sullen in spirits and feeling blue. If this is so, then I wonder what's my trouble.

I feel no love, hate, anger, fear, shame, embarrassment, shock, sympathy, pride, etc. I have been this way seven months or more. At one point I felt so bad I wanted to commit suicide.

Everything I tried to do was illogical. For example, putting bottle tops upside down, washing my face with a dry wash cloth, putting clothes on backwards, cooking backwards (trying to fry food before I turned on the fire).

I am 25 and have a seven-month-old child. My obstetrician says some women become depressed after the birth of a child. Others say this condition can be caused by marital problems—of which I have many. At present I live alone with my child, while my husband is "doing his thing" with other women.

I am miserable. Nobody can imagine just how much, unless they put themselves in my shoes. I have tried every possible way of getting myself back to normal. I've eaten well-balanced meals, seen doctors (except psychiatrists), taken medicines, moved, returned to work, gotten plenty of rest, talked about my problems, gone back to school to work on a master's degree, gone on trips, cried, and prayed, and prayed and prayed.

Nothing has helped. I remain emotionless. My greatest emotion used to be love. I loved everyone, especially children. Now that I have a child of my own, I haven't been able to feel one bit of love for him. How about that? A mother who simply is unable to love her own child.

Sometimes I just want to kill us both for I can't leave my baby without parents. Then again I think if we die, I'll never know what a mother's love is like. But if I live, I'll have to suffer indefinitely. As you can see, I am desperate. What have I left undone?

Post-partum Blues

This is what many depressed patients describe as a "living hell." And you can understand why this is so. I advised this young mother.

I agree that she had left something undone in her quest for recovery. In patients with a similar history and symptoms I believe that psychiatric consultation (and treatment) is not only invaluable—but often life-saving. If a patient remains in the dark pit of depression for months, nature—and the family physician—have been given sufficient time to bring about improvement. But every day that depression remains unresolved, is a threat to the life of the patient. Suicide is always a possibility.

After-birth depressions, although uncommon, should not be underestimated when they occur. If they persist for weeks and months, psychiatric management is imperative Whether the treatment is simply psychotherapy or shock therapy or the administration of mood pills to help the patient climb back up to normal will depend upon the psychiatrist's judgment.

This young lady's case had a happy ending after a series of shock treatments followed by psychiatric counsel. If her parents had not insisted that she see a psychiatrist, it is possible (and perhaps likely) that she might have committed suicide.

A Lonely Battle

People who have never suffered deep mental aberrations can't possibly imagine how lonely a battle such patients engage in day after day just to stay alive. When one has a pain, others flutter around him trying to alleviate it. When one is in a depression, those who surround him (family or friends) sometimes begin to look upon him as a bore and a trial.

There are various degrees of chronic anxiety and depression.

For example, here is a woman too frightened to leave the house to go shopping for groceries.

Here is a man who can't work in an office building because he is afraid to go above the second floor.

Here is a woman who no longer can go to church or to the theater because she is in panic when closed in. She sits on the aisle seat so she can jump up and run out when the fear oppresses her.

Such unhappy people may go on in chronic anxiety for years. In most cases I have seen, at last it wears out sufficiently for the patient to engage in normal ways of life again.

But the depressed patient is something else again: "The world has ended for me, I am so depressed I don't care what happens any more. I suppose I'll just have to wait around to die or do something drastic."

In most patients the family physician is able to manage the patient with chronic anxiety. Even in such cases, he knows there is a time to ask for helpful advice from a psychiatrist. But when he is confronted with the problem of deep depression, time is of the essence for survival. Not tomorrow, but today is the time to seek help. Self-destruction is always around the corner for the deeply depressed. Prognostication is imperfect. We have no specific set of rules or measurement which will tell us: "This patient is safe. We are sure he will not self-destruct." Deep depression is a challenge for which the patient deserves all the help he can muster.

Mother Is Depressed

Menopausal depression, sometimes called "involutional melancholia," is amenable to treatment. The patient playing the leading role in the following case history improved after referral to a psychiatrist who put her on hormones, tranquilizers and energizers. In severe cases, the use of electric shock therapy is the only treatment that will help.

> My mother is very depressed and is acting strange lately. This has been going on for months and getting worse. The other day she even hinted at suicide—for the first time. She always complains of being tired, even though she doesn't have much manual labor at home or at work. I can't conceive how anyone can be so tired *every day*. All she takes is three vitamin tablets a day and a B12 shot once a month. Perhaps she isn't getting the right treatment. Perhaps she is tired because she is bored.
>
> My father has been dead quite a few years. She is only 48. I can't communicate with her because she is so sensitive. I've suggested a hobby. She says she is too tired. She thinks I don't care because I don't tell her every day that I feel sorry for her. This, I think, would make things worse. What do you suggest?

Children Become Depressed, Too

As parents we are often unaware that one of the most difficult periods is adolescence. Change of life in a mature woman is often less trying than change of life in her teenage daughter. Lack of communication between mother and daughter often intensifies the problem of "growing up." With so many youngsters the mysterious uncharted area of "sex" dominates their thinking as teenagers.

I'm a 15-year-old girl, not bad looking and have
a pleasant personality. I live with my mom,
younger sister and step-father. My father's dead. I
never knew him. My mom and step-dad don't get
along. What hurts me most is the fact that they
don't respect each other. My life is actually boring.
I don't go out with boys too often. My main
source of entertainment is in school. My grades are
pretty good. Boys like me but I never had a steady
boy friend in my entire life. Not that I haven't had
a chance. I think marriage could be a beautiful
thing except for the sex part of it. This has been
worrying me for a long time. The older I get the
more terrified I become. I like boys very much but
the minute I think about the facts of life between a
man and a woman I stop liking boys. Perhaps it's
because I haven't matured. This is like a nightmare
to me. I wish I could talk to my mother about it,
but she'd only laugh or tell me to forget it. Lately,
I've become very much depressed. I feel very blue
all the time. My classmates notice it. They shy
away from me. At times I feel so bad that I've
occasionally thought of committing suicide. You
may think I'm being dramatic, but I'm not. I mean
it. I hope somebody can help me.

In her case, a long talk with her family doctor brought her
out of a trying episode in her "change of life." After she
confessed her problems to him, acting as emissary, he was
able to open the lines of communication between her mother

and herself. As she said later, "I never knew it could happen, but life has become rosy all over again."

Lack of Family Love

I don't know what to do any more I've been depressed for the past month and I can't get out of this mood. I'm a confused 20-year-old girl. I'm not dating anyone. All of my girl friends have boy friends. I have it set in my mind that I'll probably never be married. That's what keeps me depressed, knowing that I'll be an old maid and having people laugh at me. I just know I'll never find anybody. There are days when I wish I didn't have to wake up. What's the sense of living if you can't be happy?

I think if somebody offered me a trip around the world, all expenses paid, it probably wouldn't excite me at all. My friends know me as a quiet girl, which I am. I never gave my future and marriage much thought. But now that I see most of my friends getting married, I'm beginning to wonder about it. I live at home with my parents. They're old-fashioned. I'm not close to them at all. I know I never will be. They never were very interested in anything I ever did. There never was any love in our family. No kissing or hugging. I have a married sister who also admits we came from parents who never showed love or understanding.

I know that I shouldn't feel this way. I tell myself that it's wrong, and to think positive, and that there's hope for me. But it just doesn't sink in. I just can't overcome being depressed, and not caring about anything or anybody anymore. I know people get like this but I never thought I would.

Note: Happy ending. Engagement within three months, Marriage within a year—and they "lived happily ever after."

Loving Kindness Helps Depression

Sometimes doctors fail in curing severe depression. At such time both family and patient feel hopeless. But sometimes help comes from another source: loving kindness from another human being.

I have had doctors, priests, psychiatrists, hospital confinement for my severe depression. All were unsuccessful. Then I met an extraordinary human being. Loving everyone without reservation. Radiating love for you or me each day. For the next door neighbor and the guy at the end of the block alike. For the grocery clerk and for the little old lady strolling down the street. No one is a stranger to this human being. She's always there, with a smile, ready and willing to help and be truly concerned at the drop of a hat.

And this is not her profession. I've never heard her speak about the Bible, human dignity or "love for your fellow man." She has a family of her own and all of its responsibilities. Yet, makes time for hearing, seeing, feeling—whenever anyone else is in trouble.

I may have recovered without her help, but I doubt that I would have stayed well. Until I met her I was certain that no one cared. I had refused to go into the hospital again. But on her urging I did. She used to look upon the shell of misery and desolation that I was, and would waken hope within me by her smiling face, eyes of concern and love shining forth.

At first I couldn't respond, I was so depressed. But this human being kept at me like a friendly puppy and wouldn't let me withdraw completely from life. This human being sought out my company when I know I was unkempt and not good company.

I couldn't understand. Nevertheless, for the only time in my life I found I didn't have to be anything, say anything, contribute anything. My company was enjoyed. For this human being saw right past my crippled state of mind. Unadorned, I was enough.

Now I have been well for many years. We are still friends. I have come to know and love what this marvelous person represents—and not actually the person herself. She is the truly compassionate being. I have been privileged to witness a resurrection! My wish is that every nervous and depressed person is fortunate enough to discover (or be discovered by) one like her.

Look to God for Help

From another source comes this advice. I have known many depressed patients who at last found relief after turning to God.

I have a friend who was in a very bad depressive
state. She could not respond to any affection, even
to loving her new baby. I was just like her seven
years ago. I told her, as I did, to look to God. And
ask Him what she can do for Him (not what He
can do for her.)

As in my case years ago, finding God again
brought her love, laughter and faith. Now she
knows what it feels like to walk on the sunny side
of the street again. I wish many other unhappy
people would try this remedy.

Thoughts and Afterthoughts on Chapter 15

1. Many apparently well persons suffer from emotional
upheavals called depression.

2. Review case history of patient who feels "no love, hate,
anger, fear, shame, embarrassment, shock, sympathy, or
pride."

3. Young mother says post-partum blues are a "living
hell." After-birth depressions, although uncommon, should
not be underestimated when they occur.

4. People who have never suffered deep mental aberrations
cannot possibly imagine how lonely a battle such patients
engage in day after day just to stay alive.

5. In most cases the family physician is able to manage the
patient with chronic anxiety; but he must know when it is
imperative to ask for psychiatric help. Self-destruction is
always around the corner for the deeply depressed.

6. We have no specific set of rules or measurement which

will tell us: This patient is safe. We are sure he will not self-destruct.

7. Menopausal depression, sometimes called involutional melancholia, is amenable to treatment. In serious cases only electric shock therapy will help.

8. Parents are often unaware that adolescence is the most difficult change of all. Even young children may become seriously depressed.

9. A family's loving kindness often helps. So does prayer.

10. A mild degree of depression is a normal emotion. At times we all suffer from it. In other words, various degrees of "the blues."

11. Years ago depression was called melancholia. There have been suggestions for its cause and relief all the way back from the time of Hippocrates. It was in 1630 that Robert Burton published his famous book: *The Anatomy of Melancholia*.

12. Surveys show that approximately 8 per cent of men and 16 per cent of women will have a depressive illness during their lifetime. And studies show that, before the use of modern treatment to control and cure depression, it was usually a self-limited disease lasting about six months.

13. It is important that every case of depression should be studied carefully by complete medical history and physical examination. It is common after such illnesses as hepatitis, influenza and mononucleosis. Depression can occur with, and be overlooked in, peptic ulcer, Parkinson's disease, rheumatoid arthritis, and following major surgery.

14. Differentiation between depression and schizophrenia is sometimes difficult; but the latter shows a much more intense withdrawal from reality.

15. A cardinal symptom of depression is sadness. And the patient is preoccupied with his physical and mental state. In

its early stages depression may be difficult to differentiate from anxiety state.

16. Typically, depressed patients feel worse in the morning; their mood gradually improves as the day wears on. Sleep disturbances are common: difficulty in getting to sleep; wakening too early; complaining of terrifying dreams.

17. Depressed persons often act as if they want to inflict pain on themselves. They lose all their drives of self-preservation, their maternal and social instincts, and their search for pleasure. Humor no longer amuses, and the depressed patient has frequent crying spells.

18. The depressed patient does not expect to improve. He feels helpless and that nobody can help him.

19. Depression may be inherited. Both heredity and environment play a part. According to some psychiatrists, if both parents are severely depressive, half of their children will suffer, too.

20. In severe depression the psychiatrist will decide whether to use anti-depressant drugs or electroconvulsive therapy—or other treatment. Fortunately, depression adequately treated, responds and brings the patient back into the mainstream of life.

16

The Will To Die: Suicide

Suicide is a depressing topic. But so is heart disease, cancer, disabling arthritis—or any other threat to the human being. Anything potentially helpful is worth printing.

Suicide Note:

To the blissfully innocent Dr. Steincrohn: I hate life. I wait for death. You don't seem to realize how really little it means when a human being dies. And how many (too many) are born to replace each death; breathing air, eating food, taking up room and space, sleeping in a warm comfortable bed, suffering, being disappointed, hurt, dragged down—spiritually, emotionally, mentally.

The whole cycle is meaningless. The efforts spent in living, the wasted energies, the enthusiasms spent, the high ideals trampled on just to scratch out an existence. The good intentions, all gone now. All for nothing.

The sum total of one life: NOTHING. Of course, this isn't necessarily the same sum total of ALL human life. Some lives mean something. They contribute something even though only self-love, self-care. At least it's something. These humans want to live.

Your life, Dr. Steincrohn, is dedicated to helping those who want life and want to live it as comfortably as possible. But if a person discovers that all roads lead to a blank wall, such a person should have the respect and dignity from others, and be allowed to choose to end that life. Any way they choose.

I want to be left alone! I am so sick of being expected to say and be and do according to some script. To have a certain measured attitude, be in certain moods, feel certain feelings—so that I may be rated "acceptable" and "adequate." I go to my clergyman and he says, "Don't you know it's a sin to contemplate self-destruction?" For your penance, say: YOU SINNER. You unspeakable, wretched sinner.

I can just see your answer in print, Dr. Steincrohn: *"This woman needs a psychiatrist."* In your blissful innocence do you think this will help? It's too late.

I went to a social worker, not being able to afford the transportation to a doctor. He was a good listener—until he heard "suicide." Then he got frightened. He transferred me to a hospital for a few weeks. This solved nothing. I came home to the same situation I left behind. Everything that puts you into this condition remains. Most of all you are still you.

Professionals panic at the word "suicide." They

don't want the responsibility of a patient who breathes that word. Clergymen speak it as if it's a dirty word. Doctors shy away from it. My parents simply call it "talking silly" and say, "Don't you realize all the trouble you're making for everyone?"

But I am infinitely patient (living 20 years with a man who is a vegetable proves that). I will plan very carefully. Planning for the youngest of my six children, planning for me. I will die alone. Nobody at me. Nobody shoving a very bad script under my nose to say, "Speak these words—act this way— react that way"

(Signed: A NOBODY)

Comment: No signature. No address, except a postmark somewhere in New Jersey. No way of getting in touch with her family to warn that she wasn't being "silly." Yes, her prediction was correct; I would recommend a psychiatrist, and right away. Her depression is (was?) deep and dangerous. (I don't know whether or not to write about her in the present or past tense). Many can be saved from committing suicide if their threats or actions are not written off by the family as "being silly."

In reply to this note of desperation I received many letters of advice from readers. For example:

Dear Dr. Steincrohn: This is for the woman in New Jersey who is going to commit suicide after her children are taken care of. Lady, you are lying to yourself. You want to live, but you haven't the courage to do it. You sit back and say you are ready to die. Why don't you get up on your two hind feet and fight? Go to another psychologist or psychiatrist. If they cop out when they hear the word "suicide" walk out and go to another and yet another—until you find one who has the courage to help you find yourself. Such people exist.

I have found such a one here in California. Get angry, get out, and live—don't just sit there feeling sorry for yourself. Relatives, can be wrong, priests, can be wrong, and so can psychiatrists.

Don't let people who don't understand ruin your life while you sit by and whine about it. I speak from experience. I have been there twice— and am now out of my depression for years. But if I should slide back again I shall fight it out all over again. Like yourself, I wouldn't think of leaving six helpless children behind. When you're dead their burden will turn them into six miserable imitations of human beings. Nice going! You sign your letter as NOBODY. Forget it. Use that head bone, lady, for something positive—like living!

Mrs. S.

Another Note (in part) from Indianapolis

Mrs. NOBODY—please reconsider. Life is a great gift. True it doesn't always come in a gilded package, but we can rewrap it if we really want to. I was going to end my life with pills that cost $8.08. A pretty cheap cop-out don't you think? Fight. There is hope. My prayers are with you. And you might say one for me, too.

Mrs. P

Comment: Hopefully, Mrs. NOBODY is now Mrs. SOME-
BODY. Practically every large city has a suicide-prevention
center. Perhaps she has already asked for help. I have this
suggestion for such helpful agencies: that they become a part
of a national organization with *one* name easily remembered
and available in telephone books. For example, in one city it
may now be called *Lifeline*—in another, *Save-A-Life*. What is
a depressed out-of-towner to do when he needs help during a
severe depression? Or an in-towner who hasn't heard the
name of the suicide-prevention agency? I doubt that severely
depressed persons will take the time to call the information
operator.

Suicide still remains one of our great national problems. It
is tragic, not only for the patient, but for the bereavement of
family, friends and community. Therefore, every doctor
should understand how to manage the suicidal patient. First,
it is important that he be able to recognize the potential
suicide.

Whenever he treats a severely depressed patient he should
think of suicide lurking in the shadows of the patient's mind.
Perhaps we can lower the statistics which say that about one
in every six severely depressed patients commits suicide.
Many more try and do not succeed. In some countries suicide
kills as many as do automobile accidents.

Family and physician should respect all attempts at committing suicide—even though the early gestures have patently
been to call attention to oneself. For it is true, that if laughed
at and his attempt minimized in importance, the patient will
make a more serious effort next time—and succeed.

Patients do not commit suicide to punish themselves or
others. The real reasons are feelings of being a burden to
one's family, overwhelming and insoluble problems (like in-

curable illness, for example) and inability to get out of an intolerable situation. The patient simply thinks he will be better off dead. He looks for surcease.

Doctor and family should suspect suicide if the patient suddenly becomes peaceful and seemingly contented; or if he seems to anticipate death by making out his will; or if he asks how many pills of this or that are lethal; or simply says, "Well, one of these days I won't be bothering anybody any more." When such "hints" appear, early and vigorous treatment may be life-saving.

Ernest Hemingway

Never having met Ernest Hemingway, I cannot tell you about the man himself. But I write about life and death, so I am not so far off base. Having read practically everything he ever wrote, I believe I know him as well as anyone.

Although many years have passed since the gun blast went off that was heard around the literary world, I still think about him occasionally. Unconsciously (accidentally) or consciously, he squeezed that trigger. Having seen many active men reduced by illness to the final desperate act, I try to imagine how he looked, acted and thought as he picked up the weapon.

At my bedside table is a copy of *The Short Stories of Ernest Hemingway*, published by Modern Library. If you are interested in how Hemingway thought during those last few moments, turn to page 193 and read the end of his short story called "Indian Camp"—written when he was still a young man. I don't want you to put off reading it, so here it is:

"Why did he kill himself, Daddy?"

"I don't know, Nick. He couldn't stand things, I guess."

"Do many men kill themselves, Daddy?"

"Not very many, Nick."

"Do any women?"

"Hardly ever."

"Don't they ever?"

"Oh, yes. They do sometimes."

"Daddy?"

"Yes."

"Where did Uncle George go?"

"He'll turn up all right."

"Is dying hard, Daddy?"

"No, I think it's pretty easy, Nick. It all depends."

They were seated in the boat, Nick in the stern, his father rowing. The sun was coming up over the hills. A bass jumped, making a circle in the water. Nick trailed his hand in the water. It felt warm in the sharp chill of the morning.

In the early morning on the lake sitting in the stern of the boat with his father rowing, he felt quite sure that he would never die.

I have a feeling that Hemingway lived his life in the awareness of death. And every day of his living he walked with a chip on his shoulder and dared death to knock it off. For him there was not only death in the afternoon, but also in the morning and in the evening.

Hemingway was like another wonderful human being who always lived in awareness that some day he would be dead.

In his book *Charlie,* a biography of his close friend Charles Mac Arthur, you will find these words by Ben Hecht:

"From the day I met him at 19 till he died at 60, he had his eye on mortality. He was born without the illusion of permanence."

Some people still believe that Hemingway's end came by accident; most think otherwise. Each of us has the right to his own belief. It won't change things. If he did take his own life, why did he do it?

Again, let Hemingway speak—as he will in many ways for many years to come:

> "Why did he kill himself, Daddy?"
> "I don't know, Nick. He couldn't stand things, I guess."

Thoughts and Afterthoughts on Chapter 16

1. Suicide is a depressing topic—but potential patients must be dealt with as carefully as we treat those with heart disease, cancer, or any other threat to the human being.

2. Reread the case histories of the potential suicide and the letter from the formerly depressed patient who tried to help her.

3. Any severely depressed patient is a potential suicide.

4. The family doctor and the family should call for psychiatric help early.

5. This (among many) tips should not be overlooked when given by a depressed patient: "Well, one of these days I won't be bothering anybody any more."

6. Reread the significant early story by Ernest Hemingway on suicide.

VI
Philosophical Shock-Treatment of Anxiety

17
How To Be
a Happy Hypochondriac

We are all hypochondriacs, differing only in degree.

At some time in the past, present or future each one of us will become apprehensive about his body. It may range from a curiosity about what makes a finger feel numb right up to the top of the list: actual fear of death. One cannot escape it unless one is a moron.

Fear of loss of health—in other words, of sickness or death—is at some time in his life the natural reaction of the normal man or woman. The one who says, "I don't care when I go," is infantile. He is a little man who in waking dream rides a wild white horse as the conqueror of his fears and the captain of his soul. Actually, he is really a scared little boy who whistles at high noon as well as at midnight. Although he talks dangerously, he lives meekly.

I have observed this breed of braggarts who quake in fear within themselves when illness or death shows its head. How they change their tune. Don't be one of them. Admit your fears to yourself and to your doctor. There is nothing to be ashamed of in admitting you want to live. Practical experience in the treatment of thousands of human beings has convinced me that no person, whatever his position, creed, occupation or color, is immune to hypochondria.

At some time in our lives we get scared—good and scared. It is a normal reaction to threats against our health. Yesterday I visited a fearful man who had suffered a coronary attack. Anyone could see that he was anxious to come out of it alive. Yet, a week earlier (while still healthy) he was one of those who said to me, "I don't care when I go."

Most of us will live longer if we have honest apprehension rather than spurious fatalism.

"Am I a Hypochondriac?"

A hypochondriac is one who has excessive concern about his health. Undoubtedly, many thousands of persons worry unnecessarily that they have heart disease, cancer or something else. Yet, it may also be true that many who think that something may be wrong are actually correct. Here is an interesting case history:

> *Dear Dr. Steincrohn*: I am 53. On doctors' advice I began taking hormones about a year ago. One month later I developed diarrhea which has persisted since—in spite of various special diets and medicines.
>
> During the past month my blood pressure has gone up slightly and my pulse gets rapid and irregular at times. I have pain in the left chest, and also a feeling of pressure below the breastbone. Both aggravated after eating.
>
> Even if I take a cookie and a cup of tea I feel as if I have eaten a big Thanksgiving dinner. I'm often nauseated and have heartburn. I have had swelling of the face, abdomen, knees and ankles during the past week.

Am I just a hypochondriac, or is there some way I can find out what is wrong? I like to be outdoors working among my flowers and making things for my home, children and grandchildren. But now all these things have become a tremendous burden and are no longer fun. I did not expect to become incapacitated at least until 70 or 80.

Mrs. E.

Comment: I have known hypochondriacs with similar symptoms, and many more. But the diagnosis of a neurosis should not be made until all investigative efforts come up negative. Although it is true that some people can be ill without symptoms, it is also evident that others with many symptoms can be ill, too.

I don't know when you had your last physical examination, but I would think it's time for it. Swelling isn't an imaginary symptom. Neither are nausea, diarrhea, heartburn, fullness after eating, rapid pulse and chest pains. I'd want to know how your gall bladder is working. Have electrocardiograms and X-rays of your chest. See what a GI series and a lower bowel examination show. I could go on. Feeling as badly as you do, you deserve the "diagnostic works." Not until everything comes back A-OK should you even consider, yourself to be a hopeless hypochondriac.

"My Husband Is A Hypochondriac"

Dear Dr. Steincrohn: My husband is a hypochondriac. I tell him that it's a shame to bother the doctor with every little thing—when you consider

how many serious diseases there are, and so few
doctors to take care of them. Don't you agree?

Mrs. D.

Comment: If I said *Yes*, it would go against all my prin-
ciples regarding the importance of preventive medicine and
the need to fight procrastination. You speak of "every little
thing." Just what do you mean by that? Who is to say what is
little or big—inconsequential or serious?

For example, the "little lump" apparently unimportant
when you feel it today, may turn out to be an inoperable
cancer within a few months. It's a "little thing" now but a
life-shortening matter within weeks. Who's to say? The
patient? That's too great a responsibility for a well-meaning,
but medically untrained, person to take on.

I keep saying that procrastination is disease's greatest ally.
So you see, Mrs. D., I'm on your husband's side. Surprise?
How many "unnecessary" times does he see the doctor a
year? Three? Six?

Well, for his peace of mind, and the chance that he may
one day get there early enough to save his life (and you from
being a widow), I think being checked at intervals is worth
the time and money spent.

'If He Catches Cold You'd Think He Had an Incurable Disease'

Dear Dr. Steincrohn: How can one go on living
with a spouse who constantly complains about one
ailment after another. The doctor never finds anything, and believe me—during the past 25 years
—my husband has had all the tests and X-rays
anyone could have.

If he catches cold you'd think he had an incurable disease. He's worried and actually frightened for days that it may turn into pneumonia or
lung abscess. If he ever had a severe illness we'd
both probably crack up. When younger I could
cope with this problem but now I can't. I might
add that my husband is never too sick to work or
go where he wants to.

Mrs. S.

Comment: I can imagine how you feel, but unfortunately
you have come to the wrong one for advice. I happen to have
great compassion for those bedevilled souls who suffer from
hypochondria. Frankly, I have more sympathy for your
husband than for unhappy bystanders.

Nerves can be as bent or broken as bones. (And usually
hurt more). People tend to have more sympathy for a man
with his leg in a cast than for one whose days are filled with
unnecessary apprehension and anxiety.

I wish I knew how to enable you to "cope" with your
problem. All I can suggest is that you try to develop patience
and sympathy. I assure you that your husband would rather
not be abnormally fearful. At least be thankful that he
musters enough emotional and physical strength to go out
and work and provide for his family. This requires more guts
and forbearance than you realize.

Hundreds of thousands of nervous and anxious people
pray daily that they may become less burdensome to themselves and their families. Those of us who are more fortunate
should try to help by putting ourselves in their shoes and
being more patient. Think it over, Mrs. S.

Maybe You're Not Really a Hypochondriac

Dear Dr. Steincrohn: I'm in a dilemma. I know I
ought to see my doctor, but I keep putting it off.
It may seem like a silly reason, but I hate to bother
him because he may label me a hypochondriac.
Having known a few friends who were in that
category—always complaining about "little things"
and scared they'd die—I vowed I'd never be a
candidate for that classification. To come to the
point. I am 52, and feel completely healthy except
that for the past few months I've been having
indigestion when I walk. Gas seems to fill my chest
and press on me. I stop for a few minutes and the
pain-pressure goes away as if by magic. No other
complaints. I get to the office and forget about it.
My wife says it may be heart trouble, but I tell her
she's trying to make a hypochondriac out of me. If
I went to the doctor he'd laugh me right out of his
office. Don't you agree that too many people
bother doctors for silly complaints, and take up
their precious time?

Mr. D.

Comment: As one who is especially interested in preventive medicine I think you've come to the wrong one for an
opinion. I am biased. I believe that whatever the complaint,
nothing is unimportant and "silly" until it has been investi-
gated and proved innocent. Even at the risk of making a
hypochondriac out of you, I must say your wife may be

right. I think it is important that your doctor have the opportunity to look you over; to make certain that the "gas and indigestion" is not due to coronary disease causing anginal attacks.

Possibly your trouble may be due to a faulty gall bladder. But this is all guesswork. It is your own doctor's job to diagnose and treat you. Therefore it is important for you to see him early—whatever the symptoms—so he can get down to the nitty gritty of diagnosis and proper care. Forget about the shame of being a hypochondriac. Some time ago I wrote that it makes better sense to be a live hypochondriac at 80 than a dead superoptimist at 50. Remember, it's *your* health and *your* life—no complaint should be considered "silly" unless examination proves it is entirely innocent.

Things I Hate to Hear ("He Ought to Be in a Nut House")

For some who consider themselves sane (as judged by ordinary standards) there is an irreverence for those unfortunates who may have some mental aberration. It is an unnatural ego and one with lack of compassion that looks upon another who has mental problems and says, "He's nuts! He's cracked! He belongs in a nut house."

To such people I say, be thankful. Beware. Each one of us has a breaking point. Nobody knows when mounting, unbearable pressures may throw us into the tailspin of a nervous breakdown—that unenviable term which encompasses everything from a neurosis to the more serious psychosis. (More about this in another chapter.)

What I am saying is that we should have some compassion for those mentally ill. We write our best wishes on the cast of the one with a broken leg; let us be equally kind to those with a bent or broken mind. "Nut house" is the vilest of expressions. It bespeaks of lack of sympathy and human understanding. According to some statistics, one-third of all hospital beds are taken by mental patients. It is not a minor problem.

Recently a wife said:

> Why can't friends understand what the family goes through when one of its members is a so-called mental case? Why is there a certain element of disdain—as if one makes this choice of illness rather than having a heart attack (which brings friends and neighbors flocking in sympathy?)
>
> My husband has now left the hospital. Tranquilizers and energizer drugs have restored him to more than a shadow of his former self. He can now work. He socializes. He has lost his depression and is to all intents as normal as he was before his breakdown.
>
> Yet, the other day I heard a friend whisper to an acquaintance that Bill has just come out of the "nut house." I felt like hitting him over the head with my most precious vase."

Comment: I wish she had. It might have knocked "nut house" out of his mind forever.

Ahha! Club

> *Dear Dr. Steincrohn*: I'm a hypochondriac. I admit it. When I get symptoms, I'm scared of dying. But my doctor tells me I'm all right, and

there's no sense coming back to the office. My family laughs at me. Isn't there someone to turn to?

Mrs. O.

Comment: A few years ago I had the urge to write a book *about* hypochondriacs—and *for* them. I recall that my working title was to be: *How To Be a Happy Hypochondriac.* But my publisher dissuaded me. He said, "It's difficult to imagine anyone walking into a bookstore and having the courage to ask for a book by that title." Instead, I wrote a book on heart disease. To this day I'm sorry I didn't follow my impulse. In observing many thousands of patients like yourself, Mrs. O., I have concluded that most hypochondriacs are unhappy. They are sick and tired of complaining daily to their family members, friends and business associates. At last they become conscience-stricken and completely frustrated in constantly enumerating their complaints and discomforts (real or imagined).

Although they may not have been struck down by chronic illness, they continue to suffer in their own distinctive ways. Their fears are real; their anxieties unyielding.

Unfortunately, some doctors become impatient as they listen to recurring complaints from apparently healthy people. They say they'd rather expend their precious and limited time in treating really sick patients. They say they have "no time to fool" with people who have nothing wrong and still live scared.

But what are the hundreds of thousands of hapless hypochondriacs to do? Shall they try to get through the day just by taking pills and potions? And bending the ears of unwilling listeners with their tiresome complaints? Where can they go to find sympathetic understanding?

Here is an idea, Mrs. O. Perhaps getting other hypochondriacs to listen will help. "Ventilation" of problems, as psychiatrists say, is important. How about a few hypochondriacs getting together to form a local group to "swap symptoms"? Why not call it the AHHA! club (Always Happy Hypochondriacs Anonymous). It might soon burgeon into a national organization.

Nothing is so helpful to a worried hypochondriac as finding a willing ear. The AHHA! may be one answer. Am I being ironic? Is this a tongue-in-cheek suggestion? Far from it. I have never been more serious. I believe there's a need for AHHA! You have the opportunity, Mrs. O., to do something about it.

But before you take action, Mrs. O., I think it only fair that you read the following letter from a hypochondriac who does not favor AHHA! clubs.

Dear Dr. Steincrohn: Being a charter member of Hypochondriacs, I just had to make a few comments on your column. First of all there's no such thing as a "happy hypochondriac." We can only be happy when our symptoms, fears, aches and pains are gone. Then we laugh at ourselves, feeling very foolish for our behavior. But when they strike, we become the same bundle of nerves, anxiety ridden, and silly messes all over again. It is difficult to overcome fears by rationalization.

I take pills to calm my anxiety, pills to lift my depression, pills to stop colitis, pills to prevent nausea and vomiting—and then become a wreck wondering what this lethal sounding combination of pills will do to me.

Yes, I think a club might help. Maybe it would

be reassuring to have someone to call when a chest pain strikes. But it is more helpful to have a professional assure us. For example one told me "It is important to emphasize to patients their utter lack of responsibility for their condition. It is as foolish for them to blame themselves for being the way they are, as for the wing of an airplane to scold itself because it is not a fuselage." Knowing that something in the course of our lives has caused this condition; and that we did not purposely become whimpering infants through our own efforts or desire, will help ease much of the guilt which accompanies the malady known as Hypochondria.

I'm very lucky to have several excellent, very patient doctors. But how about the rest of the population? There would be nothing more maddening than to be told: "It's just your nerves!"

I realize it must be frustrating to doctors to waste time with us when so many sick people are languishing in their waiting rooms. But if they don't take the time to examine and reassure us, then we will wind up with a quack (who will listen) or maybe even in a mental hospital.

And let's not forget two harmful possibilities of hypochondria. That the doctor may dismiss something as "nerves." (knowing your history of constant complaining) when it just might turn out to be something really serious. A friend of mine had a ruptured appendix and almost died of peritonitis because her doctor said, "Oh, just another one of your bellyaches!"

The other is that we nervous people eventually become so embarrassed and tired of complaining, sometimes stop mentioning any symptom or discomfort we experience that might help make an early diagnosis. The delay in treatment might be crucial. Another friend knew she had a small lump in her breast. She kept this news from her doctor because she just knew he would say, as he always did. "Now there you go worrying again about something that isn't important." She died of cancer.

Finally, fellow hypochondriacs, let's take pride that when real illness strikes (if I represent the typical hypochondriac) we are the stalwarts of society. For example, this past year I had two major operations, second degree burns covering my back, a bad case of influenza, and a ruptured tubal pregnancy. I never complained or babied myself. (But let me get a twinge near my heart and hysteria sets in.) This martyrdom when we really get sick is probably to show the world we're not the babies they think we are. But I can attest that real pain is never as terrifying as imaginary distress, even though it may be much more severe. Come to think of it, maybe an AHHA! Club would help after all. Many's the time I wish I might capture the ear of a really sympathetic listener.

Mrs. M.

Talk Health—Not Disease

I recall a medical student, when I was a junior, who could walk toward three or four of us and disperse the group as quickly and surely as if he had pointed a shotgun at us.

Although we were sorry for him, we soon learned to avoid him for self-protection. If ever he got hold of your ear he would not let go until he had poured into it a few dozen choice symptoms he had picked up since the last time he had cornered you. (I am thankful I have become more compassionate and understanding as the years went by.)

For example, if he left a demonstration on cancer in the clinic, he was sure to have some of the predominant symptoms. And if he had been studying about tuberculosis, a harmless cough would be sure to throw him midway between agitation and despondency.

A lecture on heart disease? He would be sure to buttonhole you and say, "Just how do you feel when you climb the stairs to your room? Do you get tired and short of breath, too? Does your heart palpitate?" Then he would look at you intently—as if his entire future depended upon your answer.

If you denied any such symptoms he would be sure to say that he was certain that he had heart trouble. If you said, "Well, yes, I get a little tired, too," his face would light up with relief. He would not say, as you might expect, "That's that. I guess my symptoms are normal ones that anyone would get while exerting." Instead, he would say, "Well, I guess both of us are coming down with heart trouble. Misery loves company."

Our unhappy co-student was a Grade Z hypochondriac—right down at the bottom of the list. We all wondered what kind of doctor he would make. We used to say he'd probably spend more time reciting his own complaints than listening to his patients'.

Fortunately, and I say it advisedly, he did not complete his medical education. He flunked out. Instead, he went into business and made a success of it. In fact, he was my patient for years. During this time I found him far from being a hypochondriac.

"You know," he said to me in my office, "I guess I wasn't cut out for medicine. Just being near sick people and studying about disease all the time had me really scared. As soon as I was no longer exposed to disease, I became a normal individual again. The smartest thing I ever did was to give up medicine."

Then he lit a cigarette, took a deep puff and said with a wise smile, "And don't think I didn't realize how you fellows used to run whenever you saw me. I've forgiven you all long ago. I had it coming.

"But the shoe's on the other foot now. Even I can't listen to anybody talk, talk, talk about his sickness or his operation. Why don't people realize that they'd be better off talking *health* instead of *disease*? They'd not only have more friends—but they'd actually feel better."

So there you have it, coming right out of the horse's mouth—so to speak.

How *Are* You?

Too many of us are triggered into a long dissertation about our health whenever we hear such a simple, routine (and probably impersonal) question as, "How've you been?" The innocent inquirer is bowled over by the sudden, unsuspected rush of words that describe our last bout with the virus—or how we "almost" had double pneumonia.

Repeat a similar performance again, and, like the boy in medical school, I guarantee that your friends will begin to steer clear of you. When they see you coming, they will make it their business to find some interest on the other side of the street.

Whenever *you* are asked the simple question, "How are you?" just say, "Have a slight headache."—and drop it by turning the conversation elsewhere. Or, if your friend says, "I hear you've been sick," you can say, "Oh, I was laid up for a little while. Fine now." (And again drop it like the proverbial hot potato.)

Besides, people aren't really interested in long recitations of other peoples' troubles. They will tell you they have enough of their own. Don't open your spout of sad tales until you get to your doctor's office—and hope he has the time to listen. That's the proper place to let them gush out.

For years I have been advising patients to keep their illness an intensely personal thing—between their doctor, their family, and perhaps a few trusted friends. Otherwise they lay themselves open to questions. People will always be asking (whether deeply interested or not), "How *are* you? How do you feel *today*? Better?"

They keep reminding you that you are an invalid. They don't let you get well—even though they may mean well. One day when the world seems to be your oyster they will say, "You look kind of pale and drawn today. Don't you feel well?" If you are human, you will react like anybody else; you will begin to wonder if you are well or sick.

You see, often you innocently bring on such intemperate and superficial interest in your physical condition yourself. And you pay for it.

Without question, all of us would be healthier and happier if we resolved to talk *health* and not talk *disease*.

Make these resolutions:

1. If you have been having symptoms see your doctor. Tell him all about them and then leave them in his office.

2. Don't discuss your recent operation or illness with friends or family. Don't bring it up like a daily weather report.

3. Unless you are careful you may soon be carrying around a symptom "in every pocket."

4. Remember that illness should be a personal thing. If you broadcast it, you will never rest in peace. All you will be hearing is, "How *are* you today?"

5. Think *health*; not *disease*.

6. Be thankful you're *vertical*! It's a God-given gift to be able to get out of bed every morning.

Yes, There Is Hope for Hypochondriacs

Here is a suggestion on how to overcome anxiety, given to me by a recent dinner companion. Learning I am interested in people who suffer from "nerves" in some form or other, she volunteered (and asked me to pass it on sometime to others who disbelieve) that anxiety is curable. She was so convincing I asked her to write it down so I might incorporate it in this book.

> There are a few things that I've found very helpful—and believe me I had a rough time of it for a few years. One doctor advised: 1. Leave my husband. 2. Read and read on the subject of anxiety.
>
> I did not leave my husband, but I started to read—everything on neurosis, anxiety; the good and the amateur, the difficult and the stupid. After a while I could understand most of it. I think the Menninger books the very best. But as I read on

and began to realize that I was not alone (the A.A. theory), and even more important, that it was not fatal, I began to see light. I also developed a profound understanding of others, and a tolerance to my friends, family and children.

While I was reading (and I hasten to add that too much introspection is self-defeating—too much focus on oneself) I got busy with my hands and learned to create something. I did needlepoint, and worked with flowers, and found great joy in refinishing old furniture—hours of sanding, and staining and polishing, until finally something useful was produced. I had a feeling of "I did that!" It's an ego builder.

Another important point is that we've got to do something for other people: while the volunteers may not make the world go round, it's mandatory to get out around others. For example, as an aid in the hospital we see very quickly how comparatively well off we are—and particularly, that our problem lies in *our hands*.

Yes, there is hope for hypochondriacs or any other form of anxiety. You can beat most of it yourself. You *can*. It's like walking through a dark tunnel for months or years and at last seeing there's really a light at the other end. So I say, keep walking. Hang in there, Luv!

Philosophy of Champions

A few years ago I went straight to the source. How do real champions overcome anxiety? How do they face up to the big A? How are they able to function when practically inundated by a threatening torrent of anxiety when in the ring with an opponent? How do they survive emotionally? How do they withstand the anxieties which prick them every day for weeks before a bout?

Yes, I admit they are pros. They are paid for what they do. But so are we every morning we get up to gird ourselves against the world. I think the philosophy they expressed to me will help all of us neutralize (at least a little bit) the anxieties which overburden us every day.

I visited Floyd Patterson, a kindly man with all the attributes of a gentle man, in spite of his tigerish qualities when inside the ropes. I asked him, "Mr. Patterson, how do you train to overcome anxiety? Especially after the memory of that knockout in your first fight with Johansson? What do you do to wipe out the little devils who must be trying to stick little spears of anxiety into your mind? Can you sleep? Can you eat? What you tell me may be of tremendous help to many people who suffer from chronic anxiety, to those who have lost faith that they will ever be able to hold up their heads and live their lives without nagging fears."

Here was Patterson's philosophy: "I have no room for fear. I do not think of it; not that I am trying to run away from it. And I am not trying to build up my confidence by talking this way; it is a part of me. My days and nights are taken up with preparing my body so that it will be in top physical condition on the day of the fight. I think only of winning; never of the possibility of losing.

"I do my job, live day by day, and have faith. I guess you can call it positive thinking as much as anything else. I don't allow myself to think negative. If you want the secret that may help your patients, perhaps you can find it in that last statement: Don't think negative!"

Later on that same day I sought out another gentle, soft-spoken man. I asked Joe Louis, "How do you train for a fight? Not your muscles, but your mind, so you won't be scared?"

Like Patterson, he thought for a moment, and then said simply, "I was so busy getting myself ready, there was no time for fear. I was always confident—not in a boastful way—that I would win. My manager used to say to me, 'just fight one round at a time, Joe. Then the next one, and the one after that. Until you win.' In that way there's no time for fear. One thing at a time. People who think too far ahead can get themselves into a tizzy."

"That's the secret," Joe continued, "When you think only of winning, nothing can scare you. Too many people think of losing—and that makes them scared of life."

Still later I talked to another champion.

He said, "There's a difference between being careful and being scared."

Who said that? Plato? Freud? Shakespeare?

No. It was Sonny Liston, former heavyweight boxing champion of the world, as he leaned against a railing, placidly gazing at the Atlantic from his training quarters. He did not seem so huge, yet he oozed power. You felt it as you stood next to him. He reminded me of a panther stretched out in sleep—relaxed, yet potentially powerful and dangerous.

What especially impressed me was his handshake. Similar to Joe Louis's and Patterson's greetings, I came out with all my bones intact. It seems the bigger they are, the gentler they are with your hand. Somewhat like a large dog that plays with a puppy, or a father with a small son, an unconscious spirit of protectiveness for the weak takes over.

After we had been talking for a while, one of Liston's handlers came along and said, "Sonny, I'm sorry to have to break this up, but we have an appointment to keep in a few minutes."

I have always respected Liston for what he said next. He turned to me as if he had all the time in the world. He said, "The doctor here is trying to find something that will help some sick people get well. I've got time for that."

I asked him, "When you get into the ring are you scared? Are you worried that you may have to be carried out? Like some sick people feel when they go to a doctor?"

"Never," he said. "I always make up my mind to be careful. There's a difference between being careful and being scared."

I had what I had been waiting for. He sensed it, we shook hands again, and he ambled off to his appointment.

Liston's answer was a fitting one for those people who go through life courting disaster because they are afraid they will be labeled hypochondriacs. For those who think it silly to visit their doctor because they are "not sick enough to bother him."

I recall the many coronary patients who thought their trouble was simple indigestion. They didn't want to show they were scared so they weren't careful.

The answer seems to be that when illness strikes, whether it seems trivial or otherwise, there's no shame in finding its cause and treating it. Be careful. (You can take it from a champ.)

Sonny Liston made his contribution to preventive medicine when he said, "There's a big difference between being careful and being scared."

So did Louis and Patterson—all great champions—but also great philosophers in their own way. All having learned the secret of overcoming unnatural and excessive anxiety. Advice freely given with the hope that they might help those among us who live up to our necks in anxiety.

In a recent book I also listed the names of some phobias which haunt the anxious, filling them with layers of fear that are often difficult to remove. "Reasoning them away" proves ineffective. In many cases, psychiatric help is the only way to bring them relief.

As I believe that no book written for the anxious patient would be complete without considering such phobias, here is a short reconsideration of the problem.

"Last year you mentioned the scientific names of a long list of phobias. I have misplaced the source. Would you please repeat this information? I'm sure the world is full of people who are scared, especially these days. It would bring them some measure of comfort to know that they are not alone in suffering from these awful anxieties. Take me, for example. I'm afraid of mirrors! That makes it pretty tough for a woman."

Each one of us has his private worry or anxiety. Often our best friends don't know. We don't tell because our fears either seems so silly or because they actually scare us to death—almost. Friends might laugh outright or think we were spoofing. Yet, there is such an abnormal fear. We call it *Eisoptrophobia*.

Not long ago a friend confessed her fear of cats. She said; "Is there actually such a thing as fear of cats? I grow cold with fear when I see one. Once I came into a home that had three cats and I rushed out in panic."

I don't know how much better I made her feel when I said that William Shakespeare was reportedly afraid of cats, too. I think it is natural for every normal person to be afraid of something. The difference is that some of us scare more easily than others. People have always been afraid. Otherwise, the human race would never have survived. Fear is as natural an impulse as hunger. One of the baby's first emotions is fear. What makes fear abnormal is its intensity and the unusual phobias which induce it.

Incidentally, the scientific name for the fear of cats is *ailourophobia*. And here, at last, is a list of scientific names for many fears you probably haven't even heard about. It will prove to you that man is a bundle of nerves. It will help you to be sympathetic towards those whom you may have ridiculed in the past.

Achluophobia (fear of darkness)
Agorophobia (fear of open spaces)
Algophobia (fear of pain)
Arachnephobia (fear of spiders)
Astraphobia (fear of airplanes)
Blonephobia (fear of needles)
Cheimophobia (fear of cold)
Demophobia (fear of crowds)
Elektrophobia (fear of electricity in any form)
Eremiaphobia (fear of solitude)
Eretophobia (fear of pins)
Ergophobia (fear of work)
Graphophobia (fear of writing)
Gymnotophobia (fear of nudity)
Hematrophobia (fear of blood)
Ideaphobia (fear of thought)
Kinesophobia (fear of automobiles)
Mechanophobia (fear of any kind of machine)
Misophobia (fear of contamination)
Nosophobia (the fear that you have all the symptoms of all the diseases you read and hear about)
Ochophobia (fear of vehicles)
Oikophobia (fear of home)
Pnigerophobia (fear of smothering)
Pternonphobia (fear of feathers)
Pyrophobia (fear of fire)

Rypophobia (fear of dirt)
Siderodropomophobia (fear of railway trains)
Sitiophobia (fear of drinking)
Thalassophobia (fear of sea)
Thermophobia (fear of heat)
Xenophobia (fear of strangers)
Zoophobia (fear of animals)

Knowing about this long list of human fears will make you a more tolerant and sympathetic human being. Here you will find something that fits you, family members or friends.

You will understand (and not think it silly) why an otherwise courageous man doesn't want to fly; why another would rather fly than ride in a car; why some women who fear dirt are such enemies of house dust; why some housewives can't pluck a chicken, why others fear lightning.

Whenever you meet a person who seems afraid of the "silliest" things, think of this list (still incomplete). Not only will it make you more compassionate, it will give you a better understanding of your fellow man. And it will also test your sense of humor.

Candles on the Birthday Cake

Here for example, is a mild form of *Misophobia* (fear of contamination).

Some time ago I wrote a newspaper column on the technique of blowing out the candles on a birthday cake. (Blowing across it rather than down.) A number of readers had sworn off eating cake during such celebrations because of the danger of getting germs from the star of the occasion.

Last night I went to a birthday party. Right after "Happy Birthday to You" came the cake. I watched the guest of honor take a very deep breath and blow so hard right down on top of the cake that you could see the chocolate tremble and shake. Nevertheless, in the face of danger from millions of unseen bacteria, I sat down with the rest of the happy gathering and had my cake and ice cream.

But as I ate I wondered if there wasn't some truth in the assertion that blowing down on a birthday cake is, if not bad manners, at least showing unconcern for any sensitive guests who may be present to help celebrate. Many so believe:

> I have an important question for you. Please do not hesitate to tell me the truth even if you think I am wrong.
>
> I am extremely fond of the traditional birthday or anniversary party. The hostess prepares an enticing, delicious cake. On top are a number of colorful, cute little candles. Everybody sings Happy Birthday. A wish is made.
>
> Then comes the climax of the ceremony—the blowing out of the candles. A youngster often makes a half-dozen unsuccessful tries before the flames are extinguished. But the grown person most often accomplishes the job in hand by taking a deep breath and blowing right down on top of the cake.
>
> At my own birthday parties I never blow out the candles with my own breath. I use a small bellows. I would feel terrible to breathe on my own cake and then pass out my germs to unsuspecting guests. Shall I keep on with the bellows? Will people say I'm ruining a wonderful tradition?

A small bellows? Why not? But wouldn't flicking out the lights one by one be as effective? Or simply blowing across the cake than directly down upon it? But I wonder whether "antiseptic" birthday parties might not take away some of the spontaneity and fun of the occasion.

The Missing Dentures

Recently I heard of another kind of phobia. I do not believe there is a scientific term for it.

> At last I have joined the large group of Americans past 50 who have lost all their teeth and now are classed as being "without a tooth in their head"—except for their dentures. I admit that my smile, although a bit artificial, is much prettier than it used to be when I had my own crooked front teeth.
>
> Nevertheless, I have a phobia. What to do at night? Sleep with my dentures in or out? My dentist says the choice is mine. Some prefer to let them soak so impersonally in a glass of water at the bedside. Others, like myself, would rather wear them while they sleep.
>
> But my problem is this. I have this silly fear that some night my denture will come loose and I'll swallow or choke on it. My dentist says there's little danger because my own false teeth fit snugly. He says that only in a loose, ill-fitting denture is it possible that one will have any complications. I'll be grateful for your opinion.

The dentists I have asked, give me a reply similar to that of your own doctor. The choice is the patient's. So it seems evident you need not have a water glass at your bedside. You can sleep in peace.

However, I think you will be interested in an exception which proves the rule. (There are always exceptions!) The following case history was reported to the Editor of the *Journal of the American Medical Association* by Charles E. H. Bates, MD of San Francisco:

An 83-year-old man was seen in consultation because he complained of a wheeze. Although an X-ray film revealed that there was a "foreign body" in the upper part of his esophagus (swallowing-tube between mouth and stomach) the patient did not complain of pain or trouble in swallowing. He had just finished a full dinner in complete comfort. The patient did not appear senile. He complained that he had lost his upper bridge two months before and couldn't imagine what had happened to it.

Further studies on the X-ray film indicated that the missing bridge was caught vertically in the upper part of the esophagus. The following morning, under general anesthesia, Dr. Bates (using a laryngoscope—a hollow, lighted tube) was able to grasp the missing denture with forceps and remove it with little bleeding.

The patient had no further problems and recovered uneventfully. This case was remarkable in that there were no symptoms other than the wheezing. As the doctor describes it:

"We have all removed foreign bodies from the esophagus, such as plates, bridges, and other objects, but there have usually been signs of obstruction, pain made worse by swallowing, choking, and general alarm. Professional advice is immediately sought. Remarkably, this patient had no complaints or symptoms whatsoever and did not know that he had half swallowed the bridge."

This case history is an example that no fears should be

considered to be "silly"; either by patient or physician. What *is* silly is to keep quiet and suffer in desperation.

Thoughts and Afterthoughts on Chapter 17

1. To some degree, we are all hypochondriacs.

2. Fear of loss of health is the natural reaction of the normal man or woman. Do not be ashamed of wanting to live.

3. Most of us will live longer if we have honest apprehension rather than spurious fatalism.

4. The diagnosis of "neurosis" should not be made until all investigative efforts come up negative.

5. Complaints about "little things" may often be "big clues" that lead to recovery.

6. Nerves can become as bent or broken as bones. (And usually hurt more.)

7. Whatever the complaint, nothing is unimportant or "silly."

8. Each one of us has a breaking point. Nobody knows when mounting, unbearable pressures may throw us into the tailspin of a nervous breakdown—that unenviable term that encompasses everything from neurosis to psychosis.

9. Therefore, we should have compassion for the mentally ill.

10. The AHHA! Club.

11. Talk health—not disease.

12. A grade Z hypochondriac.

13. Illness should be an intensely personal thing—between patient, doctor, family, and perhaps a few trusted friends.

14. Reread the six practical tips on how to be a happy

hypochondriac.

15. The philosophy of champions in overcoming anxiety.

16. Reconsider the Phobias.

18
"Someday I'll be dead..."

Most of us live life "catch-as-catch-can." Relatively few have a working philosophy. We work and relax without plan or format. But there are exceptions. For example, consider John Smith:

> Everything I do, I do by plan. I plan my happiness, my eating habits, my sleeping habits, everything. I never worry.
>
> I never have suffered from insomnia and never will. However, I suppose I am subject to this malady as is everyone else. But I control it, defeat it, as you prefer.
>
> It's very simple. I never think of getting into bed unless I'm sleepy! And this entails going to bed at the oddest of hours. Sometimes I'll go to bed at 6 P.M., sometimes at nine, other times at midnight, at two A.M., even as late as four or five A.M. It matters very little what time I go to bed, as I always wake up on time. I do not use an alarm clock. So much for all that.
>
> There is another practice I follow. I will not, under any circumstances, get into bed and think of

my obligations. This I refuse to do. I think of
nothing that has happened during the day—
nothing.

I plan it this way and I live up to my plan. I also
go to bed with a clear conscience every night. On
those few occasions when sleep is slow in coming I
get up and read a book or newspaper. When my
eyelids begin to droop, Zingo, I'm in slumberland.
No tossing or squirming. Just good old glorious
sleep.

And be it three or eight hours, when I wake up
I'm ready to go. I can't wait to get out of bed and
sail into that busy, bustling, noisy, pushing, mael-
strom of humanity. (Fortunately I am one of those
who can get along on a few hours of sleep if
necessary.) I plan my happiness, too. I've got tons
and tons of that.

I asked this unusual man for his secret formula. What was
his philosophy of life? What was the driving force that
propelled him from day to day with such assurance and
fulfillment?

He told me that although he doesn't believe in God, that
on the morning of his 70th birthday he woke in amazement
and said: "It doesn't seem possible I've reached the biblical
years. Thank God."

He does not recall how early in life he became aware that
it is circumscribed—that humans are not mortally perpetual.
He does recall, however, that from the early years on, he was
certain that he would never reach the age of 30. And what
would bring him down by 40? And by 50? 60? 70? Scores of
possibilities reinforced his conviction that he was not long for
this world.

Yet, he was not a hypochondriac. Nor did he go to bed at night thinking he might be dead by morning, nor did he wake with the belief, "This day I may die." Instead, his was an unconscious feeling that man is not mortal.

Like Ben Hecht's friend "Charlie" MacArthur, he realized that something in his genes had deprived him of the fatuous belief that we are here forever. Like "Charlie," he "was born without the illusion of permanence—he had his eye on mortality." It was for this reason he was especially delighted and amazed that he has survived until the biblical 70.

He was not a morose man. Thoughts of death, like layers of earth, did not blanket his enthusiasm for life. In fact, he was as excitable as a boy during periods of elation, and calmly philosophical during adversity. He was affectionate though undemonstrative.

Especially sensitive to pain himself, he had an inborn, natural empathy for the feelings and hurts in others. Therefore, he was extremely tactful to prevent rubbing emotional sores. He was compassionate for the anxious, the frightened and the suffering—because, unconsciously, he knew that all of us are brothers and sisters on the inevitable journey to the land called Oblivion.

Her Husband "Lives Scared"

A wife complained:

> My husband is a worrywart. He's the perfect example of the person who "lives scared." He won't face up to the fact that some day none of us will be here. I tell him to stop worrying but it does no good. He's scared of life. He's scared of death.

He gets over one fear and then he finds something
else to worry over. Otherwise, the doctor says he's
perfectly healthy. But he keeps asking the doctor
"vas is los" with him.

I told her that anxiety is a peculiar thing. You find it
everywhere. That's why the sufferer deserves sympathy instead of jibes. As his wife, he was turning to her as a last
resort. He was confiding his fears in her, but probably
stomping them down all the while he was at work trying to
earn a living under great anxiety pressures.

I have known football stars who were afraid of a scratch. I
recall a champion boxer whom you couldn't get into an
elevator without inviting a chop on the jaw.

Fears, phobias, worries—to some degree victimize each of
us. Thousands of apparently healthy persons suddenly have
an attack of acute anxiety (it seems to come out of nowhere)
and for many months or years later they are so anxious and
scared that they cannot even summon enough courage to
attend church or sit in a movie. Chronic anxiety has taken
over.

Now, worry is a form of chronic anxiety state. You find it
in many places. For example, there's the millionaire who is in
daily fear that he will become poor. There's the respected
president of a large organization who is in constant fear that
he will lose his job. There's the man who worries about his
own health and that of his family when all are well. In other
words, he reasons, "things are too good, something bad is
bound to happen." There's the man who has an occasional
heart skip who is certain he is going to die soon of heart
trouble. There's the one who is always worried about having
cancer.

We medical men try hard even though we know people

can't turn off worries like they do the water in a faucet. But we try to help make life more livable and enjoyable.

Evolution (Once Upon A Time)

Each anxious patient is a problem unto his own. We can't treat all worriers the same—cover them all with a comfortable blanket that shields them from the intemperance of life. Sometimes we must resort to kind understanding; at others, to an actual shaking of the patient's shoulders and using shock treatment, such as, "Someday I'll be dead. Someday you'll be dead. Someday we'll all be dead.

"Your trouble is being intensified by an introversion that excludes the possibility that today is here and now, and that tomorrow may never come. The result is you only think of you and you and you. Everything else—people and things— are secondary. All this does is exaggerate and build your anxieties to tremendous proportions.

"If you could get yourself to believe that you are over-rating your importance, you would worry less. Perhaps you should worry more about the fact that you are on earth as a temporary visitor—and you will automatically worry less about how you feel today. Just as an animal is supposed to be able to smell out fear in people, so does life seem to single out those who live scared, and scare them even more.

"Think it over. When you learn to think less of yourself as the only important person (to yourself) in the universe, when you are able to consider that you are only the small grain of sand on the beach, perhaps you'll stick your head out of your shell, and begin to live and take advantage of what each day offers."

Once I talked like that to a patient and friend. He stalked

out of the office. For the time being I lost both friend and patient. But he returned a week later thanking me for having driven some sense of proportion into his head.

Stand Off and Look at Yourself

Until a few Martians (or any other of our celestial neighbors) swoop down here in a spaceship, until they can prove that they are exceptional and really "out-of-this-world" superbeings, until such time, man as we know him, can pride himself on being the most wonderful collection of living stuff in existence anywhere. Such confidence and awareness of the entire human race rubs off on the individual. It is one way to combat undue anxiety.

Stand off and look at yourself. If all you see in your mirror is a nose, eyes and a mouth, then you do not explore deeply enough. For you are gazing upon a most complex, unpredictable, unfathomable mechanism whose inherent wisdom and potentialities for changing this world for the better are beyond our present understanding and comprehension.

Ourselves being men and women, we cannot truly see ourselves. We hope somebody will hold up the mirror so that we can see and understand ourselves in a bright flash of instantaneous revealment. No one person can ever hope to do this service for his fellows. But thousands through the ages have tried and still try to hold up the image of man so that he may see himself.

Uncounted sculptors have chipped away at marble; as many painters have applied the paint to canvasses; and perhaps more writers have tried to fashion the true image of man. But none has come up with the finished job.

As we look we see ourselves in faint outline. That outline

has become clearer, but only slowly and imperceptibly. For man, patience is the sine qua non of existence. We must accept the fact that it will take man a few million more years to fully realize his wonderful potentialities.

Still, even in the present, imperfect state—anatomically, physiologically, psychologically, and spiritually—we are a wonder of wonders. The act of living itself in the marvelous form of man should give pride to the most crestfallen. People who suffer from anxiety have, in fact, lost perspective. They have lost confidence in themselves as human beings.

Evolution

Thereby hangs a tale: the story of evolution. It will profit you to know a bit about it if you suffer from anxiety. In your darkest hours this story should lift up your heart. In your moments of pride, it may spare you a fall.

Arnold Bennett said; "The most important of all deceptions is the continual deception of cause and effect—the deception of the cause of evolution. When one has thoroughly got imbued into one's head the leading truth that nothing happens without a cause, one grows not only large-minded, but large-hearted."

Recently I spoke with an anxious man who, in the course of our conversation, jumped out of his chair to bring me a small volume. It was a traceable history of his own family tree. He was understandably prideful of the pictures of his parents, grandparents and great-grandparents. As I remember it, he traced his lineage directly back to the sixteenth century. Unfortunately, he was more proud of his lineage than of the inherent strength of his nervous system. He lived scared instead of living in perspective which would have lessened his daily anxieties.

I was tempted to bring a brighter focus on his past so that he could see himself in a truer light. But I decided not to interfere with his complacent view and pride in his family. I might have showed him a quote from Stuart Chase who wrote: "If each of us could trace his family tree back for enough generations, we should all find the same great, great, great-grandfather."

To this day I'm sorry I didn't. I should have said, "See here. Forget about your family tree; it's really no different from anybody else's. What you should do, instead, is focus on your anxiety. The trouble with you is that your mind is filled with only yourself. You are unaware that someday you'll be dead—just like the rest of us. If you could begin to look outward instead of morosely inward all the time, you'd find that anxiety would not threaten every waking moment of your life."

I wonder how much it might have helped. Each one of us should see himself in perspective. We'd each not only be a better but a happier human being for it.

Historians of Life

Paleontologists are the historians of life. They not only study the fossils but correlate the findings of all other scientists in related fields who are unraveling the mystery of existence.

Here are some of their findings—only fragments, perhaps, but enough to give you a better look at yourself as a human being, a better evaluation of your true relation to yourself, your neighbors and your world, giving an even better perspective than you might get on looking down from a high mountain peak or comparing your insignificance to the rolling waves in open sea.

For example, there is proof that the earth as it exists today is about two billion years old. A good guess is that it is close to three billion. It is possible that life began way back there, but there is no proof. However, there is sufficient evidence that life began one billion years ago. The study of fossils proves this. Rapid evolution did not begin until about five hundred million years ago. According to geologists, that would be the Cambrian epoch or period.

At that time man was not even a gleam in the eye of existence as we know it today. Much came before: there were the protozoa, single-celled animals too minute for the naked eye to see. There were the sponges; the worms; the marine forms sometimes called the "moss animals"; the starfish; the sea urchins; the snails; the clams; the octopuses; the anthropods, including insects, crabs, spiders, scorpions; and coming closer, the vertebrates, which include fishes, amphibians, reptiles, dinosaurs, birds, and finally, mammals.

(Are you becoming less anxious? Is this recital of your "family tree" giving you a true sense of what you are and where you are in this universe of ours? Are you beginning to wonder what's the sense of worrying away a short existence?)

Mammals? Man is a mammal, but not the only one in that category. Consider your fellow mammals: bats, kangaroos, rabbits, mice, whales, elephants, giraffes, horses, cats, dogs and monkeys. In fact, thirty-two orders or classes of mammalia are recognized, of which only eighteen survive today.

A subdivision of these mammalia is called Primates. That is where you and I fit in as we gaze upon one of your fellow primates, the monkey or ape, behind the bars of his cage in the zoo. But differ we do. Man's most distinctive characteristics are flexibility, intelligence, socialization and individualization, according to anthropologist George Gaylord Simpson. (Another characteristic, anxiety. Man is the most worrisome of all primates.)

Man and ape branched off the life tree in the Miocene epoch about 28 million years ago. They went on developing through the Pliocene and Pleistocene periods. That brings us up to what is called the Recent period (beginning about 20 thousand years ago).

Stuart Chase in *The Proper Study of Mankind* puts it well:

> Our most remote forebear, according to Linton, was probably a small tree-dweller, ancestral to both men and apes. During the Miocene age, some members became too large for trees and took to the ground, still on all fours. In the latter half of the Pliocene, one branch reached the human level, but in the form of a very primitive gentleman indeed.
>
> He gave rise to a number of species, one of which finally developed into modern man. Language probably began then. This species exterminated its competitors, overran the earth, and in due course began to differentiate into the various races which we know today—brown, yellow and white. If we could piece together the story of how a small group, starting probably in Central Asia, gradually spread around the whole globe, it would dwarf all migrations in human history! . . .
>
> How did these remote ancestors of ours get over to Japan, to the Phillipines, across the watery wastes of the Pacific to one island after another? How did they make their way from the mouth of the Nile down to the Cape of Good Hope? What

was their rate—a hundred miles a year, or ten miles
a century?

I wonder how our friend with his little blue book about his
ancestors of a few hundred years back would feel on reading
all this. I should be disappointed if he were disillusioned. I
should like to believe that he would still treasure his known
family line as before.

Nevertheless, I should also like to believe that this new
aspect of his origins would make him a less worrisome and
anxious human being. Not only would he become more
tolerant of his fellows, more prideful of the strides man has
made, more hopeful of mankind's future (especially in moral
development: fewer wars, less cruelty etc.) but also less afraid
in the present.

It is my conviction that the person who lives as if he will
be here forever is the most likely to suffer from anxiety. And
that the one who is brave enough and honest enough to say
to himself, "Someday I'll be dead," lives in less anxiety.

Long ago Marcus Aurelius Antoninus wrote: "Consider
when thou art much vexed or grieved, that man's life is only a
moment, and after a short time we are all laid out dead."
(This is one of the most effective antidotes against anxiety.)

And Lajos Zilahy said, "Man fears something, and most
often it is death. Frequently, however, he fears life, and this
is the more dangerous species of fear. The fear of death leads
toward life, but the fear of life conduces to death."

But of all the antidotes against anxiety I believe that the
following is the most impressive and effectual. There would
be less anxiety in the world if it was read every day (as one
takes a nerve tonic):

To every thing there is a season, and a time to
every purpose under the heaven:

> A time to be born, and a time to die; a time to
> plant, and a time to pluck up that which is planted;
> A time to kill, and a time to heal; a time to
> break down, and a time to build up. . . .
> —Ecclesiastes, III: 1-3

Are you anxious? Try it for a least a month of days. My own experience with patients attests to its helpfulness to formerly depressed and hopeless people steeped in anxiety.

Something Sydney J. Harris wrote also confirms my belief that "awareness" is an antidote against anxiety: ". . . we must learn to live both as if we were going to be immortal and as if we were going to die tomorrow. A sense of immortality provides the continuity on which society depends; and a sense of imminent death makes us live each day as if it were our last, so that we do not forfeit goods in the present for a probable future. These are the basic existential paradoxes in human life; if we cannot resolve them, and accept them, there is no 'consolation' to be found elsewhere—not in Mozart, nor in the galaxies, nor in any anodyne." Can you learn to say to yourself, "Some day I'll be dead?" I consider such "shock therapy" the master step in the tortuous journey to neutralize anxiety. You will learn to believe that Tomorrow is the first day of the rest of your life.

Thoughts and Afterthoughts on Chapter 18

1. Read and reread this chapter on evolution. It will at last give you the perspective you need in relating yourself to yourself. I have found that anxious patients are so bound up within themselves that they lose sight of the people and the world around them. There is nothing so enlightening as the

revelation that our personal anxieties, as measured against the history of mankind's millions of years, are indeed trivial. By some peculiar chemical reaction, this realization helps anxiety-ridden sufferers to bear up under their burdens until such time as they improve sufficiently to return to the normal way of life. As our personal sense of importance diminishes, somehow our bundle of nerves loosens and relaxes.

VII
Antidotes Against
the Poison
of Chronic Anxiety

19
How To Overcome Fatigue, Tension and Insomnia

Fatigue

Fatigue is the common enemy of man and woman. All adults suffer from it at some time in their lives. So do normal children—but they sleep it off in one night and become as active and energetic as ever. Mainly, there are three causes of fatigue: physiologic, psychologic or pathologic (or combinations of all three).

A teenager runs a mile race which leaves him exhausted. He rests and recovers. Next day he feels fine. This is but one example of physiologic fatigue. You might find it in a salesman who climbs up and down stairs day after day. Unable to find time off from these daily excursions, he develops chronic physiologic tiredness.

A housewife complains:

> I'm always tired, trying to bring up a family of four children and take care of my husband. We can't afford a dishwasher so dishes pile up in the sink. Laundry remains unwashed and unironed. Meals are late.
>
> Fatigue and nervousness become so overpow-

ering that I'm always bickering and fighting with a
wonderful husband. What shall I do? If this goes on
much longer, our marriage and everything wonderful in it will come tumbling down over our heads.

I said, you're still a young housewife. There are two areas
which deserve investigation. Is your trouble pathologic or
psychologic? Let's consider the second. Perhaps you are one
of the many who are procrastinators by nature. Putting off
your problems only increases their severity.

Do you plan your day? Or does this "putting-it-off" ten-
dency only compound your work? If so, much will depend
upon taking honest inventory of yourself. Daily unremitting
stress leads to fatigue. And it's time that thousands of men
and women relieve chronic fatigue by the simple process of
planning ahead—and by fighting procrastination.

Print this motto on a card and look at it every day: DON'T
PUT OFF UNTIL TOMORROW (OR, BETTER STILL, THE
NEXT HOUR) WHAT NEEDS DOING RIGHT NOW.

As for a possible pathologic cause, everyone knows that
illness can cause fatigue. Sometimes all that is necessary for
improvement is rearrangement of diet, with adequate vitamins and minerals. Is it hypoglycemia? Quite often, simple,
secondary anemia is the reason, and this condition is allevi-
ated by removal of its cause and by taking iron medication.

However, if your fatigue is stubborn, it is your job to visit
your doctor, and it's his job to rule out the possibility that
there is a pathologic cause such as unsuspected tuberculosis,
myasthenia gravis, diabetes, heart disease, or one of scores of
other physical involvements that may be the culprit. The
main thing to remember is that daily fatigue, which causes so
much anxiety, should not be accepted with equanimity. It
deserves investigation and vigorous treatment.

Living Day by Day

"A gigantic sacrifice of the present to the future is always going on." Arnold Bennett said that in his book *How To Live on 24 Hours a Day*. I recommend it to readers as one of the most provocative books for helping to shape a fruitful way of life. Especially to the husband of the woman who made the following complaint:

> Some people act as if there is no tomorrow. My husband acts as if there is no today.
>
> All he thinks of is how much money he will have by the time he is 60. He is only 38 now, but if ever a man killed himself by the way he lived, my man is a perfect example. Meanwhile he is making an anxious wreck out of me.
>
> He works in his small factory at least 14 hours a day. Gets there at 7 A.M. and doesn't leave until about 9 P.M. When he gets home at 9:30 he is too exhausted to eat his dinner. So he has got into the habit of drinking two or three "doubles" of scotch on the rocks in the evening. I've been told he puts away at least three martinis when he goes to lunch with customers.
>
> He smokes at least two packs a day. He hasn't had a vacation in over six years. (Neither have the rest of us.) He's always exhausted. He's irritable. We have no fun at all. The children don't know they have a father. He has never even played "catch" with our two younger sons. When I try to talk this over with him, not trying to nag, he says, "Who am I doing it for? I want security for you and the kids." Don't you think he is throwing

away today for a tomorrow that may never come?

Arnold Bennett answered that much better than I can. I wonder if her husband has taken time for his own physical inventory. I'm sure he does so in his own shop periodically. How about his own body? Chances are he says, "I haven't got the time." If he is to reach his pinnacle at 60, financially secure and "sitting on top of the world," he'd better *take* the time. An unsuspected ulcer may be boring in; or symptomless high blood pressure; or beginning emphysema or lung growth; or the giant killer, coronary artery disease.

In addition to getting him to read Bennett's book I also suggested she obtain a copy of my recent book *Don't Die Before Your Time*. (Nash Publishing Co., Los Angeles, California). Between the covers of the two of them, he might find the spark which would touch off his will to live—his desire to side with Self-Preservation rather than with Self-Destruction. I was not trying to use "scare" psychology. I told her it is simply true that men who live like her husband play a long shot that they will survive until 60.

Death Is as Tragic in Bed

Death is as tragic in bed. Not as dramatic, perhaps, but just as heart-rending to family and friends. Especially when it might have been prevented. Whether the cause is accident or disease, apparently needless death is what intensifies our sorrow.

Here is an example:

My husband died in his sleep last month. In addition to natural bereavement I have been suffering from guilt. I believe I had a part in it by standing by and letting him get so exhausted. He was only 49. He was a "go-getter" in business until about a year before he died. He worked at least 12-14 hours every day.

Then he began to baby himself. Occasionally he wouldn't go to work at all. He refused to help around the house as he used to. He complained of being too tired. Wouldn't even hang a picture or mow the lawn. He was a good man. Never drank or smoked. But suddenly got quiet. After a while the children and I began to think of him as being lazy and useless.

Well, to make a long story short, our doctor later told us that he had been sick with angina. But he had kept it from us so we wouldn't worry. Promised the doctor that he'd tell me, but he didn't.

I feel guilty because I gave up on him without trying to find out the real reason for his fatigue. Although I might not have helped him live longer, I would have shown him I was on his side and not against him. Accidental death must be a horrible experience for those left behind, but quiet passing can also be terrible.

I hope you tell my story, how I suffer these guilty feelings, so you may be able to save some wife somewhere from feeling as I do. If your man suddenly changes his way of life; if he complains of always being tired, better suspect that he may be sick. May be keeping it from you. Be patient with him, otherwise you'll never forgive yourself.

This sad story underlines what I have often suggested; when one family member is ill, the others should know.

"Keeping it from them" is not saving them unnecessary worry and anxiety. Instead, it overloads them with guilt feelings that remain as a burden for the rest of their lives.

I cannot recall one patient who suffered from chronic anxiety who did not complain of fatigue. The two are practically inseparable. Prolonged anxiety ends in fatigue which often leads into depression. Conversely, prolonged fatigue often ends in anxiety. It follows that one way to prevent anxiety is to lessen daily exertions that produce tiredness and to smooth out eruptive emotional upheavals that end in exhaustion and "being spent." Emotional exhaustion, like many accidents, can be prevented. Much depends upon patient and physician—but it is the patient himself who actually fights the lonely battle.

Tension

Most of us are aware of the common causes of tension: anxiety about health, finances, interpersonal relationships at work and at home, and the degree of communication (mostly the lack of it) between parents and children. Our success in overcoming such abnormal stresses depends upon our ability to recognize them for what they are and to face up to them.

As often happens, however, it is the day-to-day unconsidered tensions which at last add up to uncomfortable stress. For example, consider this advice to an harrassed business man:

I might say don't crowd your appointment book. Don't try to live 30 hours in a 24-hour day. Don't do this, don't do that. But I'll make it simple. I'll just give you some advice on how to use the telephone. From what I hear, you'd better review your telephone habits. Are you the abject slave of the telephone bell? Thousands of businessmen are. They jump when they hear it. Something in the nature of the telephone ring releases their adrenalin and throws them into immediate action. They "race" their secretary in response to the ringing.

Do you belong to this club? Do you jump up to reach for the receiver long before the echo of the very first ring has disappeared? Do you drop whatever you are doing? Are you its slave?

I have known people who are slow in answering a question in normal conversation, who let their mail lie around unopened for days, yet become tense and have this compulsion to answer the telephone bell. Over a long business day this abnormal response to the commands of the telephone at last builds up a large reservoir of tension that doesn't do the heart, blood pressure or ulcer any good.

So here is one tip for a simple way to prevent tension: resolve not to be the slave of your telephone. Do not drop whatever you are doing to answer the phone. If you have a secretary, let her bunch your calls, and then answer them at your leisure. If you are alone, then get into the habit of letting the phone ring at least a few times before you lunge for the receiver. Don't be like the old-time fire horses who nervously pranced at the sound of the alarm. You would be surprised at how many tense and nervous patients have been helped by this apparently trivial suggestion.

One man said, "Since I stopped jumping up to answer the phone, I feel as easy and restful as I used to be when taking tranquilizers."

(Incidentally, how loud is your phone? If possible, cut down the jarring intensity of its ring to a pleasant tinkle. This will reduce tension, too.)

The Big "T"

Tension—I call it the big "T"—is what I have believed for years to be close to the number 1 cause of heart attacks and other illnesses. I have observed so many instances in practice, that I am stubborn enough to keep maintaining that it is perhaps even more of a threat than high blood cholesterol, hypertension, lack of exercise, diabetes, obesity, gout—which I admit, are unquestionably important contributing causes for heart attacks. Nevertheless, stress or abnormal *tension* is often the match that lights the fuse.

"My husband is only 42. He has just come through a life-and-death struggle after a heart attack. An examination only a few months before, showed that he was in excellent condition. I believe the reason for the attack was intense worry and tension after he lost his job a few months ago. He couldn't sleep, couldn't eat. He kept on worrying and worrying on how he could support us. Is it possible that this tension might have been the cause?"

Yes, I believe it's possible. Abnormal stress and tension pour extra adrenalin into the blood stream and whip up the circulation and may ultimately strain an apparently normal heart and arteries.

According to a report by a Yale University researcher, Dr. M. Harvey Brenner, who read his findings at an annual convention of the American Heart Association, "Economic downturns are associated with increased mortality from heart disease, and conversely, heart disease mortality decreases during economic upturns."

In other words, it seems he blamed increased heart attacks during recessions on tensions caused by unemployment and loss of income. Loss of ones job and concern about it—night and day—puts abnormal stress on the arteries and the heart.

We doctors keep telling our patients about the dangers of moonlighting and overwork. The other side of the coin, unemployment, is often worse, and not only for the heart. Other conditions affected by increased tension are asthma, ulcer, high blood pressure, mental breakdowns, diabetes and hyperthyroidism. Daily abnormal tension is the enemy. It is important for his good health that man (including woman) can work to his heart's content—and not to his heart's discontent.

Perfectionists Suffer

I am sorry for perfectionists. Somehow they look at the world with astigmatic eyes. They don't seem to realize that it is too much to expect perfection in the next fellow (even if the "fellow" happens to be your wife).

Here is a wife whose husband insists that she have dinner on the table by the time he opens the front door. And Lord help her if his 3-minute breakfast eggs turn out to be 3½. X-rays showed that she already had an ulcer of the duodenum. I had him in my office during his complete physical checkup. I said, "You're not only an ulcer-getter but an ulcer-giver. You've given one to your wife as well as to yourself. You have created an environment of tension. Why don't you face reality? Nobody and nothing in this world is perfect. Forget about expecting perfection in everything and in everybody you meet." He came to his senses, declared a truce in his search for perfection—and both ulcers healed. I suppose another way of saying "don't be a perfectionist" is, learn to forgive. This philosophy often helps more than medicine.

Here is a business man who worked 16 hours a day simply because he could not comfortably delegate any of his work to other officers in the company. He demanded perfection in others he could not find in himself. Result? After many years of suffering this daily tension he developed hypertension and diabetes—and an overactive thyroid to boot. Not until he "gave in" a lot and realized that seekers of perfection in others are the target for every kind of devastating illness did he improve. He now says, "What a fool I was." (You notice, the past tense?)

And here is a secretary who has become, as she says, "a nervous wreck." Whenever she takes shorthand or does her typing she is mortally afraid she will make a mistake. When she does, and these are rare occurrences, her boss gets red-faced, seems as if he's going into a convulsion of anger. The only way I could help her was to advise that she find other employment. Otherwise, her perfectionist boss would surely drive her out of her mind.

(As one harried worker put it: "A perfectionist is one who takes infinite pains and then gives them to every one else.")

Resentment is "Slow Poison"

Have you ever been so angry you couldn't sit down to eat? Your stomach turned on itself as if someone took a wrench and tightened a nut? Then, after a few minutes—having let out your resentment against your boss or someone else—you felt your stomach relax and were able to swallow. This is a common example of "fast" resentment. But when slow anger turns into "slow" resentment that eats into you day after day, you are now at the mercy of the slow poison called daily tension. If you are a "resentee," you're only harming your-self—making yourself miserable and nervous.

There is a moral: if you can't change the one who is producing or affecting your nervousness or illness, then it's up to you to change your own philosophy and learn to accept it. (Not easy, I admit.) But if you don't, resentment and tension will eat a hole in you somewhere—or tighten up your bundle of nerves.

Temper: Keep It In or Let It Out?

Man's his own worst enemy. How often have you heard it—and how true it is. Even though forewarned, he kills himself in one of many ways. Threats against his very existence arise in himself. Warned against excessive smoking—and heart trouble or cancer—he keeps on. Like the man who stands in an open field during a storm, he shakes his fist at the heavens and dares lightning to strike him down. He dares the law of averages to single him out for a heart attack or an inoperable "lump" in his lung. Likewise, the chronic alcoholic "dares" cirrhosis of the liver; and the reckless, speeding driver "dares" self-annihilation in an auto crash.

Such are but a few of the common (and well-recognized) methods of self-destruction. Others are not so evident. For example, consider how repressed tensions result in outbursts of temper. Although "keeping temper bottled up" is certainly not good either, temper outbursts can lead to sudden tragedy.

My husband who is only 42 has already had a severe heart attack. His blood pressure remains over 200 and his kidneys are bad, too. He gets

attacks of angina. Our doctor strongly advises him
against getting excited so much. He says his arteries
are too weak to withstand such extra pressure on
his circulation. Do you go along with that? My
husband goes into the most terrible rages that leave
him almost gasping for breath. His face turns pur-
plish-red and the veins bulge in his neck. He's on
tranquilizers. He has been warned. But nothing
seems to help.

I told her that as she and her doctor predicted, he's likely
to kill himself in a tantrum some day. Recently I mentioned
the case history of a renowned English heart specialist who
also had bursts of rage. He correctly predicted his own
demise: "My arteries are at the mercy of my bad temper. One
day I shall die in an angina attack brought about by myself."
Some time later, at a medical meeting, while in violent
disagreement with a colleague—he dropped dead.

To prevent inbursts and outbursts of tension it is important to develop a philosophy of equanimity. I have observed
such character transformations in many similar patients. It
prolonged their lives. Self-control, although admittedly difficult to attain, may be one of the most important life-saving
measures. Bottled up anger, resentment and daily tension are
not good for the body and the mind; but sudden outbursts
may be worse.

Productivity of Contentment

Better than hypnotism, tranquilizers or any other therapy,
is developing a philosophy that will counteract tension and
its by-affects. It does not seem likely, but some of the most

serious cases of tension I have observed have been in people who were no longer working—who were suffering the daily boredom some undergo when cut off from their usual activities.

My friend is 61. He has recovered nicely from a serious operation, but still has a problem: facing retirement. He has been advised to sell his business and move to Florida or live in some other equable climate. Previously distressed and made ill by cold, northern winters and sharp temperature changes, his doctors are convinced he should make this precautionary move.

He is still laboring under the irksome distress of indecision. Shall he or shall he not, he keeps asking himself. Yesterday, he put something into words that dug straight down into the core of the problem which besets many men of his age. Shall they retire or not?

He said, "Fortunately, my investments will keep my wife and me comfortable until we get our bearings. But one thing bugs me. I hate to live an unproductive existence. I've seen some of these retired people. All they do is play golf or cards or go fishing or just sit around gabbing. They don't do one constructive thing all day."

I asked, "Don't they seem happy?"

He said, "It's remarkable. Few of them are bored. They seem to be enjoying themselves. But where is their productivity? How can they sit around from day to day without doing something constructive or worthwhile?"

I have known many men who began to "wither on the vine" after retirement. They did so because of psychological rather than physical reasons alone. They got this "nonproductivity" guilt complex. It brought on tenseness and dissatisfaction. They forgot their previous contributions to society.

For example, my friend admitted that he had worked hard

(in school and out) since the age of 10. He had been a successful businessman, a civic leader, a friend to the needy and a respected citizen in his community.

I said, "You've worked hard and given of yourself for a half-century. Isn't that sufficient contribution?

"Your children are married. Your life has been spared from serious illness. Don't you owe yourself and your wife a few years of ease? Are you concerned about loss of productivity in your life? How about the productivity of contentment?"

He liked the phrase "productivity of contentment." He admitted that many men like himself could chew on it a while and perhaps see themselves in better perspective. He said it should ease the conscience of any retiree. Especially one who has labored hard and long—and is forced by illness (or even by free choice) to live in this new world, free from the usual personal tensions. I am happy to say that he retired to the productivity of contentment.

Insomnia: Get All the Sleep You Need

How much sleep do you need? Napoleon said, "Six hours for men, seven hours for women, and eight hours for idiots." True or untrue, I admit to needing the latter. Anything less than seven or eight hours of sleep nightly for a week, and I become inefficient, irritable and tired.

I am not alone. Most people are affected by loss of sleep, whether it be by loss of an hour or two or by nightly insomnia which robs them of their rest.

For example, in my recent book on sleep problems, I wrote the following dedication: "Dedicated to tossers, snorers, groaners, pillow-punchers, sleep-talkers, clock-watchers, twisters, turners, counters-of-sheep; to worry-ridden, tension-filled insomniacs, lying there wide-eyed night after night; to 100 million Americans who have said, are saying or will say: How'll I ever get through tomorrow?"

Napoleon, and others like him who profess not to need much sleep, often get more than they realize. I've heard it said that Napoleon used to snatch quite a few naps while on his horse. And Edison, who supposedly got along on only four hours of sleep nightly, was a renowned day-napper.

The other day a patient said, "My wife keeps saying she's one of those people who were born without the need for much sleep. On the face of it, she's right. She gets to bed late and is often up before six.

"But lately I've observed her sleeping habits more closely. She naps at least an hour in the afternoon. And when we're both watching a two-hour movie at night, most of the time she sleeps through at least one-and-one-half hours of it. Add up such naps and you discover that she's getting at least eight hours of sleep out of the twenty-four. Yet, she prides herself on needing very little sleep."

What's wrong with getting a good night's sleep? What's wrong with taking a nap every afternoon? Why are some people ashamed to admit that they need enough sleep to keep them fit?

The next time somebody comes along bragging about how little sleep he needs, observe him carefully, if you get the opportunity. Chances are he will be asleep astride his horse or while sitting in front of his TV set.

Let's get over our Napoleonic complexes regarding sleep. Ask yourself: "How much do I really need to keep me fit and contented?" If you need at least eight hours, let them call you an idiot—and turn over into delicious slumber.

Too Much Sleep Dangerous?

Lately there have been some more "Thou shalt nots" in medical articles warning against the dangers of sleeping too much. According to this new theory, if you sleep longer than eight hours or so every night you are more liable to have a stroke or heart attack. This is a far from convincing theory. I still believe you will be healthier and enjoy life more if you get your personal quota of sleep. You will note I said "personal quota." For it is true that some of us get along very well on 6 hours nightly, while others need at least 8 hours of sleep. And some as many as 10 hours before they feel completely rested. After reading about the warning against too much sleep a reader wrote:

> *Dear Dr. Steincrohn:*
> I am in my late 60s. All my life I have required at least 9 hours of sleep at night. In addition, I take a half-hour nap in the afternoon. I've been perfectly healthy all my life. Now I'm troubled. I've read that too much sleep may be dangerous for people my age. Do you suggest that I set the alarm two hours earlier and get only seven hours?
>
> Mrs. B.

Comment: Sell your alarm clock, give it away or throw it into the yard. Under no circumstances, let it be the instrument for getting you out of bed so much earlier than you've been accustomed to all your life.

Continue with your present sleep-quota. There is too much

sleep interruption as it is. For example, consider the sick patient actually aching for a good night's sleep while he is in the hospital.

How many times have you heard the hoary joke: "I can't get any sleep. The nurse comes in to wake me up to give me a pill to go to sleep." Or, "They wake me up to take my temperature." Or, "Why should they be cleaning my room at six oclock in the morning and wake me up so early?"

So go the complaints from patients. We are coming to realize that the hospital is no place to get a good night's rest. There have even been some recent complaints in medical journals by doctors that their patients, seriously ill and in ICU (intensive care units) are deprived of necessary sleep because of so many interruptions. I could go on and on.

Be thankful, Mrs. B., that you are a sound sleeper. Keep on with the regular quota that has helped you keep healthy for over 60 years. Don't let every new (unproved) theory throw you off schedule.

"Restless Legs"

All are not sufficiently fortunate to be able to choose whether they shall have eight hours or more. They sleep so fitfully and gradually have such a deficit of sleep that they become nervous, tense and exhausted. For example, consider "leg jitters." You don't have to be a neurotic to suffer from it. I have observed this syndrome in well-balanced, calm persons. Nevertheless, it is the first lieutenant of insomnia. Ask the person whose legs are uncontrollable and jump around like a nervous frog's, and you will understand why leg jitters cause so much unhappiness and discomfort.

The typical patient says:

My legs are driving me crazy! I dread going to sleep. I used to sleep like a baby, but for the past year or two I have been fortunate to get one good night's rest during the week.

I just settle down when one of three things happens. I either get prickly sensations all over my legs as if ants were walking up and down, or a very nervous feeling which I call the heebie-jeebies, or cramps which seem to lie in the calves of my legs. Is there a remedy?

This patient is not alone. Since Dr. K. A. Ekbom of Sweden described *Restless Leg Syndrome* in 1944, both doctors and patients have been aware of this awesome and nagging condition. Thousands of people, however, still suffer from it unaware that it has a label—"restless legs."

It drains them of their energy because they lose sleep. It is not a serious illness, it doesn't shorten life, but how it disturbs one's rest! It can waken one out of deep sleep. It may recur, on and off, for weeks at a time and then disappear for months.

Patients give varying descriptions of their discomforts: "My legs simply will not keep still"—"Something is pulling or stretching my legs"—"Something keeps creeping up and down"—"It feels as if my whole leg were full of small worms"—"It spoils my life. At times it makes me hysterical."

Patients have told me that uncomfortable sensations are worse at night. Leg jerks may also come on while at a lecture or the movies. They may have to get up and leave. They can't relax and sit still at a card game or at a dinner party. Their legs suddenly begin jerking and thrashing out dangerously at unwary bystanders.

Is there a remedy? Nothing specific. But here are some

procedures that have helped some patients:

1) Prolonged soaking in a hot bath. 2) Stick feet out from under the covers. 3) Pour cold water on feet before bedtime. 4) Sleep with socks on or use a hot water bag or heat pad. 5) Take a cold shower. 6) An aspirin or two before bedtime often relaxes some patients. 7) Occasionally, tranquilizers or sleeping pills help. 8) Your doctor may try other drugs. 9) Beware of using narcotics.

What works for one may not help another. Self-experimentation is often the only helpful answer. Thankfully, as I have said, restless legs are not a menace to health nor do they shorten life—but sufferers will tell you "they sure take the joy out of living."

Sleep Habits of Children

People are funny. Parents are people. Parents are funny. At least, so they may often appear to their children. In bringing up our children we are influenced by what we've heard, read or experienced ourselves as youngsters. For example, consider sleeping patterns. Often we inflict them on our offspring, deaf and blind to their protestations.

One patient says:

> I've brought up six children who have grown to
> be happy adults. Why? Because my husband and I
> recognized that each one of us has a personal
> "rhythm." When one child wanted to stay up a
> little later than usual, we did not force him to go
> to bed—or else. When one wanted to go earlier, we
> didn't force him to pry his eyelids apart to stay
> awake.

I have a neighbor who has the idea that sleeping time should be measured by the ticks of the clock. Whether her little girl is sleepy or not, she actually forces her to drop whatever she may be doing to go to bed. She tells me the child often lies there for hours crying and whimpering, but she has never relented and let her stay up a little longer. Don't you think that sleeping rules should be more elastic?

Many a grownup night owl, I believe, is the end-product of parental over-strictness when he was young. It is rebellion against his inability, in childhood, to stay up a little longer. The child becomes an adult, now able to make his own decisions, and mentally thumbs his nose right back at the hands of the clock. He is the one who is wide-awake at 1 or 2 A.M. when all others at the party want to go home to bed.

Over-restrictiveness is the mother of neurosis and character quirks. Parents should not be too strict with their youngsters, acting like drill sergeants when bedtime draws near.

The child who is not sleepy, who wants to finish a game he is playing or see the end of an interesting TV play or who just wants to feel grown up sitting with his parents or other siblings a few minutes after accustomed bedtime, should be given this delightful dividend at the end of the day. Parents should also remember that some little children require less sleep than others. Sleeping patterns vary because individuals vary. The trouble is that we forget that children are individuals.

Do You Hate to Go to Sleep?

Most children hate to go to sleep; so do many adults.

Youngsters hate missing wakeful activities; but adults hate going to bed because they suffer physical or emotional discomforts.

A *businessman*: "I hate to go to sleep because I suffer from insomnia. Night after night I toss and turn. I read for hours in early morning. I keep looking at the clock. Hoping that there's still time enough to get a few winks of sleep, or mostly, hoping it's close to morning so I won't have to keep fighting insomnia any longer."

A *secretary*: "I'm afraid to go to sleep. I'm afraid of the dark. With all you hear about burglaries and rape how can anyone find any rest? I have been sleeping better since I installed a night-light."

A *teacher*: "Whenever I lie down lately, I get heart skips. My heart seems to turn over in my throat. My doctor says the skips are harmless, but I still get scared. They don't bother me much during the day. That's why I hate to go to sleep."

A *physician*; "I should know better, but I won't check on my cough. I smoke three packs a day. I know I must have emphysema but I can't quit. At night it's worse. Sometimes I have to jump up from a deep sleep to catch my breath. Maybe I have a little heart weakness, too. But I'm too chicken to find out. And me, a doctor!"

A *housewife*: "I know why I hate to go to sleep. A lumpy mattress. It's so old and uncomfortable anybody would need an anesthetic to sleep well on it. Yet, it's my fault. For my birthday, my husband gave me the choice between a new fur coat or new mattresses. Like a fool I chose you know what."

To come up with the battered statistic that we spend one-third of our lives in bed is like driving a tack with a sledgehammer. Yet most of us remain deaf and dumb to the doctor's insistence that it pays off in well-being to get sufficient rest at night.

As one who requires a good night's sleep myself, I can

understand what a nightly trial it must be to look upon your bed as enemy rather than friend. It is too bad that so many surrender to insomnia. My experience with many nervous and anxious patients has convinced me that, in many instances, a minimal effort on their part might have transformed them from victims into victors.

Do you hate to go to sleep? *Do* something about it. You will find it more rewarding than continually complaining about insomnia.

Are Sleeping Pills Bad?

A patient asks:

> Are sleeping pills bad? I suppose I'm being ridic-
> ulous, but I refuse to take them. I consider them
> nothing but dope. And I sure don't want to be-
> come a dope addict. My doctor says they will help
> my anxiety. But don't you feel that people should
> learn to get along without them?

Sleeping pills are bad as alcohol is bad for the chronic alcoholic—as cars are threats to the driver with the heavy foot on the accelerator—as too much coffee and tea are bad for immoderate users. I could go on and on. What I am getting at is evident: don't put moderation and immoderation in the same category.

You may take 3-4 sleeping pills every night to get sleep. That's bad. But your neighbor may take a pill once or twice a week on the advice of her doctor. I consider that good, not bad.

In today's paper you may have learned of a recent suicide

who emptied a bottle of sleeping pills. Or, of a wreck in which an alcoholic driver killed himself and other innocents. That is what I mean by immoderation in the use of something beneficial to the human race.

But I don't want all cars off the road because some chronic alcoholics endanger the rest of us. (Rather, I hope for the cure of the alcoholic.) Neither do I suggest that all sleeping pills be prohibited.

Under the direction of a physician, there is little danger of becoming a "dope" addict when taking sleeping pills. Never hesitate to take them if your doctor prescribes them. Just remember there is danger of bootlegging them without prescription and taking them on your own.

For those who are afraid that sleeping pills taken for many years may be harmful, the following case history should give them courage to take sleeping pills when the doctor advises them to do so.

I became a victim of insomnia 45 years ago. I was told by my friends to drink warm milk, but that didn't help. I was losing so much sleep and energy that I visited one of our largest and best-known diagnostic clinics out West. I went through a three-day, thorough examination. The doctors couldn't find anything organically wrong. They prescribed a barbital. Told me I may have inherited my insomnia from my mother.

I found immediate relief. I slept better. Later other doctors prescribed similar pills over the years. I take one or two at bedtime. For the past ten years my dear wife has also been troubled with insomnia. She takes a pill before bedtime every night, too.

I am now 79 and my wife is 78. I do not believe
that either of us would have made it if we hadn't
taken pills to give us a good night's sleep. We have
lots of pep. At the age of 78 I drove myself and my
wife across the United States without any trouble
at all.

We've made it a rule not to take the sleeping
pills unless doctors have given us prescriptions and
said it was OK to take them. Luckily we've had
broadminded and sensible doctors. They have said
that elderly people troubled with insomnia should
not be afraid to take prescribed pills. As I've said,
they've been actual life-savers for both of us. I
think too many people are unnecessarily scared of
taking sleeping pills. Why not if the doctor says
they're OK and gives you a prescription for them?

Some Practical Tips

If you suffer from sleep loss, it is possible that you can
help yourself better than the doctor can—if you use a little
self-study and introspection. Perhaps the remedy is simple.
Perhaps you need just an extra hour of sleep nightly (going to
bed earlier or getting up later). Experiment. Find your niche.
Do you waste precious hours watching early-early TV shows
(late at night, that is)? Do you spend too many evenings late
at poker or bridge sessions, lodge meetings? Is there any
wonder you are tired and irritable during the day?

Sleep is as essential as food, water and oxygen. Chronic
sleep loss can be devastating—especially to the nervous system. Fatigue and tension are tied in with loss of sleep.

Check your bedding, your mattresses, your pillows, your

room temperature, your ventilation. Are you uncomfortable in a double bed? Then a twin bed may solve your insomnia problem.

There have been hundreds of suggestions on how to get a good night's sleep. You will find them in books written about the sleep problem. I suggest that you read them. Somewhere, buried in those archives, may be a simple suggestion that may transform you from an insomniac into one who wakes refreshed morning after morning. Insomnia is often the refuge of people who would rather complain about their insomnia than find a cure for it.

Whatever the solution, experience proves that relief from insomnia is one of the most important steps in overcoming anxiety.

Thoughts and Afterthoughts on Chapter 19

1. Fatigue is the common enemy of man and woman.

2. Use this motto: DON'T PUT OFF UNTIL TOMORROW (OR, BETTER STILL, THE NEXT HOUR) WHAT NEEDS DOING RIGHT NOW.

3. If your fatigue is stubborn visit your doctor for study.

4. "Some people act as if there is no tomorrow. My husband acts as if there is no today."

5. Death is as tragic in bed.

6. I cannot recall one patient who suffered from chronic anxiety who did not complain of fatigue.

7. The day-to-day unconsidered tensions add up to uncomfortable stress.

8. Resolve not to be the slave of your telephone.

9. Tension is the big "T." It is perhaps our greatest threat.

10. Economic downturns are associated with increased

mortality.

11. Perfectionists suffer.

12. Resentment is "slow poison." It can eat a hole in you somewhere—or tighten your bundle of nerves.

13. Man kills himself in many ways. Temper is one of them. Develop the philosophy of equanimity.

14. Accept the "productivity of contentment."

15. Eight hours of sleep nightly is not for "idiots." Some need more—some need less. But too much sleep is not dangerous.

16. "Restless legs" is a common cause of insomnia.

17. Children are people, too. Their sleep habits should be respected.

18. Sleeping pills aren't "dope."

20
Overcoming Bad Habits—
Finding a New Way of Life

First the egg or the chicken? Do bad habits cause anxiety, or does anxiety cause bad habits? Undeniably, each is in some way an integral part of the other. Perhaps it is less important to know which came first, and more important to recognize that there is an interrelationship.

Obesity: "I'm Tired of Being Fat"

Normal-weighted people look upon the obesity problem as a joke. Never having had to do battle with calories, they think that all this talk about dieting is being overdone. Blessed with the ability to eat whatever they want without becoming fat, they do not realize how this problem disrupts the lives of so many.

> Please help! I'm tired of trying to lose weight. I'm medium build and weigh over 175 pounds. I've tried diet pills, shots, fad diets, doctors' diets. I've even joined diet clubs.
> The first time I joined I lost 19½ pounds. You win a trophy when you lose 20 pounds. Well, I lost

that trophy by one-half a pound. Then I regained those 19½ pounds and even added 8 more. I hate being fat. I've been trying to lose weight since I was 13. I weighed 175 then. I went to a doctor and lost 30 pounds. Now, at 26, I'm back where I started 13 years ago.

What can I do? I'll bet I've lost over a thousand pounds altogether. I'm married and have two children. My husband tells me I'm too fat, then turns around and buys me candy! I get very depressed when I am fat so I eat to feel better. It's a vicious circle. (Help!)

I make jokes and say, "I can't wait until I'm a grandmother so I can eat all I want and get fat." Why do the pounds keep accumulating? Life doesn't seem worth living anymore. If I had all the money I've spent trying to lose weight I could buy a new home. Besides, my husband is getting disgusted with me. I can't go on like this much longer."

I told this unhappy woman, as I have told many who are overweight, that the "cure" of obesity narrows down to one word: *motivation*. Without it, fat people flounder around helplessly in a sea of calories. What do I mean by proper motivation? You'll have to ask yourself, "Just why do I want to lose?" For vanity's sake? To overcome your depression? Look and you may find a real hard-core reason which will give you the will to look food straight in the eye and toss it away uneaten.

I asked her what bothered her most. She answered, "Fear of losing my husband who says he hates me fat." I said, "You don't have to look hard to discover your motivation. There it

is: you want desperately to save your marriage. Picture yourself as divorced and alone with your children. Is that the
pretty picture you want to frame your life in at the age of
26? All you have to do is to remind yourself every morning
that you must stay thin to save your marriage. Dividends of
personal satisfaction will come later.."

Within months this unhappy girl was down to 135 pounds.
"It was easy," she said. "And I accomplished it all without
going on any crazy, new-fangled diet. Just ate less."

100 Pounds Overweight. For most people, being overweight is one of the minor problems of existence. They say,
"I've been putting on some weight lately. Guess I'll just have
to cut down a little." So they go through life up an down one
or two rungs of the obesity ladder—not especially concerned
about the problem. ("What's an extra five or ten pounds
anyway?") But there are too many others for whom excessive appetite and increased weight is the bane of their way of
life.

I have been terribly depressed by my weight.
I've been to a couple of doctors, but their only
advice is to push myself away from the table. I
have four children and a husband who works afternoons. It seems I spend half of my life fixing,
preparing, serving food and invariably stuffing
myself all the while. I seem to be gorging myself to
keep my nerves calm.

Whenever I try to diet, I get terribly weak,
extremely nervous and very hard to live with. I've
had my thyroid checked. There's nothing wrong
with it. I get so depressed over being heavy, I feel
like literally slitting my throat to keep from eating
that extra portion of bread, pie or cake. But some-

thing seems to say, "Go ahead. Eat it. You'll feel
better." I know just how drug addicts must feel.

I must admit that while food is being consumed
I feel pretty good. But as soon as I've finished
eating I feel like killing myself for having eaten it. I
try to keep very busy, but even then there's one
hand reaching for a snack. I hate being fat. I hate
myself for being so emotionally unstable. I can't
seem to cope with it. I'm every bit of 100 pounds
overweight. Can you help?

(In her case, regular attendance at one of the nationally
known weight clubs was the answer to her problem. Some
people need to be with "comrades in misery" before they can
generate the will to overcome obesity.)

Tension causes nibbling

I lost my husband quite suddenly about three
years ago. In about 2½ years I have gained 45
pounds. When I told my doctor how little I eat, he
smiled and said, "Sure you do." I know he doesn't
believe me.

I work in an office and in my home and never
stop running. I'm as active as any 48 year old can
be. I look awful and have never been as heavy as
this in all my life. Isn't there some medicine that
may help?

Your doctor smiles because most of us believe that when
there is a weight increase the reason is usually an increase in
calorie intake. Some people eat more than they realize. They
will use their will power when they sit down for their regular
meals; but unconsciously stuff themselves between meals. In
plain words, they nibble all day—and far into the night.

Perhaps you are a nibbler, too. The sudden death of your husband, like an explosion, set off a daily, recurring tension which causes you to take in an extra load of calories which pile on the excess weight. You say, please tell me what to do? My first suggestion is that you look to your complete food consumption during 24 hours. Write down every mouthful or peanut-sized bite. Your extra 45 pounds can come only from extra calories, and your job is to be a detective and run down the clues. But even when you find the "leaks" in your diet, you may need some help. Not until you overcome your tension will you overcome your nibbling. In many instances I have helped patients who had a problem similar to yours by prescribing tranquilizers for a while. By lessening anxiety, their nibbling decreased, too. Such medication is often overlooked as a crutch to lean on until tension decreases and calorie intake lessens.

"Don't Do as I Do. . ." We doctors have a responsibility to set a good example to our patients. Otherwise, we make it more difficult for them to overcome their difficulties. Consider these three short notes:

Dear Dr. Steincrohn: Yesterday my doctor blew smoke in my face while he was telling me to quit smoking. How can a doctor expect his patient to be apprehensive about lung cancer or emphysema when he sets such a bad example himself?. . . Mr. P.

Dear Dr. Steincrohn: My doctor must weigh close to 300 pounds, yet he gave me a long lecture on why I should lose about 20 pounds. He said that overweight people are more prone to get coronary attacks, diabetes, gall bladder trouble, and a host of other ailments. Although my major in college was psychology, for the life of me I can't understand how he had the nerve to give me such advice.. . . Mrs. U.

Dear Dr. Steincrohn: When I am in his office, our doctor is

so tense he can't seem to sit still long enough to listen to me
or to talk for any length of time. Yet, he keeps stressing the
need for me to live a more relaxed way of life. I can't
understand how he has the nerve to give me such advice. . . .
Mr. C.

This hoary saying has supported thousands of doctors
since the time of Hippocrates: "Don't do as I do, do as I
say." It is a bewhiskered admonition, a feeble, inexcusable
way of setting a good example for the patient. Like striking a
match before a young child and saying, "Never fool with
matches. They are dangerous."

How much more effective it would be to be normal-
weighted when we tell patients that fat can kill prematurely.
Or have a sign in the waiting room: PLEASE DO NOT
SMOKE—and not smoke ourselves. Or, sit in our consultation
room, relaxed and attentive while the patient relates his
history and we tell him that tension is one of our most
formidable enemies. I know that doctors are human and are
as fallible as their patients. However, if we hope to achieve
the best results, like good parents we should set good examples for those we treat.

Long gone are the days when people looked upon their fat
brethren as "happy-go-lucky" individuals. We know enough
about the problem of obesity to realize that beneath the
smiles and apparent jollity, like the rumblings of a volcano,
lie the frustrations and emotional sores which produce a very
unhappy human being. Anxiety in itself is a taxing problem.
Why overtax yourself with obesity? It is the most curable
disease—at the mercy of most patients without the help of a
doctor.

Lost Weight and Regained Her Mind

Here's how I lost weight and regained my mind.

I have a cup of coffee with my husband in the morning. At noon I have a piece of knockwurst sausage or a piece of Polish sausage, which I really prefer for its flavor, and drink a glass of skimmed milk. For dinner I have everything and anything I want. Loads of lettuce and tomatoes, salad with garlic dressing made with oil and spices, all kinds of vegetables, and all the meat, fish or chicken I desire. If I get hungry between meals I take care of the craving with skimmed milk or tomato juice. I have lost 20 pounds on this diet. I have been off tranquilizers which I have been taking for 10 years.

I couldn't feel better. We have two sons, 10 and 11. My husband says I am a different person since I lost weight. He gets a kick out of my energy and spunk. My 10-year-old couldn't keep up with me shopping one day. I'm jolly and have lots of fun, enjoy reading, take care of three beds of lilies in the back yard. My kids enjoy me because I am patient and understanding.

I had an unhappy youth, in and out of state hospitals for 13 years since I was 23. Some doctors didn't think I'd make it.

When I was a child Mom couldn't express affection for me. And she used to criticize Dad all the time. She told me I should never get married. I grew up on a farm, but was not permitted to know anything about sex. When I was in my teens I couldn't believe that intercourse could possibly happen. I couldn't believe I had female parts. Boy, did I have a lot to learn, and unlearn.

I was 35 when I married. Met my husband in the state hospital. He was there two years. So you see it's almost 15 years since we were married. Neither my husband nor I have had any breakdowns since. And our two boys are as normal and happy as you'd see anywhere. We're a closeknit family.

I hope, Dr. Steincrohn, that some day you will tell my story, for two reasons. The first is this: anyone can lose weight if they put their mind to it—even though it seems to be a peculiar diet like mine.

And second, it is not inevitable that a broken mind cannot heal. In our cases two broken minds joined to make two healthy ones. And we're bringing up our youngsters in such a way that their minds won't bend or break either. I pray that many other "hopeless" men, women and children read or hear you tell our story. What better way to bring faith to the anxiety ridden—and worse?

No better way.

Tobacco

Hazards of Smoking. Whatever their ages, patients tire of hearing doctors say, "Don't do this" or "Don't do that." I'm as guilty as the rest of my colleagues. But hear my confession. Doctors tire of playing little gods. Like parents who are constantly saying "no" to protect their progeny, medical men become frayed around the edges after day-in and day-out negation. We wish we could be saying "yes" for a change.

Although I can say "no" emphatically, I am occasionally lenient with the bad habits of the elderly. For example, if a 70- or 80-year-old is apparently healthy, I do not take his pipe, cigars or cigarettes away from him. The calendar has proved that he is the exception that can get away with a bad habit. Why not let him enjoy it?

Nevertheless, I am strict—whatever the age—if I believe that the habit of smoking is a threat to the health and life of the patient. I'll say "no" to youngsters as well as to oldsters, without remorse.

Consider the complaint of this 75-year-old patient:

> It's a little late to correct mistakes of the past. I have been smoking for 59 years—cigarettes for 52 years. Friends and relatives used to send me cartons while I was in the Army.
>
> Until 10 years ago I was convinced that smoking never harmed me. At 65 I could easily climb stairs two at a time, and fast, with no discomfort. But coughing and phlegm began to bother me and led me to have a bronchogram taken.
>
> And POW! What a sudden change. Because of shortness of breath I am nearly incapacitated. I've lost weight and appetite. I'm very nervous. I have that awful feeling of exhaustion after the slightest exertion. Isn't it true that when you take away cigarettes to prolong life it's like sounding the death knell to freedom and the love of life as I have known it? Because the medical profession was 50 years late in discovering the hazards of cigarette smoking, why should I be accused of self-destruction?
>
> I've cut down on my smoking from three packs to one and one-half a day. Telling me to quit just like that is like telling a man he has to quit eating. Have you got the nerve to say "no smoking" to a

man who has smoked so many years?

I said: If you had no symptoms at 75 I'd say go on. Enjoy yourself. But in your case age is no excuse for continuing a bad and destructive habit. You are suffering from emphysema. If you continue to rationalize I suppose I won't be able to convince you that you do not deserve a medal for smoking "only" one and one-half packs a day. That's like taking less poison. Yes, I have the nerve to say don't smoke at all. Quit. Otherwise, I'm a little god who has fallen down on his job.

Pipe Smoker's Personality. Another patient said:

> I know how often you have preached against tobacco in any form. I'm aware that too much smoking—or any at all—can intensify anxiety, cause emphysema or lung cancer, lip cancer, throat cancer, heart disease and so many other of the killers that stalk man from the time he was born.
>
> And I also know that you have often told me that pipe and cigar smokers should not be absolved of guilt where tobacco is concerned. In other words, that cigarettes are not the only threat to the arteries and lungs and throat.
>
> But I wonder what you think of the psychology of the man who smokes a pipe. Is it true, in your opinion, that the man with the pipestem forever in his mouth is really reverting to childhood and mother's nipple? I'm a smug nonsmoker, but I've always been curious about those smug pipe smokers.

There are many theories. What it comes down to is one's own beliefs in the matter. For example, I've found it to be true, quite often, that the cigarette smoker is more edgy, more nervous and chronically anxious than the pipe or cigar smoker. The extreme of the anxious person is the one who lights cigarettes end to end—the chain smoker.

On the other hand, the pipe smoker is outwardly, at least, the more composed, even-tempered bloke. When his pipe goes out he calmly relights, undisturbed by the need for keeping his tobacco lit.

He fondles his pipe. He rubs it against his nose for the natural oil so he can shine the bowl until it glistens. The pipestem is forever between his lips. He sucks on it, even when it is unlit. Even when there is no tobacco in the bowl. In fact, I've known some pipeholders—who never smoke, just suck.

In my opinion, the inveterate pipesmoker is not free from anxiety. He is the fellow who needs continuing reassurance—like the infant who continually sticks his thumb in his mouth. You might call a pipe smoker an adult thumb-sucker.

Whenever I see these self-assured TV personalities who never appear before the camera without leaning on the support of a pipe, cigar or cigarette, I know they are in reality less assured than they appear to be. If you took away their "smoke" they'd stick their thumb in their mouth.

Mind you, I do not say this in any spirit of condemnation. As a former cigarette, pipe and cigar smoker, I recall how often I lit up for a feeling of security rather than for the urge to enjoy tobacco.

Frankly, most analyses of human traits are speculative and unfair. So don't be so smug, Mr. nonsmoker. If a man insists on fondling his pipe, let him satisfy his oral pleasure. It's better for him than going around with thumb in mouth. Or, is it?

Undoubtedly, the ubiquitous habit of smoking often

causes anxiety and is often the result of it. People get nervous when they smoke too much—often to the point of becoming nicotine-stained habitués. Those who say that "smoking calms my nerves" are taking a balm which heals only the superficial sore—beneath it is the larger ulcer. For the most part, smoking causes tenseness and irritability and sleeplessness. Even the "calm" pipe smoker is not exempt.

A Gamblin' Man. "Why should I quit?" asks this man.

> I smoke like the proverbial chimney. My wife calls me a chain smoker. I am more than that. I'm the kind of smoker who never takes the cigarette out of my mouth until it has burned down to about a half inch from my lips. I eat about three packs a day. I am 36 and extremely healthy except, I must admit, nervous as a jumping frog. But I have no cough or other symptoms. Yet my wife worries about me. Isn't it true that some of us are immune to the so-called poison we call tobacco? Why should I quit when I enjoy it so much?

I agree that some of us are immune. But we have no test of knowing which ones are susceptible to disease. Russian roulette, anyone? That's what it amounts to. A gamble. Your wife has good reason to worry. I know that statistics aren't likely to convince you that her fears are warranted; yet they may be of interest to you:

For example, a recent study by Drs. G. Z. Brett and B. Benjamin of London, England, of fifty-five thousand English workers showed some striking results. They called your type of smoking the "drooping cigarette habit"—in which smokers do not take the cigarette out of their mouth between puffs. Such smokers had the highest mortality rate from lung cancer: 14 times greater than that of nonsmokers and ex-smokers. They also found that heavy smokers had death rates 3 times that of light smokers and 8 times that of nonsmokers.

Congratulations are in order (and I'm not being sarcastic) on your present "extremely good" health—except for your nervousness. How long will your good health last? No doctor can prophecy. But I think you must admit that you're a "gamblin' man."

Alcohol

Social Drinker or Chronic Alcoholic? The pressures of existence increase. The "bomb" is there in the background, forever threatening—consciously and unconsciously. It discolors our thinking and our emotions. Hundreds of thousands try to lessen the tensions of business and family life by taking a drink. And too many of these so-called social drinkers totter on the edge of a cliff overlooking a deep chasm we call chronic alcoholism. They do not realize that they are in danger of taking a precipitous fall some day.

What is wrong you say with taking an occasional drink? If you are over 40 and limit your intake to no more than an ounce or two before dinner (except on very special occasions) then I advise a daily drink. It promotes conviviality, increases appetite and relaxes the person about to sit down to dinner after a hectic day.

But suppose you consider yourself a social drinker simply because you have never missed a day of work because of overdrinking, or never have had any lost weekends. Suppose you take "only" two or three martinis for lunch—and perhaps a beer, too. In midafternoon you take a shot or two. Also on the train home on the 5:15. And then a double

double of scotch or bourbon before dinner, and raise a few that same night (and on other nights) at cocktail parties.

My reply is that I disagree. You may be a social drinker in your own mind, but my diagnosis is that you are a hairsbreadth away from chronic alcoholism.

Review your drinking habits as an overweight patient writes down his caloric intake over a period of 24 hours. You may be surprised what your total intake of liquor is.

If you have the tobacco habit, I advise: *quit*. If you have the social drinker habit, I advise: cut down. If you can't cut down, then cut out. Your nerves and general health are bound to improve.

Even Beer Is a Threat to Some People. Hard and soft liquor—people keep on making distinctions between the two, as if the first is harmful and the second innocuous. "One can't become a chronic alcoholic if he sticks to beer alone" is the common concept about this malt liquor. Here is an example of what beer can do:

> I am a 65-year-old-woman who can't get away from her husband for five minutes since he retired three years ago. Can't even shut the bathroom door. Why? Because he's afraid of being alone.
>
> When he worked, he drank only in the evening. Now it's the first thing after breakfast. He claims that a half-dozen cans of beer in the morning and a half-dozen more in the evening are the only things that keep him alive. I know he also sneaks beer he doesn't talk about.
>
> He is overweight, has ulcers, heart trouble and high blood pressure. He is so filled with anxiety he says that drinking is the only thing that keeps the ulcers from getting worse and gives him courage.

He is so afraid of being alone I am a prisoner.

He claims I don't want him to enjoy life when I ask him to give up the booze. Also that I want him to die when I suggest I'd like to go shopping by myself once in a while. He's sure I want him dead, yet I love him and have no desire to be a lonely widow.

But I'd rather be dead myself than go on seeing him suffer. Wouldn't it be much better for his health if he gave up the beer drinking? What can I do? I feel I'm drowning—and going down for the third time. If I could only convince him that he isn't what he calls himself: "a social drinker."

Another Complaint.

No one believed me when I said that my former husband was turning into an alcoholic on beer alone. This very same "soft liquor" caused hell in our household, emotional damage to me and to my children, and my marriage ended in divorce. My teenagers begged me to get a divorce, but I procrastinated "for the sake of the children." Then I found that our son had turned to LSD and marijuana. Since the divorce this has ceased and my son is once again an honor student.

I only wish someone had told me earlier about the group called Alanon, established to help the nondrinking partner, and about Alateen for teenagers. Perhaps years of misery and much emotional damage might have been avoided.

Such are only a few indications of what damage both hard and soft liquor may cause to the individual and to his family.

Anxiety is invariably a by-product of alcoholism.

If you suffer from the "A" of anxiety, perhaps the double "A" of (AA) Alcoholics Anonymous is the answer to your problem.

Caffein

A Patient Says She Can't Break the Coffee Habit

> I have been a very heavy coffee drinker for 30 years, drinking at least 12-15 cups daily. I cannot break myself of the addiction. I believe it causes numbness in my extremities, nervousness, irritability, forgetfulness, exhaustion and absolute inability to function. What shall I do?

Perhaps the following case history will help:

> I am a 39-year-old woman, home during the day. Without realizing it, I developed a habit of taking a dozen "coffee breaks" daily in addition to my usual quota at mealtimes.
>
> I never gave this a second thought until I examined my own state of mind and physical condition. I was amazed to realize that I have been unreasonably jittery and fatigued. So much so that I have had all I could do to stay awake evenings after dinner.
>
> I decided to try an experiment. Maybe it was the coffee? I limited myself to two cups a day. On this regime for only a week, I've already notice that I'm much more calm and nowhere near as tired as I was before. It's almost unbelievable! I'm thrilled over this improvement.

Another patient says:

> So help me I don't understand how my friend
> gets any work done. There's a coffee machine in
> our office. She takes at least a dozen coffee breaks
> a day. No wonder she's nervous. Isn't there a limit
> to how much coffee one can drink?

I can understand the reasonableness of taking a coffee
break in midafternoon to break up the accumulated tensions
of the day. But in some establishments, coffee breaks begin
as early as 10 A.M. Are coffee breaks overdone? Are they a
valid excuse to drop (or not begin) work in hand? Or, are
they really necessary oases for refreshing body and spirit? Do
they guarantee increased working efficiency?

My own feeling is that employers unnecessarily lose many
millions of man (and woman) hours of labor yearly. Translate
that into money lost, and you'd find it's large enough to
nibble away substantially at the national debt. Sometimes I
can't understand why employers appear to accept this open-
faced embezzlement so placidly.

But forgetting about employers, how about the
employees? They get off less easily than they think. Many an
overweight problem is due to several "coffee and ———'s"
during the day. And it is a potential producer of unnatural
anxiety.

Think of the nervousness coffee breaks engender—instead
of the sought-for relaxation. The caffein stimulates the pituitary gland, which in turn stimulates the pancreas, which puts
out more insulin. Result? Many chronic coffee break addicts
have a sharp fall in blood sugar. Unrecognized hypoglycemia
(mentioned earlier) causes nervousness, fatigue and lack of
efficiency.

I have often suggested a brake on coffee breaks—and

retired to a bomb-proof shelter. I need protection from coffee fanciers who'll soon be looking for me as a target. (My wife, included.)

For example: "We agree that a dozen coffee breaks a day are excessive. In our office this could never occur. We are lucky that management allows us even two a day. If our boss had his way, these two would probably be taken away. We just hope that he leaves us in peace for the two coffee breaks that we are allowed. We? A group of overweight, overworked, underpaid, nervous, fatigued, inefficient, coffee-drinking embezzlers."

Cholesterol

Do You Suffer From "Cholesterolophobia"? Are you afraid of cholesterol? Does your conscience bother you when you take butter on your hot cakes? When you eat ice cream? Have you given up eating cheeses? Steaks? And many other foods that contain saturated fats?

Well, there may be a good reason for it. On the other hand you may be depriving yourself unnecessarily. For you should know that cholesterol is an important constituent of many body cells. It is manufactured by the liver. If you didn't eat or drink one bit of cholesterol, it would be present in your system.

"Then why all the talk about rigorous control of cholesterol intake?" you ask. "Isn't it true that it causes heart attacks and strokes?"

The answer is that just because it is at the scene of the trouble doesn't automatically label it as the guilty cause. It is true that cholesterol is often found in weakened heart and brain arteries. But it is possible that the fats, called "lipids" have a hand in atherosclerosis, too.

Too much cholesterol in the blood is reason enough to cut down on saturated fats, just to play safe. But not knowing definitely that cholesterol is the actual cause of heart attacks and trouble in the brain arteries (and elsewhere), there is no logical reason why you should become what I term a "cholesterolophobe." Especially when tests show that your heart is all right and your cholesterol blood levels are normal.

Many healthy persons worry unnecessarily about fat in their diets. If you are overweight, better cut down. If your doctor finds good reason for less saturated fat intake, follow his advice. But if you have had a recent checkup and are pronounced healthy, I suggest you live like a normal human being. Don't be a cholesterolophobe. That's one sure way to take the joy out of life.

Vitamins

Too Many Vitamins? Of late, thousands of Americans have not only become diet-conscious but vitamin-conscious to such an extent that they are very anxious that they may be depriving themselves and inviting illness. I know many who have actually developed a fixation on vitamins.

> I admit I'm a health nut, therefore a vitamin nut. I'm one of those persons who believes that health and longevity depend more on proper vitamin intake than upon anything else. You would be correct in assuming that it has almost become a phobia with me. When I don't feel quite right I keep asking myself, "Have I been taking too many vitamins or not enough." Are vitamins really that important? Can they be harmful?

Important? Yes. You would soon know if you were deprived of essential ones in sufficient amounts. For example, children in Denmark without Vitamin A during World War I soon developed eye troubles which frequently caused blindness. Fishermen suffered from night blindness due to Vitamin A deficiency until they made up for it with a diet high in butterfat, fish liver and fish oils. In many parts of the world where there is shortage of vitamin A—rich foods (like butter, cheese, cream, liver, eggs, green leafy vegetables, yellow fruits and vegetables) people may suffer abnormal growth and development. Vitamin A is also important in maintaining the efficiency of the membranes that line the nose, ears, mouth, lungs and digestive tract. But people should remember that they can take too much vitamin A. It may cause headache, nausea, vomiting, loss of hair and skin diseases. Many patients get into trouble by taking huge doses of vitamin A with the hope of getting well "fast."

Of course vitamins are important. For example, vitamin B1, commonly known as thiamine, will definitely prevent (and cure) beriberi, a vitamin deficiency disease. We know that vitamin B2, known as riboflavin, is essential for healthy skin and proper eye function.

Vitamin B6 is necessary for a healthy nervous system. Another B-complex vitamin known as B12 will save the pernicious anemia patient. Another, niacin, will prevent or cure pellagra.

Vitamin K is necessary for normal clotting function of the blood. Vitamin C (common in citrus fruits) will prevent or cure scurvy. Vitamin D (in fish oils and in sunlight) will prevent rickets.

So it is evident that everyone needs a sufficient quantity of vitamins. But there is a catch. Too many become too vitamin-conscious and actually nervous about the importance of a "proper diet." Millions are spent needlessly for vitamin products. If you have a varied diet consisting of meat, fish, fowl, milk and eggs; vegetables and fruits; breaks and cereals —chances are that you will not have a vitamin deficiency. If your doctor believes you are a normal person on a normal diet why spend money on vitamin pills? Special foods rich in vitamins and minerals are superfluous. For the majority of us the answer to the vitamin problem is inherent in what I have told you: eating a normal, well-balanced diet. But if you still admit you are a diet-nut then I suppose the only one who can talk you out of it is your own family doctor.

I have had difficulty in convincing highly enthusiastic food faddists that there isn't sufficient proof that Vitamin C, for instance, (as recently recommended in large doses) will surely prevent the common cold or the almost equally common cases of allergy. Or, that large doses of vitamin E will overcome sterility, decrease the likelihood of miscarriage, and lengthen the life span. It seems to work on mice, but that's a long way from proving it will be helpful to humans.

"Mood" Pills

A patient said, "A friend of mine went to her doctor because she was depressed and he said he was going to prescribe some mood pills for her. Just what are they?"

There are many kinds. We call them psychotropics. Is your friend "up"? Then he may want to bring her "down." Is she "down"? Then he will prescribe medicine to bring her "up."

For example, here is a patient who is depressed. The doctor will try to find the reason and correct it. Meanwhile, he will prescribe pills that will give her spirits a lift . In other words, a change of mood from low to higher. But here is another patient who can't relax. She can't sleep well. She is wound up. What to do? As in the first patient, it's important to discover the reason for the tension and anxiety. But meanwhile the patient needs to be quieted down. So the doctor has her take tranquilizers during the day and a sleeping pill before bedtime. He wants to change her mood from one of hyperactivity to one of more normal calm.

One estimate is that nearly half of all adults in the United States have used mood-changing drugs at one time or other and that about one in four still uses them. In order of their common use they are tranquilizers, sedatives and stimulants. I favor the use of indicated mood pills only under a doctor's direction.

Too Many Tranquilizers?

Within the past 18 months I have seen an internist, a neurologist and a psychiatrist. I have been trying to rid myself of nervous tension. I have consumed tons of tranquilizers. I've been in the hospital for a rest, during which time I had chest X-rays, ECGs, thyroid scan, G.I. series, barium enema, blood and urine tests. I've also had a glucose tolerance test for hypoglycemia. Everything checked out normal. I really wish they had found something—even if it was serious. I'm still fighting anxiety. My doctors tell me to keep on with the tranquilizers until I feel much better. Meanwhile, they allow me to sleep well, to go to work every day and carry on almost like a normal human being. My question is this: will I hurt myself by keeping on with tranquilizers for so long?

Be thankful for the new "energizers" and tranquilizers available to us in treating anxiety patients. Admittedly, they may only serve as temporary crutches to support the emotionally sick. But you will agree, as in your case, that they at least allow you to sleep and work.

Somehow, tranquilizers make some people feel conscience stricken. Perhaps they should feel so, if they do not take them under a doctor's direction. But if prescribed by a physician, and under his constant care, most of us should feel thankful for these temporary supports which allow us to go about our daily business—waiting for the day when we can get around normally without having to pop pills into our mouths as a routine part of our daily schedule. Tension is one of our greatest problems these days. Any "legitimate" way to neutralize it serves a valuable purpose.

Self-treatment Dangerous

Picture this man. There are thousands like him. He takes barbiturates to put him to sleep. Groggy and confused in the morning, he swallows a few amphetamine tablets to wake him up. Day after day he is in a boxing ring of his own making: he allows himself to be knocked out by one pill and picked up from the canvas by another. And chances are there's not even a referee (doctor) present to make decisions. Our man has decided to take barbiturates and amphetamines on his own.

Here is an example:

> It all began innocently enough. I lost my mother and was so upset that our doctor prescribed barbiturates for me to take; I got hooked. He refused to

prescribe any more, but I bootlegged them. Went
from doctor to doctor to get my supplies. Then I
began to take amphetamines, too. I had to in order
to stay awake and keep my job. My only reason in
telling you is so you can warn others not "to
begin" bootlegging. Although I have at last kicked
the habit, it has been a horrible experience getting
"unhooked." Almost like being a dope addict and
having to take the cure.

As I have been saying, such medication is not "dope"
when taken under a doctor's direction. Patients should not
refuse tranquilizers or sleeping pills to help them get over
some rough spot in their lives. But it is necessary to keep
repeating that self-treatment may be harmful. If you get
"hooked" you invite continued drowsiness, tremor of hands
and lips, confusion and loss of judgment, poor muscular
coordination (dangerous while driving), deterioration in
appearance, loss of job and loss of friends.

The barbiturate habit is easy to begin, easy to maintain,
but quite difficult to break. Why invite a knockout by hitting
yourself on the chin?

People Are Funny. But people are funny. Some don't take
the treatment their doctor prescribes. Instead of suffering
from "self-treatment" they suffer from negligence.

Everyone's heard the expression "stand up and
take your medicine." My husband will not take his,
sitting or lying down. Let me explain. We are in
moderate circumstances. He goes to the doctor
quite often because he's a worrywart. He himself
admits to being a hypochondriac. But what I can't
understand is this. He'll go to the drugstore, have
his prescriptions filled, take the medicine home,

and put the bottles or boxes on the shelf of the medicine cabinet—and not even open them.

What bothers me so much is how he can spend so much for medicine (you know how expensive it is these days) and not take it? It is driving me nutty. I think it would do the same for any other wife who wants a new dress once in a while but can't afford it because her husband throws the money away on unused medicines. How do you explain it?

You have a lot of company. In thousands of medicine cabinets throughout the United States, dust gathers on unopened bottles and boxes of medicines. Ask patients why they didn't take their medicine as directed and one gets various replies. Some will shrug their shoulders, as if they forgot to take it. Others will say, "I felt better after I had the prescription filled, so why take the medicine?" What it all adds up to, I think, is that many patients go to their doctor only for reassurance, rather than for treatment.

For example, one man who has been complaining of tiredness is concerned that it may be due to something serious. His doctor looks him over carefully and gives him a clean bill of health. He also prescribes a tonic to help recovery from his fatigue. The patient goes through the motions of filling the prescription, but doesn't take his medicine. All he wanted to know was that he is all right.

Or, consider the woman who suffers from anxiety. She is worried that she is going to have a nervous breakdown "like my cousin had." The doctor assures her that it isn't hereditary and prescribes tranquilizers. The bottle stands unopened. She feels better just knowing her nervous condition isn't serious.

Of the two bad habits—self-treatment or ignoring medica-

306 _Antidotes for Anxiety_

tion—it is difficult to judge which is more harmful. A good rule is to rely on the judgment on your doctor (with or without consultation) and follow his advice rather than make your own decisions.

Finding a New Way of Life

To be able to untie a taut bundle of nerves it is essential to find a new way of life. To be able to face up to yourself honestly and ask: "Am I nervous? If so what is causing the anxiety? Shall I try to master it myself or ask for professional advice early?"

Many will not admit they suffer from anxiety. The first step in finding a cure is to say to yourself that you are unnaturally nervous. It is possible that you may help yourself by discovering the cause in your environment (job or home)—and by changing the environment or changing yourself.

But it is more likely that you need the help of a compassionate, understanding physician to guide you through the dark tunnel until you see a light at the end. The longer you procrastinate, the longer you will suffer emotional distress. Anxiety can be a stubborn ailment, but it is curable. You can find a new way of life by rereading these pages. Somewhere here are specific antidotes for your own special kind of poison we call anxiety. _Faith_ heads the list.

Thoughts and Afterthoughts on Chapter 20

1. Do bad habits cause anxiety, or does anxiety cause bad habits?

2. Obesity is no joke. It is a serious problem. Its cure depends upon proper motivation. No one can reduce without it.

3. Tension causes nibbling. Many of us do not realize we are nibblers when we become anxious. Fat brethren are not "happy-go-lucky."

4. She lost weight and regained her mind.

5. The hazards of smoking are well known. The ubiquitous habit of smoking often causes anxiety and is often the result of it.

6. Are you a social drinker or really a chronic alcoholic? You may believe that you are only a social drinker yet be a hairsbreadth away from chronic alcoholism. Review your drinking habits honestly. Even beer is a threat to some people.

7. Caffein may cause nervousness, irritability, forgetfulness, exhaustion and absolute inability to function. How many coffee breaks do you take daily?

8. Do you suffer unnecessarily from cholesterolophobia?

9. Vitamin deficiency is unlikely if you take a normal diet.

10. Tranquilizers and other mood pills can be quite effective—but only when prescribed and supervised by your physician. Self-treatment is dangerous.

11. It is possible to discover a New Way of Life with the help of a compassionate doctor and your own resolve to feel better.

Parting Note: A Summing Up

You have good reason for disappointment if you opened these covers with the hope that you would read a definitive book on Anxiety, an erudite dissertation on Freudian concepts of the conscious and the subconscious. As you must realize by the time you have come to the end, my purpose has not been to define and explain Anxiety on the plane of professor to pupil, but to talk to you (across my desk) as physician to patient. It is often easier to write a dry, encyclopedia of informative items than just talk simply and informatively—"from me to you."

My work in writing this book has been fruitful if I have been able to convince you that Anxiety is not a personal problem, but a universal enemy of every living individual.

If you accept it as a natural phenomenon of life, then you will not look without compassion on your neighbor or family member who suffers from unnatural Anxiety. You will not label his fears as "silly" aberrations.

You will recognize your own degree of fearfulness, and measure it (with the help of what you have read here) against what is considered to be normal Anxiety.

You will, after such assessment be able to face yourself more honestly when you shave in the morning or "put on your face" in the evening.

In other words, when you become really anxious—more than you can seem to bear, you will hesitate to call for help from your doctor simply because you think it's "silly to bother him."

To help you see yourself as you really are, here is a summing up of what you have already read. I'll list the main points, and then consider them again, briefly, one by one. As in advertising, reiteration is a powerful force in influencing the mind and emotions.

Here are the main factors, in review:

1. *What is the condition of your bundle of nerves?*
2. *Do you grow anxious in your doctor's office?*
3. *Choosing your doctor should be an important decision.*
4. *Are you certain that your symptoms are not hiding behind anxiety?*
5. *There are commonsense ways to live with coronary disease—and without it.*
6. *Are you certain your heart trouble's not imaginary?*
7. *Hypoglycemia is often overlooked.*
8. *Maybe your thyroid needs a tune-up.*
9. *Faulty breathing can exacerbate nervous feelings.*
10. *Cyclic tension is more common than realized.*
11. *Hysterectomy is "just another operation."*
12. *Both males and females have their "change."*
13. *Everybody gets the "blues."*
14. *"Nervous breakdown" is a wastebasket term.*
15. *Major depression, although serious, can be helped.*
16. *The will to die (suicide) can often be neutralized.*
17. *How to be a happier hypochondriac.*
18. *Have your eye on mortality.*
19. *There are ways to overcome fatigue, tension and insomnia.*

20. *Take true inventory—and you can find a new way of life.*

If, instead of skimming, you have read the book carefully, you will recall most of these factors. Nevertheless, a brief reconsideration of each will, I hope, give you a better conception of how to manage your anxiety.

1. *What is the condition of your bundle of nerves?*

Are you taut or relaxed? The answer depends upon how tied up you are by your nerves. If your bundle of nerves is tightly constricted by anxiety, it is time to do some loosening. You know how wearing tight shoes, a tight girdle or a tight collar can produce unnecessary and unrelieved tension during the day. Then consider how a too-tight bundle of nerves, suffered not only for one day but for months and years can deaden the spirit and joy of living. The answer is evident: complaining about nerves without constructive measures to help yourself will only intensify and prolong your anxiety.

2. *Do you grow anxious in your doctor's office?*

Which one among us is so brave that he (or she) doesn't have feelings of anxiety when confronted by a doctor in his office? It is natural to be afraid of what the verdict will be. A heart guilty or innocent? Lungs free of serious impairment, or harboring incurable illness? Everybody's scared. Not so much of the examination itself as about what the doctor will say. Therefore, do not consider yourself some sort of coward when confronted with illness and the need to have an examination.

3. *Choosing your doctor should be an important decision.*

Many play roulette with their lives by choosing a doctor

simply by running their fingers over the Yellow Pages in the telephone book. In an emergency, any M.D. is a welcome sight. During sudden danger we do not ask for the qualifications of the man who dives in to pull us out of a whirlpool. But under ordinary circumstances, the choice of doctor should be more than a routine browsing among members of the medical profession. Somewhere, if you seek, there is just the right doctor for you and yours. It pays to choose your doctor when there is no pressure of family illness to influence a too hasty judgment.

4. Are you certain that your symptoms are not hiding behind anxiety?

Although it is not always easy, try to be frank with your doctor. I have known so many patients who came complaining of "indigestion" or of "headache" or of dozens of other symptoms which were only screens behind which to hide their anxiety. As a result they underwent expensive diagnostic examinations (X-rays etc.) which might have been prevented if they had come right out with an admission that they were depressed, anxious or unduly nervous. "I am worried about my son who takes LSD," for example, might have put the doctor on the true diagnostic trail much earlier. Likewise, many a headache, is due to resentment. Of course, it is true that some patients cannot pinpoint the reason for their anxiety. Nevertheless, a frank admission that nervousness is their main concern can prevent months of unnecessary suffering.

5. There are commonsense ways of living with coronary disease.

Perhaps more than any other, coronary disease instills fear. This is a natural reaction to statistics which give it the jealous role of being number 1 in the list of killers and maimers of the human race. But as I have said in the chapter on coronary disease, we have ways of preventing it—and of treating it successfully so that patients may return for years to their normal way of life. I suggest that anyone who is anxious about his heart after having had a "coronary" reread that chapter and memorize the "rules" for living with coronary disease. And perhaps what is more important, learning the accepted ways of lessening the likelihood of an attack in the first place.

6. *Are you certain that your heart trouble's not imaginary?*

If it is true that three out of every four people who come to the doctor thinking they have heart disease are free of it, then you will admit there is much needless suffering and anxiety in the world. I realize that palpitation, swelling of the ankles, shortness of breath, chest pain and other symptoms may be found in actual, organic heart disease. But please believe your doctor (after a thorough checkup) when he tells you that your heart is normal—in spite of these symptoms. They may be due to something outside of the heart. Whether or not you live as a cardiophobe for the rest of your life will depend more upon you than upon your doctor.

7. *Hypoglycemia is often overlooked.*

What a relief to discover that you are anxious only because you have had unsuspected hypoglycemia. You have thought that maybe epilepsy, brain tumor, or seriously high blood pressure might be the reason for your spells of faintness, the jitters, and extreme anxiety. A *high* protein diet commonly overcomes the symptoms of low blood sugar.

8. *Maybe your thyroid needs a tune-up.*

Not too many years ago thyroid disease was overlooked simply because it was too much of a bother for patients to come into the doctor's office without breakfast to lie down and take the breathing test known as the basal metabolism examination. When the thyroid was underactive such patients could not understand why they were always so tired; when overactive, why they were so nervous. These days, when a blood test is taken for laboratory tests, usually a routine examination is made of thyroid function. As a result of this protein-bound iodine test (and others) fewer cases of thyroid inefficiency are overlooked. And thus there's less reason for unexplained anxiety.

9. *Faulty breathing can exacerbate nervous feelings.*

We call it hyperventilation. Anyone who has experienced an acute anxiety reaction tied in with faulty breathing will never forget the extreme agitation and fear that accompanies this syndrome. Anxiety is present before and after the attack. Relieving the hyperventilation is only one step in recovery. The doctor must dig deep into the patient's history before being able to reduce attacks of hyperventilation and anxiety.

10. *Cyclic (premenstrual) tension is more common than realized.*

It is still not unusual to hear some young women say, "I can't understand it. Why am I so relaxed for about three weeks every month, and then become so tense and nervous for a week before my period?" Instead of suffering these monthly episodes of distress they should not feel "too silly" to bring their complaints to their doctor. He can help by prescribing the proper medication.

11. *Hysterectomy is "just another operation."*

Gradually the fear of this operation is being obliterated. It is being accepted, although not with pleasure, as an operation on the gall bladder or on a hernia. The psychological reactions to it—its effects on "womanhood" and sex—have been discounted by increasing publicity that removal of the uterus is not the "end" of a woman's life.

12. *Both males and females have their "change."*
Men and women are brothers and sisters under the skin. Both have sex glands, and although some doctors still disagree that the male does not undergo a "change," it makes better sense to believe that his sex glands change with age as do those of his female counterpart. Call it by the name of "male climacteric," but it's the change, nevertheless.

13. *Everybody gets the "blues."*
Job blues, family blues, weekend blues—there isn't a human being who hasn't had his temporary quota of "down days."

14. *"Nervous breakdown" is a wastebasket term.*
The next time you hear of someone having a "nervous breakdown" don't jump to conclusions. Only his doctor knows if it is simply a neurosis or the more serious psychosis. A nervous breakdown may range from a sudden outbreak of temper, over in a few minutes, to months of mental illness. Whether a few weeks vacation is the cure or some shock therapy, depends upon the nature and extent of the nervous involvement.

15. *Major depressions, although serious, can be helped.*
The newer antidepressant drugs and energizers and/or the use of shock therapy can do much for patients who have sunk into major depressions. Many conditions formerly thought hopeless are now amenable to treatment.

16. *The will to die (suicide) can often be neutralized.*

The time factor is important here. And not overlooking the potential danger to patients who "talk of doing away with themselves." During a depression every such hint should be considered a warning. Early treatment by a psychiatrist often spells the difference between life and death.

17. *How to be a happier hypochondriac.*

I have changed "happy" to "happier." It is doubtful that any patients suffering from psychoneurosis are happy. Happier is only a relative term. But it is true that, with understanding by family and physician, compassion exerts its positive effects on hypochondriacs who live in continuing anxiety.

18. *Have your eye on mortality.*

Too many of us live as if we shall be on earth forever.

19. *There are ways to overcome fatigue, tension and insomnia.*

Alleviate one of this triumvirate and you inevitably decrease the discomforts of the remaining two.

20. *Take true inventory—and you can find a new way of life.*

Follow the suggestions in this book. See if it isn't true that you can untie your bundle of nerves.